The Social Work Business

Sε
dr
pι
m
ca
ac
ar
fo

its
Lε
niι
us
wι
wι

rει
ne
in
rel

Jo
Uι
vει
wι

and manager in a Social Services Department.

D1144124

The State of Welfare
Edited by Mary Langan

Throughout the Western world, welfare states are in transition. Changing social, economic and political circumstances have rendered obsolete the systems that emerged in the 1940s out of the experience of depression, war and social conflict. New structures of welfare are now taking shape in response to the conditions of today: globalisation and individuation, the demise of traditional allegiances and institutions, the rise of new forms of identity and solidarity.

In Britain, the New Labour government has linked the projects of implementing a new welfare settlement and forging a new moral purpose in society. Enforcing 'welfare to work', on the one hand, and tackling 'social exclusion' on the other, the government aims to rebalance the rights and duties of citizens and redefine the concept of equality.

The State of Welfare series provides a forum for the debate about the new shape of welfare into the millennium.

Titles of related interest also in *The State of Welfare* series:

The Social Work Business

John Harris

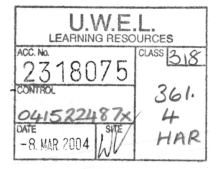

London and New York

First published 2003
by Routledge
11 New Fetter Lane, London EC4P 4EE

Simultaneously published in the USA and Canada
by Routledge
29 West 35th Street, New York, NY 10001

Routledge is an imprint of the Taylor & Francis Group

© 2003 John Harris

Typeset in Times by BC Typesetting, Bristol
Printed and bound in Great Britain by
TJ International Ltd, Padstow, Cornwall

British Library Cataloguing in Publication Data
A catalogue record for this book is available from the British Library

Library of Congress Cataloging in Publication Data
A catalog record for this book has been requested

ISBN 0–415–22488–8 (pbk)
ISBN 0–415–22487–X (hbk)

For Lydia, Seth and Vicky

Contents

Series editor's Preface

State welfare policies reflect changing perceptions of key sources of social instability. In the first half of the twentieth century – from Bismarck to Beveridge – the welfare state emerged as a set of policies and institutions which were – in the main – a response to the 'problem of labour', the threat of class conflict. The major objective was to contain and integrate the labour movement. In the post-war decades, as this threat receded, the welfare state became consolidated as a major employer and provider of a wide range of services and benefits to every section of society. Indeed, it increasingly became the focus of blame for economic decline and was condemned for its inefficiency and ineffectiveness.

Since the end of the Cold War, the major fear of capitalist societies is no longer class conflict, but the socially disintegrative consequences of the system itself. Increasing fears and anxieties about social instability – including unemployment and homelessness, delinquency, drug abuse and crime, divorce, single parenthood and child abuse – reflect deep-seated apprehensions about the future of modern society.

The role of state social policy in the Clinton–Blair era was to restrain and regulate the destructive effects of market forces, symbolised by the Reagan–Thatcher years. On both sides of the Atlantic, governments have rejected the old polarities of left and right, the goals of both comprehensive state intervention and rampant free-market individualism. In its pursuit of a 'third way' the New Labour government, which came to power in Britain in May 1997, has sought to define a new role for government at a time when politics has largely retreated from its traditional concerns about the nature and direction of society.

What are the values of the third way? According to Tony Blair, the people of middle England 'distrust heavy ideology', but want 'security and stability'; they 'want to refashion the bonds of community life' and, 'although they believe in the market economy, they do not believe that the only values that matter are those of the market place' (*The Times*, 25 July 1998). The values of the third way reflect and shape a traditional and conservative response to the dynamic and unpredictable world of the late 1990s.

The view expressed by Michael Jacobs, a leading participant in the revived Fabian Society, that 'we live in a strongly individualized society which is falling apart' is widely shared (*The Third Way*, London: Fabian Society, 1998). For him, 'the fundamental principle' of the third way is 'to balance the autonomous demands of the individual with the need for social cohesion or "community"'. A key New Labour concept that follows from this preoccupation with community is that of 'social exclusion'. Proclaimed the government's 'most important innovation' when it was announced in August 1997, the Social Exclusion Unit is at the heart of New Labour's flagship social policy initiative – the 'Welfare to Work' programme. The preoccupation with 'social exclusion' indicates a concern about tendencies towards fragmentation in society and a self-conscious commitment to policies which seek to integrate atomised individuals and thus to enhance social cohesion.

The popularity of the concept of social exclusion reflects a striking tendency to aggregate diverse issues so as to imply a common origin. The concept of social exclusion legitimises the moralising dynamic of New Labour. Initiatives such as 'Welfare to Work', targeting the young unemployed and single mothers, emphasise individual responsibility. Duties – to work, to save, to adopt a healthy lifestyle, to do homework, to 'parent' in the approved manner – are the common themes of New Labour's social policy: obligations take precedence over rights.

Though the concept of social exclusion targets a smaller section of society than earlier categories such as 'the poor' or 'the underclass', it does so in a way which implies a societal responsibility for the problems of fragmentation, as well as indicating a concern to draw people back – from truancy, sleeping rough, delinquency and drugs, etc. – into the mainstream of society. Yet New Labour's sympathy for the excluded extends only as far as the provision of voluntary work and training schemes, parenting classes and drug rehabilitation programmes. The socially excluded are no longer allowed to be the passive recipients of benefits: they are obliged to participate in their moral reintegration. Those who refuse to subject themselves to these apparently benign forms of regulation may soon find themselves the target of more coercive interventions.

There is a further dimension to the third way. The very novelty of New Labour initiatives necessitates the appointment of new personnel and the creation of new institutions to overcome the inertia of the established structures of central and local government. To emphasise the importance of its drugs policy, the government has created the new office of drugs commissioner 'tsar' – and prefers to implement the policy through a plethora of voluntary organisations, rather than through traditional channels. Health action zones, education action zones and employment action zones are the chosen vehicles for policy innovation in their respective areas. At higher levels of government, semi-detached special policy units, think tanks and quangos play an increasingly important role.

The State of Welfare series aims to provide a critical assessment of social policy in the new millennium. We will consider the new and emerging 'third way' welfare policies and practices and the way these are shaped by wider social and economic changes. Globalisation, the emergence of post-industrial society, the transformation of work, demographic shifts and changes in gender roles and family structures all have major consequences for patterns of welfare provision.

Social policy will also be affected by the demands of social movements – of women, minority ethnic groups and disabled people – as well as of groups concerned with sexuality or the environment. *The State of Welfare* series examines these influences when analysing welfare practices in the first decade of the new millennium.

Mary Langan
February 1999

Preface

In addressing the commencement, consolidation and consequences of the social work business, the book considers general trends and picks up on specific illustrations or issues mainly from services for adults. The transformation of this field of social work, through the community care reforms of the late 1980s and early 1990s, served as the proving ground for many of the developments that spread subsequently to other areas. From the outset, however, there was no intention to establish the social work business only in services for adults, as the White Paper on community care, *Caring for People*, made clear: '*The two programmes* [i.e. the Children Act 1989 and the NHS and Community Care Act 1990] *are consistent and complementary* and, taken together, set a fresh agenda and new challenges for social services authorities for the next decade and beyond' (Cm. 849 1989: para. 1.3, my emphasis).

There are certainly many indications that the trends initially associated with community care for adults are evident elsewhere in social work. The markets in private fostering and private children's homes have expanded rapidly. Work with children and families is now conducted in what are effectively care management terms, with responses to children in the form of care packages (Causer and Exworthy 1999: 97). The 'Quality Protects' programme (see Department of Health 1998a) is as preoccupied with objectives and targets as any initiative elsewhere in social work, and this is but one aspect of the changes which have taken place in work with children and families. Others have included: a preoccupation with financial concerns; the importation of management practices; the rise of a business culture focused on the centrality of 'value for money'; proceduralisation, standardisation; centralisation of decision making; greater prescription of social work interventions and redefinition of roles and responsibilities (Huntington 2000: 117–19).

Dealing with this wide range of manifestations of the social work business proved to be beyond the scope of the book and, in the end, biography won out in the selection of services for adults as illustrative of the more general developments that have taken place. Since the demise of genericism, that is the field of social work with which I have been most concerned, both in academia and in practice, the field in which I have seen at first hand the social work business develop.

Acknowledgements

Over the last few years, I have benefited from a network of stimulating discussion among the members of 'the Bielefeld gang', brought together at the instigation of Hans-Uwe Otto (University of Bielefeld), who himself has been a source of solid support and personal encouragement. Under his leadership, the gang has grown in size and has spread internationally to the extent that it is impossible to mention all of the other members, save to say that the contributions of Steve Burghardt and Mike Fabricant (Hunter College) have been inspirational, that the analyses of Michael Muetzelfeldt (Victoria University) have been razor sharp and the questions and comments of Heinz Sünker (University of Wuppertal) have often stopped me in my tracks. The opportunity to meet up again with Peter Leonard (McGill University), after so many years, has been an added bonus of gang membership.

I have gained a great deal from working, with members of the research group, on managerialism and professional discretion, a branch of the Bielefeld gang led by Stefan Schnurr (Universities of Bielefeld and Rostock), and I have valued the contact that developed out of that group both with him and with Wiebke Horn (University of Bielefeld), Sue Sunesson (University of Lund), Tommy Lundstrom (University of Stockholm), Sissel Seim (Oslo University College) and the irrepressible Linda Briskman (Royal Melbourne Institute of Technology). My original contact down under, Catherine McDonald (University of Queensland), continues to be a thought-provoking and humorous collaborator.

The Bielefeld gang originally supplied my colleague Andreas Schaarschuch (now at the University of Wuppertal). Since our first meeting, he has pushed forward ideas enthusiastically and has worked hard to make it possible for me to be in Wuppertal for a sustained period in order to work on them and to discuss them with staff and students.

My colleagues at the University of Warwick have been generous in allowing me considerable scope to follow up my interests during the writing of the book, for which I am very grateful.

Finally, and most importantly, nothing would have been possible without the unstinting emotional and intellectual support provided by Vicky (Ch. 6 in particular, would not have materialised without her) and the regular bringing down to earth that only Lydia and Seth can supply.

List of Acronyms

ADSS	Association of Directors of Social Services
CCETSW	Central Council for Education and Training in Social Work
CGC/CCW	Cygnor Gofal Cymru/Care Council for Wales
CQSW	Certificate of Qualification in Social Work
CSS	Certificate of Social Service
DHSS	Department of Health and Social Security
DipSW	Diploma in Social Work
DoE	Department of Employment
DoETR	Department of the Environment, Transport and the Regions
GSCC	General Social Care Council
HMSO	Her Majesty's Stationery Office
INLOGOV	Institute and Local Government Studies
LGMB	Local Government Management Board
LGTB	Local Government Training Board
NCVO	National Council for Voluntary Organisations
NCVQ	National Council for Vocational Qualifications
NHS	National Health Service
NISCC	Northern Ireland Social Care Council
SCIE	Social Care Institute of Excellence
SSD	Social Services Department
SSSC	Scottish Social Services Council
TOPSS	Training Organisation for the Personal Social Services

1 Doing the business

Reminiscing

In 1975, I sat with my social worker colleagues in our regular team meeting as the Team Leader summarised the contents of a memorandum from the Director of Social Services. It announced that team leaders were to become 'District Managers', with increased responsibilities for a wider range of services and with more managerial authority. Team members exchanged puzzled and quizzical glances. Most of us were amused by this strange term, which didn't seem to fit with the social work ethos in which we worked. There were suppressed giggles around the room. I said that I had come across this job title before, when I was still at school and was working for a men's tailoring chain on Saturdays. We had a district manager then, I recalled, who used to visit us once a month to check whether our profit levels were higher than in the comparable month of the previous year. I predicted confidently that a job title used in the commercial world of men's tailoring would never catch on in social work. There were approving nods and grunts of assent all round. We moved on dismissively to the next item on the agenda. (Five years later, I was a district manager.)

This brief reminiscence is the historical starting point for the book. It was my first encounter with the suggestion that social work had things to learn from the business world. Up to that point, during my time as a social work student and throughout my work following qualification, a clear distinction was drawn between social work as a non-commercial activity in the public and voluntary sectors and private commercial activities, driven by the market's profit motive. As time has gone by, this distinction has been eroded to such an extent that what we now have in existence is, I would argue, 'the social work business'. This business has distinctive aspects, just as other businesses do: for example, the business of supermarkets is obviously different from the business of car production. However, the central argument of the book is that so much of social work's ideology and management is derived from an overarching business discourse, shared by businesses of vastly different hues, that 'the social work business' is now an appropriate designation. (One of the private sector's social care trade papers is called, without a trace of irony, *The Caring Business*.) Thinking along these lines prompts other, more contemporary, reminiscences.

I am at the annual conference of a voluntary sector organisation. The chief executive, fresh back from an intensive management course at a leading American university business school, includes in his opening remarks the comment: 'We are a business. We want to be at the cutting edge. We want to be in the top 10 per cent soon and we want to be the industry leader in the not too distant future.' A succession of senior and middle managers from the organisation address the conference, stating how the parts of the organisation for which they are responsible can contribute to the mission the chief executive has proclaimed.

In the period leading to the death of my father, I am on the telephone to a social worker in my father's local Social Services Department. The conversation is a little stilted. Regardless of anything I say, the social worker pulls me back to a series of short, tersely delivered, questions about various aspects of my father's physical functioning. Some time later, I am on the telephone to a different social worker. The experience is exactly the same. In fact, I realise that he is asking me the same short questions in the same order as the social worker I spoke to the last time. This experience is repeated a third time, a few days later. These three social workers have responded to each of my calls by taking me through a scripted assessment over the telephone. I have had scripted exchanges which were more engaging and responsive at the windows of drive-through fast-food restaurants.

I go to visit a student on placement. After checking in with the receptionist, and having been issued with a security pass, I ask where the toilet is. The receptionist looks slightly flustered and says she is not sure whether I should use the customers' toilet or the staff toilet. I say the customers' toilet will be fine and am directed to a door with a large TOILET FOR CUSTOMERS OF SOCIAL SERVICES sign. I meet up with the practice teacher, who I have known for some years, and the student. I remark on the smart new telephone-answering machine sitting on the practice teacher's desk. She looks slightly embarrassed and explains that one of the 'quality standards' in this Social Services Department is that 90 per cent of calls must be answered within three rings. She, and several of her colleagues, have been taken to task for failing to meet this standard, so many of them have purchased their own answering machines and now the standard is being met.

I am working as a social worker, on secondment from my university job. I attend my induction training. I am sitting next to a new home help. We get chatting, while we are waiting for the session to start. She says that she used to work for a private home care agency. I ask why she wanted to move to the Social Services Department. She tells me that in her previous job, she had an evening call which involved putting someone to bed. She drove three miles in each direction to do this, was allowed fifteen minutes, including travelling time, to do it and was paid no travelling expenses. At that time (just before the introduction of the minimum wage) she was being paid £2 an hour. So, for being away from her home for an hour or more in the evening, she was being paid 50p, and then having to pay for her petrol. She says, 'Do I need to say any more?'

What jolted me in each of these everyday experiences, and many more which I have not recounted, was the intrusion of 'business thinking'. Different people in different settings and circumstances were 'doing the business'. On each occasion, the business ethos was simply there, as a seemingly inescapable reality through which social work had to be conducted and, as a consequence, social work appeared to have lost any of the critical edge it once possessed. This book seeks to document how that position was reached in social work and to identify some of the key dimensions of the social work business.

Constructing social work

The book begins from the premiss that the forces constructing social work lie outside of social work itself: social work is shaped by the societal context from which it emerges. Although it is clear that international markets and the global economy now exert pressures on the direction social welfare policy takes in particular societies (Deacon *et al.* 1997; George 1998; Barns *et al.* 1999), the societal context has been shown to shape different versions of social work (Harris and McDonald 2000; Harris and Yueh-Ching Chou 2001). Therefore, in this book the mediating impact of the British context is seen as central to understanding the development of the social work business. The emphasis on context is also seen as a necessary counterbalance to accounts of social work in which it is portrayed as simply an activity in which individual social workers are engaged or as a professional project with its own, internally-driven, trajectory (McDonald *et al.* forthcoming). Accordingly, in the remainder of the book, rather than thinking about social work as a phenomenon which somehow develops itself, it is positioned in relation to changes in its context; changes that led to the construction and reconstruction of social work in Britain and, in the process, to the establishment and consolidation of the social work business.

Those changes have taken place within the overarching framework of liberal representative democracy (Pierson 1998). Within this framework, the welfare state has provided the primary vehicle for the mediation of social work. The institutional and organisational processes of the welfare state have been the source of social work's legal and moral authority and have constituted the material conditions for its practice. Ultimately, social workers implement legislation on behalf of the state, as an arm of social policy, rather than as an autonomous profession. The law sets out the rights, duties and responsibilities of social workers, on the one hand, and of service users, on the other, in those socially problematic areas which have been accorded official recognition. The law not only defines the ends of social work, but constitutes the source of social workers' authority for the means by which they intervene in service users' lives in the pursuit of statutory duties. In other words, social work is not just mediated by its context in a general sense: more specifically and directly it is a mediated profession, with the state deciding who its clientele will be and what should be provided for them (Johnson 1972: 77).

In the policy, practice and analysis of the British post-war welfare state, a clear distinction was drawn between public non-commercial activities, which the welfare state was considered to exemplify, and private commercial activities, driven by the market's profit motive. The welfare state was seen as shouldering responsibilities that were intrinsically non-capitalist. Its interventions, such as social work, were depicted as being driven by a very different dynamic and as protected from the vagaries of market forces. This was the case in both social democratic accounts of the welfare state (see Ch. 2) and neo-Marxist discussions of 'non-capitalist state activities' (Carchedi 1977). As late as 1993, a book on public sector management could begin:

> In this book, we are mostly concerned with those services which are mainly or completely funded by taxation and which are not sold to customers at prices which produce profits. This is a very distinctive part of the economy because the 'normal' processes of producing goods and services do not apply. As well as public services not being run generally to make a profit, there is no competition in the

sense of firms trying to entice customers away from competitors. Because these basic features of a market are absent, many of the principles of management which apply to the private sector are absent. Other principles, such as equitable treatment and allocation of resources according to need, pervade the processes of decision-making and management.

(Flynn 1993: xi–xii)

Social work occupied a niche in this 'non-capitalist' sphere and accounting for the development of the social work business is inseparable from analysing the destabilisation of that niche and its subsequent transformation. The transformation has been largely taken-for-granted as a series of incremental adaptations to the changed context of the surrounding welfare regime (Pollitt 1990; Clarke *et al.* 1994; Evers *et al.* 1997; Flösser and Otto 1998). However, the cumulative effect of the transformation, the social work business, makes it difficult to sustain the clear analytical distinction, previously made by social democratic and neo-Marxist commentators, between public services and private sector businesses. Rather, 'social domains, whose concern is not producing commodities in the narrower economic sense of goods for sale, come nevertheless to be organised and conceptualised in terms of commodity production, distribution and consumption' (Fairclough 1992: 207). Another way of putting this is that the culture of capitalism has colonised the public sector as business thinking and practices have crossed the public–private sector divide and been transplanted into activities such as social work. As a result, social work has shifted to operating in accordance with a 'quasi-business discourse' within which the explicit or implicit assumption is that social work should, as far as possible, function as if it were a commercial business concerned with making profits.

Doing the business

The quasi-business discourse in social work does not galvanise the straightforward implementation of a neutral set of knowledge, skills and techniques, despite the frequent depiction of it as such. The discourse is the outcome of political choice or, more accurately, as will be shown later in the book, a series of political choices. Those choices have identified business thinking and practice as representing a distinctive and valuable expertise and have used that expertise as a resource in a struggle for power. In other words, expertise from business has been used to rearrange and consolidate sets of power relations in social work, as the later chapters show. However, the politics and power of the social work business are not necessarily immediately apparent. The quasi-business discourse may be a very limited way of thinking – a 'bounded rationality' – but it does not appear to be so: 'All bounded rationalities tend to conceal their own boundedness and appear to those who operate within them to be universal' (Muetzelfeldt 1994: 151). In other words, for much of the time the quasi-business discourse in social work governs the limits and form of what is knowable, sayable and do-able (Bourdieu 1991; Foucault 1991; Harris, P. 1999). As such, the discourse contributes to the construction of the social identities of social workers, managers and service users and shapes the networks of social relations in which they engage (Fairclough 1992: 64); it inculcates a 'habitus' – a set of dispositions that incline people to act and react in certain ways (Bourdieu 1991: 51). Reflecting on her experience of higher education in New Zealand, O'Connor refers to managerialism (a key component of the discourse) as having been

> gradually grafted on to us and now it is the way we plan, it is the way we do things, it is the way we speak. It is like sexism or racism before we realised. . . . It is a tribute to the power of the 'there is no alternative' mantra uttered in different ways a million times until everyone just believed it and did it. . . . Managerialism became the wallpaper of our lives.
>
> (O'Connor 2000: 4–5)

This statement captures graphically the centrality of the quasi-business discourse to the maintenance of relations of power within social work. In articulating and closing off definitions of the 'reality' of the social work business, the discourse patterns the day-to-day reality of what 'social work' now means, of what is thinkable in social work, and the terms and conditions under which social work is organised and practised. In addition, the opacity of the quasi-business discourse in social work is supported by lived experience in the wider society in which the 'business way of doing things' features increasingly strongly.

The book

In the next chapter, the characteristics of social work within the British welfare state in the pre-business era are explored. The chapter outlines the shoring up of social work's position following the implementation of the Seebohm Report (Cmnd. 3703 1968). The levels in social work's bureaucratic hierarchy are then set out as a precursor to highlighting the existence of a parochial professional culture in social work, within which social workers enjoyed a substantial degree of autonomy and discretion as 'bureau-professionals'.

Chapter 3 begins its account of the establishment of the social work business by exploring general aspects of the pressure on nation states to become more business-like and highlights the significance of the political strategies used by individual nation states to position their social welfare regimes in relation to the global economy. In this regard, the political strategy adopted by the first Thatcher government, elected in 1979, is discussed in terms of its exploitation of a perceived crisis in order to achieve major change in the British welfare state. The argument is then advanced that, against the backcloth of this wider context, the social services sphere of community care was used as the primary vehicle for the establishment of the social work business through two inter-related developments: marketisation and managerialism.

The way the social work business was run thereafter was premissed on a generic model of management, which minimised the differences between the management of capitalist enterprises and the management of public services in a new mode of 'marketised state' provision. Chapter 4 examines the diffusion of quasi-capitalist rationality, as part of a quasi-business discourse, and the consequent similarities that developed between running private sector businesses and the social work business. Managerial incursions into social work, constrained by cash limits and the intensification of competitive forces through quasi-markets, are shown to have resulted in a range of measures for controlling the activities of social workers.

By the time New Labour came to power in 1997, the context within which social work operated and the content of social work itself had changed fundamentally as a result of the establishment of the social work business. New Labour accepted the business legacy it inherited from the Conservatives and set about its modernisation. Chapter 5 identifies the origins of the modernisation programme in 'Third Way' thinking and argues that there are substantial areas of overlap between the New Right and New Labour. The modern business model, represented by 'Best Value', is outlined as a precursor to charting the modernisation of the social work business. The central significance of regulation and audit is discussed as part of the framework for reconstructing social work practice and controlling professional discretion.

In parallel with the establishment and modernisation of the social work business, a process of reform in social work education has taken place, and that reform is the subject of Chapter 6. Consolidation of external authority over social work education has reinforced, and served as another avenue for, the extension of the quasi-business discourse.

Businesses have customers, and Chapter 7 provides an account of the attempts made to create customers for the social work business, by re-imaging, or perhaps more accurately re-imagining, the people on the receiving end of social work. After considering the significance attached to the customer identity, the shift to a customer focus in the social work business is located in the Conservative reforms of the late 1980s and early 1990s and the consolidation of those reforms by New Labour. The customer base of the social work business is then scrutinised in order to discuss whether the creation of customers is a feasible and/or desirable goal.

Businesses also have supply chains. Chapter 8 reviews developments in the social work business' supply chain in so far as the voluntary sector and informal carers are concerned. Voluntary organisations have been enveloped in a new term, the 'independent sector', and have had to compete for funding against other voluntary organisations and against the commercial sector. Contractual trading relationships have subjected the sector to quasi-capitalist rationality and have eroded aspects of its distinctiveness in relation to the commercial sector. In tandem, the Conservative governments' reforms positioned caring as the core resource in packages of care. Caring arrangements in households became actively identified, publicly negotiated, carefully organised and subject to formal agreements about the scope and nature of the care provided, often with the goal of averting service provision. New Labour articulated and consolidated this shift to caring as an expression of citizenship obligation, refining its ideological basis and securing its position in the social work business supply chain.

The book concludes with an attempt to peer below the surface of the social work business, considering its personal impact on social workers, its past record and its future prospects.

2 Before the business era

Within liberal representative democratic governance regimes (Pierson 1998), mechanisms and arrangements have developed for managing the sphere of 'the social' (Donzelot 1988; Parton 1996a; Rose 1996). These include the range of institutions that came to be known collectively as 'the welfare state'. In Chapter 1 it was noted that, as part of its management of 'the social', the welfare state provides the legal authority for social work and the material conditions for its practice: social work is the operational embodiment of the welfare state's intervention in individual citizens' lives (Harris, J. 1999; White and Harris 1999). Against that backcloth, this chapter explores the characteristics of social work within the British welfare state in the pre-business era. It outlines the shoring up of social work's position following the implementation of the Seebohm Report (Cmnd. 3703 1968) The resultant levels in social work's regime in this period are then set out as a precursor to highlighting the existence of a parochial professional culture in social work, within which social workers enjoyed a substantial degree of autonomy and discretion as 'bureau-professionals'.

The welfare state in the hyphenated society

Prior to the business era in social work, social democratic commentators depicted the essence of the British post-war welfare state as lying in its distinctiveness from the market:

> A 'welfare state' is a state in which *organised power is deliberately used . . . to modify the play of market forces . . .* first, by guaranteeing individuals and families a minimum income *irrespective of the market* value of their work or their property; second, by narrowing the extent of insecurity by enabling individuals and families to meet certain 'social contingencies', for example, sickness, old age and

unemployment which lead otherwise to individual and family crises; and third, by ensuring that *all citizens without distinction of status or class* are offered the best standard available in relation to a certain agreed range of social services.

(Briggs 1961: 228; my emphasis)

The sentiments expressed by Briggs are steeped in the assumption that the services provided by the welfare state should be driven by a very different dynamic from that which drives the market. The nature of the dynamic was captured graphically in Titmuss's classic study (1970) of blood transfusion supplies, in which he argued for the moral and practical superiority of the donation principle. This distinction between the operation of the market on the one hand and the welfare state on the other was both celebrated by social democratic writers and enjoyed a broad measure of support across the parliamentary political spectrum in Britain from 1945 to 1976. In addition, identification of a demarcation line between private, commercial, market-based activities and public, non-commercial, welfare-based activities extended beyond the British social democratic tradition. For example, one of Carchedi's contributions to neo-Marxist analysis was to make a distinction between capitalist and state activities, and to further subdivide the latter into capitalist state activities and non-capitalist state activities. The basis for this sectoral classification, Carchedi (1977) argued, was that some parts of society (non-capitalist state activities) were focused on the meeting of needs outside of capitalist relations.

For social democrats and some neo-Marxists, then, private commercial and public service contexts were seen as analytically distinct. Within the public service context, Marshall (1981) argued that citizens had collective obligations for each other's welfare through the agency of the state, as a corrective to life chances based purely on market-based outcomes. If left unchecked, he reasoned, unfettered market capitalism's inability to guarantee the provision of services as of right to all citizens would lead to injustice. The inequalities of the market had to be constrained by the state in order to promote social stability, balancing the socially divisive effects of market-based inequalities by the integrative experience of social solidarity in what he termed the 'hyphenated society' of democratic-welfare-capitalism. In the hyphenated society, Marshall laid a strong stress on the hyphen between 'welfare' and 'capitalism'. There was a private *market* and there were public *services*, with the latter seen as a means of stabilising capitalism and regulating, at least to some extent, its impact on people's lives. Within this representation of public services as distinct from the market in the pre-business era, Marshall saw the concluding contribution of the twentieth century to the development of citizenship as being that of according social rights (Marshall 1950). From this perspective, Ignatieff (1991: 29) argues:

> The history of the welfare state in the twentieth century can be understood as a struggle to transform the liberty conferred by formal legal rights into the freedom guaranteed by shared social entitlement. Given the tendency of markets to generate inequality, the state was called upon by its own citizens to redress the balance with entitlements designed to keep the contradiction between real inequality and formal equality from becoming intolerable.

The post-war consensus on the hyphenated society, described by Ignatieff, resulted from the impact of the Second World War, economic collapse and a range and depth of governmental response, during and after the war, that was shaped by a conception of the state as active and responsible (Barnes and Prior 2000: 1–2). The consensus has been defined as 'the set of commitments, assumptions and expectations, transcending party conflicts and shared by the great majority of the country's political and economic leaders which provided the framework within which policy decisions were made' (Marquand 1988: 18). It underpinned the welfare state and gelled the 'totality of schemes and services through which central government together with the local authorities assumed a major responsibility for dealing with all the different types of social problems which beset individual citizens' (Marwick 1990: 45). Marshall's optimistic summary from within the post-war consensus was that welfare state provision had moved from being targeted at 'the helpless and hopeless of the population' and had been extended to all citizens through 'a convergence of principles and an integration of practices' with which all political parties concurred:

> There is a growing measure of agreement on fundamentals. It is realised that many of the old antitheses are largely imaginary. . . . There is little difference of opinion as to the services that must be provided and it is generally agreed that . . . the overall responsibility for the welfare of the citizen must remain with the state.
>
> (Marshall 1965: 97)

Marshall considered that this convergence signalled a Britain that was approaching 'the end of ideology', in an era characterised by a new understanding of community living and a willingness to share which had moved Britain from the 'naked cash nexus' to a recognition of citizens' rights (Marshall 1965: 97), thus bringing within reach his call for all citizens to be treated equally by the welfare state (Marshall 1950: 40). Consistent with this emphasis on the contribution to the hyphenated society made by the public service sector, Marshall regarded the provision of social work, through the personal social services, as one of the services which were intrinsically unsuited to delivery on the basis of principles derived from the market:

> There are some services which, with strong popular support, governments have recognised as being *intrinsically suited to organisation on the welfare principle, as public, non-profit, non-commercial services*, available to all at a uniform standard irrespective of means. They include health, education and *the personal social services. These are welfare's strongest suit and the purest expression of its identity, clearly detached from the market economy.* . . . There will always be casualties to be cared for and it will be part of the welfare state's responsibility to care for them, but, it is to be hoped, more as a personal social service than as poor relief. Welfare fulfils itself above all in those services which are its own in every sense – health, education, the personal social services.
>
> (Marshall 1981: 134–5; my emphasis)

Social work and the welfare state

In the previous section, we saw that social democratic writers in the pre-business era regarded welfare state institutions such as social work as the key to managing the tension between the democratic political system and the inegalitarian economic system. In similar vein to Marxist accounts, but reaching very different conclusions, Marshall saw welfare state services as the ransom paid by the ruling class for social stability and the maintenance of a capitalist society. Social services were regarded as the material expression of the social rights of citizenship status, which countered the social consequences of capitalism:

> By the social element I mean the whole range from the right to a modicum of economic welfare and security to the right to share to the full in the social heritage and to live the life of a civilised being according to the standards prevailing in the society. The

institutions most closely connected with it are the educational system and the social services.

(Marshall 1963: 74)

Although Marshall saw social services as closely connected to citizenship, social work joined the post-war welfare state somewhat in the shadow of its major pillars such as the National Health Service and social security. However, from the end of the Second World War the dominant professional interests in Britain saw their struggle to secure social work's legitimacy as linked to its incorporation in the welfare state (Jones 1999: 48). The range and responsibilities of social work grew through its fragmented location in different departments of local government, with administratively discrete, legislatively specific and professionally specialised services for children and families (children's departments), for people with mental health problems and learning disabilities (mental welfare services under the auspices of medical officers of health), and for older people and people with physical disabilities (welfare departments). Despite its disparate locations, social work was considered to have the potential to play a pivotal role in mediating the relationship between 'ordinary' citizens and the state:

> The social worker who does for the run of ordinary people what confidential secretaries and assistants do for the favoured few is putting a genuine professional skill at the disposal of those who may properly be called her clients and she is as essential to the functioning of a welfare state as is lubrication to the running of an engine. Without her the machinery would seize up.
>
> (Wootton 1959: 298–9)

The mechanics applying their expertise to the lubrication of the welfare state engine were professionals using their expertise in the delivery of social services (Marshall 1975: 205–6). They had a key role in identifying those citizens who required assistance and in allocating state resources to them (Alaszewski and Manthorpe 1990: 237) within social work's various organisational settings. The somewhat disjointed development of social work's spheres of influence was often represented as motivated by an evolutionary trend towards a more sympathetic approach to the welfare state's meeting of human need: 'As the accepted areas of social obligation widened, as injustice became less tolerable, new services were separately organised around individual need'

(Titmuss 1963: 21). This evolutionary trend witnessed a major mutation when social work broke out of its position as a relatively marginal and dispersed collection of roles and practices, located in separate social work services, and was transformed into a central and systematically organised element of state welfare (Clarke 1979: 127). This position was achieved through the production of the Seebohm Report (Cmnd. 3703 1968) and its implementation in the Local Authority and Allied Social Services Act (1970).

The Seebohm Report

As we have seen, for the dominant professional interests in social work the overriding goal in the pre-business era was the establishment of one discrete organisational location that would be co-terminous with professional social work. Following the acheivement of that ambition through the implementation of the Seebohm Report (Cmnd. 3703 1968), generic social work in local government Social Services Departments was the main banner under which professional social workers gathered. Structural reform of the personal social services and professional unification occurred simultaneously and, as a result, the Social Services Departments, and the Report on which they were based, were of crucial importance in shaping the nature of social work in the pre-business era.

The Seebohm Report contained a commitment to universal services, which reflected the overarching social democratic assumptions of the post-war welfare state considered in the previous section. The Seebohm committee regarded universalism as the antidote to the stigma and paternalism of administrative functions and categories of need, stemming back to the Poor Law, which the committee thought still clung to the then-existing forms of local authority social work specialisms. In seeking to overturn the Poor Law legacy, the Committee sought to transform social work by enunciating that the basis of the personal social services would be universalism:

> We recommend a new local authority department, providing a community-based and family-oriented service, which will be *available to all*. This new department will, we believe, reach far beyond the discovery and rescue of social casualties; it will enable the greatest possible number of individuals to act reciprocally, giving and receiving service for the well-being of the community.
>
> (Cmnd. 3703 1968: para. 2; my emphasis)

The universalist tone of the Report was complemented by an equally strong stress on the comprehensive nature of citizens' entitlements to social work services (Webb and Wistow 1987: 64). In contrast to the incremental accumulation of responsibilities for specific social problems by different branches of local government in the post-war period, the Seebohm committee envisaged a more generalised social democratic responsibility (Joyce *et al.* 1988: 48) for the social problems of the citizenry:

> One single department concerned with most aspects of 'welfare', as the public generally understands the term, is an essential first step in making services more easily accessible. They must not be camouflaged by administrative complexity, or their precise responsibilities closely defined on the basis of twenty year old statutes.
>
> (Cmnd. 3703 1968: para. 146)

The Seebohm Report's recommendations had the potential to consolidate and strengthen social work's position in the post-war social democratic welfare state, unshackling it from the grip of other interests, most notably the medical officers of health (Hall 1976). Sensing the increased power, status and prestige which was at stake, the political opportunity provided by the Report's publication was seized upon by proponents of the professional social work project, who campaigned and lobbied for its implementation (Hill 1993: 81), for example through the Seebohm Implementation Action Group. The subsequent unification of the institutional arrangements for social work in the form of local government Social Services Departments (in England and Wales) provided the basis for the unification of the social work profession. A generic organisational form supported the emergent notion of a generic social work task. From 1971 onwards, as previously disparate and specialised social work fields were merged after the passing of the Local Authority Social Services Act (1970), all aspects of a service user's needs were seen as amenable to the attentions of a single trained social worker. Thus, reorganisation of the personal social services and professional unification coincided in an affirmation of both managerial structures and professional claims. These developments in the pre-business era have been described as the 'high tide of social work', coming at the tail-end of the commitments of 1960s' social democracy to tackling social problems through expertise located in the state and the promotion of citizenship through solidarity (Langan 1993: 48). Whilst in this respect the Seebohm Report placed social work in the mainstream current of social democratic responses to social problems (Younghusband 1978: 35), in another respect it represented a departure from that current. One of the fresh aspects of the Seebohm Report was the influence of the rights discourse of the 1960s' New Left with, for example, the proposal for setting up 'advisory fora', with service-user representation, for social work teams. The advisory fora failed to materialise (Gyford 1991: 69) and, in the event, what emerged was a welfare state bureaucratic form of organisation was combined with a pegging out of the professional space within which social work would operate:

> In 1970 the new Social Services Departments came into being; they represented the culmination of post-war developments in social work involving, as they did, a blending of elements of profession-alism and bureaucratic organisation. Neither autonomous professionalism nor purely bureaucratic hierarchies emerged from the reorganisation. Instead the new departments were a conflation of both elements, manifesting something of the strains and complexities which such a mixture involves. This mode of organisation . . . is a hybrid, which we shall refer to as bureau-professionalism. . . . It involved a negotiated partnership between social work, attempting to organise as a profession on the one hand, and the managerial and organisational approach of the state and local authorities on the other.
>
> (Parry and Parry 1979: 42–3)

The dynamic driving the Seebohm reform of social work towards bureau-professionalism was squarely within the post-war welfare state's emphasis on public sector services for citizens, seen as superior to the operation of the market and as delivering services which the market did not, and should not, provide. It was taken for granted that the state had a dominant role to play both as the funder and the provider of social services (Pinker 1992: 273). The origins of the fusion of the roles of funder and provider in the state in the pre-business era have been seen as lying in demands for strong financial and political accountability and equity in service provision (Glennerster 1992a: 31–3; 1992b: 15–16). Accordingly, the state was viewed as the means of guaranteeing provision that was comprehensive, universal, professional, impartial and subject to the democratic political control of local authorities (Webb *et al.* 1976: 7).

The shift in mainstream social work's location to local authority Social Services Departments was therefore critical in shaping its nature in the pre-business era. In its local authority bureau-professional regime, social work brought together two key aspects of the organisation of state welfare: the rational administration of bureaucratic systems; and professional expertise in control over the content of services (Clarke and Langan 1993a: 67). Thus bureaucratic hierarchy did not necessarily represent an attack on social workers' sphere of influence: bureaucracy was compatible with considerable discretion for social workers, enabling Webb and Wistow to point to the example provided by the degree of discretion encapsulated in the survival of the therapeutic casework tradition in Social Services Departments in the post Seebohm period (Webb and Wistow 1987: 107–8). Hugman takes this argument further in identifying the possibility that social services departments' bureaucracies allowed scope for professional work not just to survive but to develop to a greater extent than previously. For example, following the implementation of the Seebohm Report, the increased allocation of resources enabled the consolidation of social work's control over its area of work (Hugman 1991a: 78). Rather than constructing an iron cage for social work, as was claimed by radical social work writers (Bailey and Brake 1975; Corrigan and Leonard 1978, Bolger *et al.* 1981; Jones 1983; Simpkin 1983), social work's location in the legislative, fiscal and organisational arrangements of the welfare state opened up its sphere of operations; the bureau-professional regime was the locus of the power exercised by social workers (Hugman 1991a: 62). This regime was stratified on a number of levels.

Levels in the bureau-professional regime

In the pre-business era, social work's bureau-professional regime was constituted on the basis of levels that were relatively autonomous from each other. These levels were:

- central government
- local government
- middle management and
- front-line management.

Central government

Central government legislation both established Social Services Departments (Local Authority Social Services Act [1970]) and, reinforced by other pieces of legislation (such as the Children and Young

Persons Act [1969] and the Chronically Sick and Disabled Act [1970]), imposed statutory duties upon them. Central government-derived statutory duties were the framework within which social work was practised. The legislation defined groups of people with 'problems' and 'needs' and, in general terms, outlined the ways in which Social Services Departments could respond to them.

Depicting the central government level of social work's bureau-professional regime in these terms runs the risk of portraying central government as simply giving instructions to local authority social services departments via legislation. However, it is clear that, in the pre-business era, there was no single coherent set of policies for the personal social services but rather streams of policy interacting, sometimes in contradictory ways (Webb and Wistow 1987: 130). These policy streams were promulgated through a variety of channels and arenas: legislation itself, white papers, policy documents, ministers' remarks and guidelines, resource planning processes. In contrast to the National Health Service and social security, social work's location in local government produced a lack of uniformity in structures and an absence of detailed national policies. Local authorities were required only to 'act under the general guidance of the Secretary of State' (Section 7, Local Authority Social Services Act [1970]) and, as a consequence, local governance led to local variation (Stewart 1983; Webb and Wistow 1987: 3). The secretary of state articulated guidance through general policy frameworks, with advice to Social Services Departments through the DHSS's Social Work Advisory Service. This Service's approach had a lightness of touch in the pre-business era, rooted in a model of reciprocity between central government and local authorities. The circular announcing its arrival gave the brief as: 'to advise local authorities, to promote the achievement of aims and the maintenance of standards and to act as *two-way channels for information and consultation between central and local government*' (quoted in Hallett 1982: 88; my emphasis).

In the pre-business era, there was, then, no notion of a direct line of command from central government dictating either the organisational structure of social work at the local authority level or the detailed policies to be implemented within and through that structure in response to legislation. Within loose overall financial controls there was room for local authority Social Services Departments to shape structures and policies within the framework of central government's legislation and general policy guidance.

Local government

If it were the case that local authorities had wide scope in the pre-business era for interpreting central government legislation, mediating between that legislation and service users (Cooper 1991), this demonstrates that social work was not only located in the social democratic context of the hyphenated society, considered earlier, but was also constructed in a local political context. Local government provided both a system of accountability for the personal social services and, as we have seen, the capacity for local choice (Stewart 1983). Local authorities were providers of services under statute but they were also political institutions which had the capacity to vary their structures, procedures and the form and level of the services they provided (Stewart 1983: vi). The internal management of departments was officer-dominated, with professional cultures of technical expertise (Stewart 1983: 18; Stewart 1989: 174; Challis 1990: 6; Laffin and Young 1990: 24). Relationships at the councillor–senior manager level in local government in this period were both deeply political and deeply professional (Cochrane 1994: 121). Webb and Wistow (1987: 63–4) suggest that within Social Services Departments, as examples of such local authority cultures, a stress on the complexity of the issues and professional autonomy was used to police the boundary between professional and political concerns. This further increased the power of senior officers and heightened day-to-day professional control.

Given that the nature of social work at the local government level was not specified in detail by central government, the latter was dependent on local government to interpret and implement legislation, with senior managers advising councillors on the policies, procedures and resources required to implement legislation in the political context of local conditions: 'The autonomy of the [local authority] employing body derives from the freedom with which they can organise their own social services' (Howe 1986: 161). Within the political process of local government, councillors and senior managers elaborated policies, allocated resources and instituted procedures to comply with statutory duties. For example, when local authorities implemented the Seebohm Report, they were not required to apply straightforwardly a detailed model of the organisational structure. Choices had to be made about the structure of each Social Services Department at the local level (Challis 1990). Further, as we saw in the previous section, in the pre-business era central government policy guidance on the implementation of specific legislation through social work was couched in general terms. Within overall legislative constraints, local authorities could make policy choices about the social work activities undertaken (and their extent and form) and organisational choices (on structures, practices and procedures).

Middle management

In the previous section, the concentration was on politicians and senior managers at the local government level in social work's bureau-professional regime. That was the level populated by those engaged in longer term policy and planning within political and financial constraints. The next section considers the front-line management level. In the pre-business era, between the front-line management level and the local government level there was a middle stratum of management concerned with the interaction between the local government level of policy and planning and the management decisions taken at the front-line level. At this intermediate level, middle managers with geographical and/or specialised responsibilities co-ordinated the implementation of policy and allocated resources, in accordance with the outcomes of the interplay between senior managers' interpretation of the social services department's legislative responsibilities and councillors' political priorities.

Front-line management

The area team was accorded a central place in Social Services Departments in the pre-business era. There was considerable delegation to this level, rather than direction of the work of area teams by centralised senior management or by middle managers. As a result, there was a high degree of autonomy, which was consistent with the proposals of the Seebohm committee concerning the importance of decentralisation and delegation:

> The important points are that the social service department can only work effectively through area teams, drawing support from the communities they serve, with a *substantial measure of delegated authority to take decisions*, and able to call on the more specialised resources, advice and support of the departmental headquarters when the need arises.
>
> (Cmnd. 3703 1968: para. 594; my emphasis)

Seebohm chose to push home the point at the press conference which launched the Committee's Report:

We attach great importance to this decentralisation, which is not just physically moving them [social workers] out from the centre and putting them into area units, but also involves *a great deal of delegation of decision-making*. I think this is the only way to make an effective service on the ground.

(Press conference transcript, 1968, reprinted in Seebohm 1989: 2–3; my emphasis)

Research findings suggested that autonomy was the order of the day for area teams. For example, in a study of a London borough's Social Services Department, Satyamurti found that team leaders did not view the wider Social Services Department as an entity to which they owed loyalty or with which they identified. There was little scrutiny of team leaders' work with social workers and they could disregard specific departmental rules without negative consequences (Satyamurti 1981: 35). Similarly, Pithouse's study of a Welsh Social Services Department found that in supervision meetings between team leaders and social workers the 'good practice' aspects of social work were looked at as much as, or more frequently than, work as viewed from a managerial point of view (Pithouse 1987: 73–4). This permissive form of supervision in social work was well-entrenched, and Pithouse (1987: 65) found that team leaders demonstrated to their teams their 'independence from higher management and their disinclination to intrude overly in the worker's day to day practice'. He stressed the existence of negotiable working arrangements in social work offices, rather than formal rules or objectives; social workers and team leaders saw themselves as definers of good practice as a result of the insulation of the area office from the rest of the department (Pithouse 1987: 47–9). Parsloe (1981: 92–3), drawing on the findings of research into the practice of 33 area teams, concluded:

Sometimes we felt that a kind of Berlin wall existed between each team and every other part of the department within which it was situated. It was particularly high and well-guarded between teams and what team members always called 'the hierarchy', which meant everyone above team leaders. . . . It was apparent that, in general, management had laid down few policy guidelines for the way teams undertook their work. Decisions about the way duty, intake and allocation were managed seemed to be made by the teams themselves. . . . Teams often appeared to make decisions in a vacuum which was seldom filled by guidance from headquarters.

Parsloe identified some of the features of the permissive culture that existed behind the 'Berlin Wall', in particular the absence of detailed forms or guidelines in relation to undertaking assessments, with no shared criteria for deciding who in the team should do what work and no shared ideas about the kind or amount of work members should undertake (Parsloe 1981: 60). She found 'little evidence of any systematic planning by supervisors to acquaint themselves with information about all the cases being supervised by individual social workers' (Parsloe and Stevenson 1978: 53) and the common pattern was for social workers to decide what they wanted to talk about in their supervision sessions. It was unusual for team leaders to even use lists of cases as a basis for keeping a check on work being done on each case (Parsloe 1981: 131).

The findings from each of these studies suggest that social workers had a substantial degree of discretion and autonomy in dealing with the idiosyncrasies of peoples' lives in the pre-business era. Parsloe and Stevenson (1978: 134) note the 'wide ranging freedom which social workers had to choose the style and content of their direct work with clients'. Their dealings were regulated predominantly not by bureaucratic procedures but by views of what constituted good professional practice (Challis 1990: 6), established through the process of supervision. Good professional practice was considered to reside in aspiring for a differentiated response to each 'client', by assessing the nature of the tasks facing her or him, making a judgement about her/his capacity and the internal and external resources available and then deciding on the most appropriate ways to seek a resolution to her/his problems (England 1986).

Parochial professionalism

Permissive supervision at the front-line management level of the bureau-professional regime was the key indicator of the existence of what might be termed 'parochial professionalism' in social work in the pre-business era (Harris 1998). This parochial professionalism had nothing to do with the grandiose aspirations to elite status and professional self-determination associated with the established professions. It was simply a way of team leaders and social workers attempting to construct a shared view of social work as a key aspect of their working relations within a bureau-professional regime. In supervision, team leaders who had been promoted on the basis of judgements made about their competence in practice stressed their seniority as practitioners, rather than their managerial position. Supervision was overwhelmingly a form of consultation on professional practice, indicating that there must have been areas of discretion and autonomy within which social workers operated (Hugman 1991a: 70). Parochial professionalism in supervision was geared to developing orientations to the personalised and discretionary nature of social workers' contact with service users, rather than the imposition of control. It gave social workers considerable discretion to define problems and the priority allocated to them, choice over their preferred methods of work and control over how they rationed their time and paced their work.

In a study undertaken in 1982, front-line managers advocated that supervision should be approached not on the basis of a superior–subordinate relationship in which they prescribed and judged social workers' practice but rather as a meeting of two colleagues. The statements quoted below, from interviews with front-line managers, give a flavour of the permissive supervision in the parochial professional culture of the pre-business era:

> My intervention would only be through consultation and discussion in the supervisory process. I try to get the individual to develop professionally. I cannot see me dropping into a situation and saying 'I'm not happy about this, this is what I want you to do'. There is a continual dialogue on cases from which decisions come.

> I see social workers as autonomous. They should accept the responsibilities they have and supervision should be sharing those situations that they feel they need to talk over. . . . You have to allow social workers their autonomy.

> Supervision is about giving people a large degree of autonomy about what they do and how they get on with their work. I can't think of an example of a worker going so obviously wrong that I've had to intervene against their wishes.

> If I was a social worker I would like to think that I was the person who knew better than my supervisor what was happening in a family situation. I would want the person to say which people had the visits. Therefore if I were to be allowed to develop in a professional way, my assessment of the situation would have to have bearing on what happens. So I don't interfere as a supervisor. I don't interfere in people's decisions because I don't find the need to.

> (Harris 1995: Ch. 7)

As the statements illustrate, these front-line managers, far from feeling that their interests or position were threatened by social workers' discretion and autonomy, represented themselves as guardians of the permissive supervision tradition in existence at that time, which carved out the space for social workers' sphere of operation. The managers saw their role as helping social workers to cultivate their craft; a craft which the managers seem to have held in high regard. As a consequence, in the parochial professional culture of the pre-business era, there do not appear to have been limitations on social workers' wide area of discretion, either from senior managers attempting to control social workers through front-line managers' supervision of them or as an outcome of any initiative by front-line managers themselves to exercise control. Rather, social workers had command over their time and, at the point of contact with service users, decided how much time to give and how it was used, the frequency with which they would meet service users, the strategy to be adopted with people with whom they were working and even, in some cases, whether they would provide a service at all.

A consistent theme is that social workers' discretion and autonomy was embodied in casework which, despite critical assault, held on to its position as the main form of practice in the pre-business era and underpinned the organisation of work in personal caseloads (Hugman 1991a: 98). As a result, as one senior manager noted, the individual social worker retained a degree of personal decision making substantially greater in terms of the consequences for the service user affected by her or his decisions than was true for most occupational groups (Bamford 1989: 155). It was this feature of social work that led Hallett to conclude that Social Services Departments represented a striking departure from the classic model of a bureaucracy because of the absence of

> a detailed system of rules and regulations for dealing with each case. Indeed, much of the activity in relation to particular cases in Social Services Departments is characterised by a high degree of discretion accorded to or assumed by the individual worker. . . . There is the discretion for the basic grade worker to decide upon the method of intervention, the aims of the work, the frequency of client contact and in many instances although not all, the decision to close the case.
>
> (Hallett 1982: 47)

Corporate management

It might be argued at this point, by any readers who lived through the pre-business era, that I have omitted a key development. Did not the establishment of Social Services Departments in 1971 occur in the wider context of the adoption of 'corporate management' in local government? Were not the organisational structures erected for the implementation of the Local Authority and Allied Social Services Act (1970) caught up in this discourse of corporatism? Benington (1976) and Cockburn (1977), for example, argue that corporate management was a system introduced into local political structures from the private sector in order to achieve centralised control, with Benington seeing its introduction as the point at which local government became big business. Both writers argue that the introduction of corporate management in local government was used to seek detailed control over all aspects of corporate functioning, and thence outwards to control the communities being served. With regard to social work, Bolger *et al.* (1981) drew on Benington (1976) and Cockburn (1977) to represent the shift to corporate management as the impetus behind the trend towards an industrial model of social work:

> This form of control, taken from capital itself, was adopted by various committees appointed to examine all aspects of public accountability and government. The overall tendency throughout was to adopt centralised and hierarchical modes of management found in capitalist enterprises.
>
> (Bolger *et al.* 1981: 57)

Corporate management was thus regarded as the means by which private management techniques had been introduced. These techniques were seen as further strengthening 'the centralised mode of control':

> The total effect of these changes in the structure of the local state was to centralise control and policy formulation . . . the centralised control of management . . . has directly reduced [local authority social workers'] autonomy. . . . The feelings of increased powerlessness experienced daily within Social Services Departments are based upon a real structural centralisation which has shifted power not only away from the base within the department, but from the Department to the Policy Advisory Committee.
>
> (Bolger *et al.* 1981: 58–9)

While it is undoubtedly the case that up until the early 1980s structural issues dominated debates about management in local government and organisational principles from the private sector were used to restructure local government, it is nevertheless important to introduce the note of caution sounded by Smith *et al.* about the degree of fit that was achieved between private industry and local government in the pre-business era. With echoes of Carchedi's sectoral classification, discussed earlier, they suggest that the non-capitalist nature of some public sector organisations meant that attempts to incorporate solutions from the private sector resulted in an 'approximate fit, contested and competing with a service ideology and wider political practices that go beyond the criteria of profitability. . . . When examining work within the public sector it is important to incorporate an awareness of its distinctive characteristics' (Smith *et al.* 1991: 2–3). This can be illustrated through a consideration of the circumstances in which corporate management was introduced, the extent to which corporatism was achieved and corporate management's attendant contradictions.

From the 1960s onwards the need to reorganise the organisational structures of local government was a source of considerable debate. Existing local authority departments were depicted as insular, jealously guarding their specialised responsibilities through senior professionals linked into national policy networks. The management of departments by professional experts and administrators was the antithesis of the council-wide approach to management sought by corporate reformers (Cochrane 1994: 144). The managerial reforms were

> aimed at creating administrative and management systems in place of what were identified as archaic and ramshackle systems which had developed over the previous 150 years and whose lack of integration presented a major stumbling block to the efficient coordination and management of public services.
>
> (Clarke and Langan 1993b: 41)

Although attempts at reform had gathered pace from the 1960s onwards (Leach *et al.* 1994: 26–9), it was the reorganisation of local government in 1974, with the setting up of new local authorities, which provided the opportunity to tackle what was regarded as petty departmentalism (Cochrane 1994: 145). It was believed that the larger authorities responsible for the bulk of service provision would result in more effective management through the public sector adaptation of private business wisdom. Large private sector corporations with corporate management systems were regarded as the best-integrated and most cost-effective organisational form. Such corporations provided the model for developing local government approaches to long-term planning and the allocation of resources (Clarke and Langan 1993b: 43–4; Cochrane 1994: 145). The Bains Report (1972), in particular, provided the basis for the management structure and processes to be adopted following the 1974 local government reorganisation. In implementing that reorganisation three common elements appeared in local government: a policy and resources committee with responsibility for authority-wide policies and bargaining about resource allocation; a reduced number of service committees and departments with wider remits, compared with the 1950s and 1960s, a trend which began with the creation of Social Services Departments; a chief executive convening a management team of chief officers to discuss authority-wide or cross-departmental issues and to advise the policy and resources committee. It was these elements, as we have just seen (pp. 25–26) that were seized upon by Benington (1976) and Bolger *et al.* (1981) as evidence of dramatic changes in the management of local government.

However, although these common elements of a corporate management approach were put in place, local structures and practices varied considerably within the framework provided by them (Elcock 1993: 153). In addition, it is all too easy to exaggerate the significance of corporate management as a sharp break with the past. Surviving within the façade of corporate management was the bureaucratic paternalism characteristic of the post-war social democratic settlement (Crewe 1982; Hoggett and Hambleton 1987), with corporate management as an outward semblance of co-ordination in the formulation of long-term strategy (Webb and Wistow 1987: 219). Even these limited organisational efforts to pursue corporate management were regarded as too cumbersome, and they were in decline by the end of the 1970s (Greenwood *et al.* 1980). Attempts at private sector corporation-style management were thus short-lived (in the sense of ongoing management of the full range of activities across the local authority), as the power of individual departments, and their links into national policy networks, were maintained. What remained was a corporate planning cycle for setting general objectives and reviewing progress towards them, which did not challenge existing local authority assumptions (Leach *et al.* 1994: 33). Leach *et al.* (pp. 70–2) concluded that the corporate management approach in local government was concerned solely with the extent to which the 'building blocks were moved about', leaving local authority strategies and cultures untouched:

The degree of real change was limited, reflecting the difference between the relative ease of changing the structure of the organisation and the much greater difficulty of changing the culture. The new positions and approaches were added to the traditional system rather than the system being transformed.

(Ibid.: 109)

In this context, the corporate planning cycle provided a site for negotiations between chief officers over resource allocation, through the traditional incremental budgetary process. On that site, the contest waged was over the allocation of growth to departments, not corporate direction (Friend and Jessop 1969; Cochrane 1994: 146–8): 'Although the language of general local government acts and constitutional discussion tended to define local authorities as unitary multi-functional agencies, the closer one moved to the practice of individual departments the less appropriate such a construction appeared' (Cochrane 1994: 151). This was particularly the case for Social Services Departments engaged in marking out their distinctiveness in local government.

The preceding discussion suggests the need for caution in any assessment of the precise impact of corporate management. However, we can go further. A contradiction bound up with corporate management's transference from the private sector into the public sector concerned its potential to further politicise local government, a contradiction unexplored in the view of local government having become 'big business' (Benington 1976) by this stage. The tendency towards greater politicisation stemmed from the attempts at greater co-ordination and integration within corporate management. Departmental fragmentation, poor co-ordination of policies and service provision and the inefficient use of resources were issues addressed in local government in this era (Greenwood and Stewart 1974; Joyce *et al.* 1988: 62): differentiation and departmentalism 'were to be matched by mechanisms capable of integrating the work of the authority' (Greenwood 1983: 167; and see Elcock 1993). As a consequence of the attempt at greater integration, there were pressures for increased acceptance of a governmental role by local authorities (Greenwood and Stewart 1974). A subsequently neglected emphasis in the Bains Report (1972) is that given to the need to shift from local administration to local government:

Local government is not, in our view, limited to the narrow provision of a series of services to the local community, though we do not intend in any way to suggest that these services are not important. It has within its purview the overall economic, cultural and physical well-being of that community and for this reason its decisions impinge with increasing frequency upon the individual life of its citizens.

(Bains Report 1972: 6)

In similar vein, the Maud Report (1967: paras 200, 607–8) had earlier called for the relaxation of specific statutory duties on local authorities in favour of granting them general competence to undertake what in their opinion was in the interests of their areas and their inhabitants. Rather than obscuring politics in corporate management (Benington 1976), it can be argued that through these injunctions to local authorities – first, to reject seeing themselves as simply carrying out the functions allotted to them by central government and then to accept that local government had a wider responsibility for the communities they served – corporate management had a contradictory tendency to prompt greater politicisation at the local level.

With the benefit of hindsight, the significance of corporate management was overrated and its implementation overstated. Even where its influence was felt, it is important to remember that corporate management was aimed at bolstering rather than dismantling the social democratic welfare state (Cochrane 2000: 123–6).

Conclusion

We have seen that, in the pre-business era, social work was firmly embedded in the social democratic welfare state, as a component in the 'hyphenated society' of democratic-welfare-capitalism:

The citizen [was] constructed as a member of a political community whose interests [were] collectively expressed by the system of governance reflected in the state. The citizen, by becoming a member of the body politic, establishe[d], along with other citizens, a general, collective or public will. This regime of governance provided the fundamental rationale for why the state undertook . . . the provision of services . . . delivered . . . by social workers. . . . The model of government operationalised in an active welfare state provided both a niche and a role for the occupation of social work.

(McDonald and Jones 2000: 8–9)

Following the implementation of the Seebohm Report (Cmnd 3703 1968), social work's niche shifted from a range of specialised social work services in local government to a drawing together of those specialisms into a local authority bureau-professional regime. That regime had a number of relatively autonomous levels. The professional discretion and autonomy of social workers were privileged through permissive supervision at the front-line management level, which nurtured the practice of social work as a parochial professional 'craft'. Thus, social work in this era has all of the characteristics of the 'public administration model': a bureaucratic structure, professional dominance, accountability to the public, equity of treatment and self-sufficiency (Butcher 1995: 2–7).

The discussion has drawn particular attention to the position of social workers as professionals in this model. Faith in the expertise of professionals, exercised through public service, enjoyed cross-party political support and was a cornerstone of the post-war social democratic consensus. The welfare state was a professional state, with professionals mediating between the state and citizens. In the absence of market forces and competition, professionals were accorded a substantial measure of 'responsible autonomy' (Friedman 1977) in the allocation of resources and the application of professional knowledge (Duff and Larsen 2000). Thus, the professional space occupied by social work in the pre-business era insulated it from the market and from political intrusion, with the professional clearly distinguished from the manager and the politician (Keat 1991). The welfare state's reliance on insulated professionals was a key facet of social work's location in the legislative, fiscal and organisational base of the social democratic welfare state, particularly following the implementation of the Seebohm Report (Cmnd. 3703 1968). In that sense, Social Services Departments did not represent the classic conflict between bureaucratic employment and professional organisation. Having a clear main organisational location for the employment of social workers in social services departments defined and strengthened their spheres of competence and jurisdiction, and protected them from encroachment by and competition with members of other professions (Anleu 1992: 23–5). The legitimacy of social work increased, as the compatibility of interest between government's and professional social work's objectives became clear. The occupational focus of the argument for a unified social work profession was achieved through organisational means, thus ensuring that 'organisation and professionalism were inescapably linked' (Hugman 1991b: 200), in three key elements of professional activity – expertise, credentialism and autonomy (Freidson 1994). Those elements were focused on the project of establishing an exclusive area of jurisdiction and expertise for social work, in concert with the construction of a field of operation within which social work was portrayed as possessing legitimate knowledge (see Ch. 6) that allowed it to intervene on behalf of the welfare state (Fournier 2000: 69–77).

The key features of social work in the pre-business era have been outlined in this chapter as a baseline against which to discuss subsequent developments in the social work business in the succeeding chapters. Chapter 3 begins that discussion by considering the establishment of the business.

3   Establishing the business

The account of the establishment of the social work business begins by exploring general aspects of the pressure on nation states to become more business-like and highlights the significance of the political strategies used by individual nation states to position social welfare in relation to the global economy. In this regard, the political strategy adopted by the first Thatcher government, elected in 1979, is discussed in terms of its exploitation of a perceived crisis in order to achieve major change in Britain. Against the backcloth of this wider context, the social services sphere of community care was used as the primary vehicle for the establishment of the social work business through two inter-related developments: marketisation and managerialism.

The post-Fordist welfare state

The framework most frequently employed to describe changes in social welfare since the 1970s has been the 'mixed economy of welfare'. This framework has been used to chart accounts of the changing patterns of social welfare delivery. Analysis of these changes within wider theoretical perspectives, which position social welfare developments in relation to economic forces and changes in the state, has been less pronounced. The post-Fordist welfare state thesis has attempted to articulate such links between economic forces, state forms and social welfare. It locates changes in social welfare within a wider analysis of the transformation of capitalist societies in response to the demands of the global economy. Although post-Fordist ideas vary significantly, they are united in their identification of distinctive historical periods in the development of capitalist societies represented by the shift from 'Fordism' to 'post-Fordism'. Within this school of thought, the analysis of the Fordist era has identified a set of socio-economic arrangements linking together the welfare state and the mass production and consumption of standardised goods and services. In contrast, the post-Fordist era is seen as resulting in the restructuring of the economy and the welfare state in the interests of flexible production and diversified consumption. This era is regarded as signalling fundamental socio-economic change, triggered by the economic crisis of the mid-1970s. The post-Fordist welfare state thesis has been the subject of much academic debate (see, for example, Burrows and Loader 1994), and its preoccupations have also entered everyday political discourse:

> [Western governments] urge us to come to terms with the fact that the competitive life is nasty and brutish and that we are immersed in a life or death struggle for economic survival. In this struggle, the old ideas which ruled the modern welfare state – universality, full employment, increasing equality – are proclaimed to be a hindrance to survival. They are castigated as ideas which have out-lived their usefulness: they are no longer appropriate to the conditions of a global capitalist economy where investment, production, labour and consumption are all characterised by flexibility, transience and uncertainty.
>
> (Leonard 1997: 113)

One of the key aspects of these developments in the post-Fordist era is the subordination of social welfare measures within nation states to the creation of conditions that will ensure international competitiveness in the global economy, with a consequent diminution of autonomy for nation states in determining social policy (Jessop 1994; Deacon *et al*. 1997; Mishra 1999). Pressures are exerted on governments by business interests to accept responsibility for national competitiveness and to see the interests of business as the same as the national interest (Flynn 2000: 33). Reappraisal of the welfare state has thus been linked to the maintaining of the conditions necessary for profitability in order to avert capital flight and to attract new investment from multinational corporations and international finance capital. Castles and Pierson (1996) see this as the emergence of a nation state convergence theory in order to account for the retreat from social welfare provision by nation states, disempowered by the global market and pursuing reforms to their welfare states in a uniform direction. Central to implementing this process of reappraisal and reform is managerialism, or 'new public management', which, it has been argued, is a European (George 1998: 28–9) and a worldwide phenomenon (Hood 1991a).

However, while the general trend in nation states' responses to globalisation may show signs of uniformity, distinctive political strategies have been adopted in relation to the transformation of social policy and of particular social welfare services in individual countries. The main body of this chapter is concerned with tracking the strategies of the Conservative governments in relation to the positioning of Britain as a player in the global economic context and the consequences of those strategies for the restructuring of social work. (The response of the Labour governments is considered in Chapter 5.)

Conservative strategy

Of all the European social welfare regimes, that of the British welfare state under Thatcher and Major was the regime most exposed to the New Right agenda of privatisation, liberalisation and deregulation. The dominating vision was of a deregulated, weakly unionised, flexible, low-wage, low-taxation economy in which the state would devote a decreasing percentage of the national wealth on public expenditure, providing the individual entrepreneur and the global corporation with open markets for their products (Lee 1997: 107–8). Three principles were of paramount importance: limiting public expenditure; the pursuit of efficiency, economy and effectiveness; and the intrinsic superiority of the market in the provision and delivery of welfare (Spicker 1995: 96–7). A fundamental incompatibility was perceived between the market economy and social welfare provision. In the cause of reviving economic growth, taxes were lowered, the goal of full employment was abandoned and the economy was deregulated (Mishra 1993: 23). In this strategic context, the central significance of Conservative rule for social work was the establishment of the social work business, making the operation of social work as similar as possible to that of a private sector business.

From consensus to crisis

During the 1960s, gross domestic product increased, public expenditure and public services expanded and average personal incomes rose, in the context of full employment, low inflation and steady, if slow, economic growth. In the 1970s, inflation increased dramatically, unemployment reached inter-war depression levels, the balance of payments worsened and the value of the pound against the dollar declined, leading to economic conditions of low growth and high inflation; so-called 'stagflation'

(Zifcak 1994: 7–8). Conditions of stagflation lent themselves to the portrayal of public services as non-productive and a drain on the wealth-producing parts of the economy (Flynn 1993: xii). As a result, the post-war consensus (see Ch. 2) came under siege, particularly in the wake of the economic crisis in 1976, following the quadrupling of oil prices in 1973 at the instigation of the Organisation of Petroleum Exporting Countries. In the aftermath of the subsequent recessions in the West, the effects on the welfare state were widely discussed (see, for example, George and Wilding 1984; Mishra 1984; Taylor-Gooby 1985). In Britain £2.5 billion had, within a single year, been added to the current account deficit, the cost of living had increased by 10 per cent and gross domestic product had declined by 5 per cent (Healey 1989: 434). With Britain's currency reserves endangered by the mounting economic crisis, the International Monetary Fund granted a loan in 1976 on condition that severe cuts were made in public expenditure and that a policy of wage restraint was introduced. As part of the expenditure cuts, the Labour government set about reducing the total amount of local government spending. Its approach was to seek to influence and consult with local government rather than to control local government directly or to intervene in the spending plans of individual local authorities, all of which was to come later under Conservative governments (Alexander 1982: 104; Elcock *et al.* 1989: 28; Rhodes 1992: 53). As the Labour government's strategy took effect, the winter of 1978–9 became infamous as the 'winter of discontent', with massive trades union action, which included social workers, in response to the curbing of pay demands and cuts to the 'social wage' through public expenditure restraint. With rubbish piled high in the streets and bodies unburied, British society was presented in the media as on the verge of collapse, under a Labour government that had lost control (particularly of the unions with which it was associated) and lacked any sense of direction.

This was the immediate context in which the first Thatcher government was elected, in May 1979. It inherited and exploited a public perception of a social and fiscal crisis in welfare provision, despite the Labour chancellor of the exchequer's protestations that the loan from the International Monetary Fund had been paid off by the time the Labour government left office (Healey 1989: 434). The Conservatives' economic policy was to control the rate of monetary growth, bring down the public sector borrowing requirement, lower taxation with the aim of providing incentives for investment and implement public expenditure cuts to allow reductions in borrowing and taxation.

Three inter-related dimensions of Conservative policy were presented as the response to a 'nation in crisis':

> a strategy of de-regulation of labour markets and promotion of a low wage, low skill economy as a means of attracting inward investment; competitive tendering and internal markets in the public sector; and the sustained legislative assault on union organisation, employment rights and collective bargaining.
>
> (Thompson and Ackroyd 1995: 618)

As a result of this overall strategic direction, by the time the Thatcher government began to turn its attention to social welfare services in a sustained way, many of the technical and political issues had already been rehearsed in the industrial sphere (Drakeford 2000: 20). The critique of the public sector was intense, with ferocious attacks on the welfare state on ideological and economic grounds. The public perception of a fiscal crisis enabled the Thatcher government to depict welfare provision as too expensive for the state's tax base to support, as squeezing out private sector investment and as undermining (through its demands for taxation support) entrepreneurial and managerial incentives. In attacking the welfare state as economically mismanaged, prone to induce dependence and needing to be trimmed if Britain were to succeed in the global economy, the newly elected Conservative government saw itself as beginning to correct the failings of the post-war consensus, in which social work was considered to be deeply implicated. The welfare state's fiscal and legitimacy crises (O'Connor 1973; Offe 1983, 1984) were focused into a sharp attack, which was characterised by antipathy to large bureaucracies and the planning of services, and an ideological commitment to privatisation and the extension of the market (Taylor-Gooby and Lawson 1993a: 1).

This critique of the welfare state predisposed Thatcher governments to take a sceptical view of social workers and local authority social services departments (Loney 1986: 142; Jones and Novak 1993). Social work was a key component in the Conservatives' depiction of the social democratic welfare state's services in the pre-business era as bureaucratic and insensitive to individual needs (Wilding 1992). In this context it has been argued that social work became the metaphor for what was considered to be wrong with the welfare state (Midgley and Jones 1994: 118), and two of social work's severest critics questioned whether social work could survive as the 'nanny state' was demolished (Brewer and Lait 1980). Other commentators saw a role for social work in subjecting the citizens of the 'nanny state' to a coercive process of moral re-armament, in order to re-acquaint them with their caring responsibilities:

> Society rightly feels that elderly parents and relatives . . . are the responsibility of next-of-kin to help. The same is true of handicapped children. . . . Neglect of these family responsibilities should be actionable by the state. . . . Social services are necessary, just as police are necessary, to maintain law and order. The logical action to take is therefore for such responsibilities to be made legally mandatory just as child battering or child neglect are penalised by the law.
>
> (Minford 1984: 133)

Although such sentiments did not find their way into concrete proposals in the Thatcher government's legislative programme, their articulation by Minford, as an advisor to the Thatcher government, nevertheless gives a flavour of the social policy debate in this period; a debate in which the welfare state was castigated as a prime contributor to Britain's economic decline through its misallocation of resources, its sapping of individual responsibility and its production of a dependent citizenry. New Right academics such as Minford were presumably useful to the Thatcher government in making acceptable its more 'moderate' views as social work came under increasing attack (Jones and Novak 1993), and four themes came to prominence:

> Firstly, that the delivery agencies of the welfare state were inefficient, wasteful and unbusinesslike with a lack of concern for efficiency and value for money; secondly, that welfare delivery agencies were provider dominated and paid insufficient attention to the needs and wants of the users of their services; thirdly, that the institutions of welfare delivery and their personnel were not close enough to their users or customers; and, fourthly, that the delivery agencies of the welfare state were not sufficiently accountable.
>
> (Butcher 1995: 7)

Consistent with these themes, four developments were identified as essential to the transformation of social work:

- the introduction of market mechanisms;
- the promotion of competition leading to efficiency gains and savings;

- the keeping of state provision to a minimum; and
- the pursuit of individualism and individual choice (Flynn 1993: 14–15).

The sense of crisis was moving inexorably towards a process of change.

From crisis to change

In the first two Thatcher administrations, from 1979 to 1987, what in retrospect look like fairly cautious moves were made to cut back budgetary allocations to social work. For example, government expenditure forecasts for 1980–81 indicated a cut of 6.7 per cent in real terms for the personal social services, but local authorities used their relative autonomy from central government control (see Ch. 2) to protect those services and hold spending at pre-existing levels (Webb and Wistow 1982). Having already been thwarted in this way by local authorities, the Conservative government was faced with massive Labour Party gains in local elections in the early 1980s. The gains threatened to continue to constrain the actions of central government. In addition, these 'urban Left' Labour local authorities experimented with new forms of decentralised provision, which were more responsive to service-user needs, as an attempt to develop policies and provision that would win the support of local people and that could be adopted nationally on the return to power of a Labour government. This brief period of experimentation was curbed by a severe reduction in the grants made from central to local government and limitations on local government powers to raise any consequent shortfall in expenditure through local taxation. (The Rates Act [1984] made it illegal for local government to set taxation rates above a level determined for each individual local authority by central government.) Having reduced the scope of local government's financial independence, central government actively pursued its policies through the Audit Commission and, in the case of social work, the Social Services Inspectorate. The Audit Commission, set up in 1983 following the Local Government Finance Act (1982), encouraged the emergence of a strong management culture (Kelly 1992) in Social Services Departments. It reinforced moves towards managerialism by suggesting that generic expertise in accountancy and management was powerful enough to question professional practice across the board (Cochrane 1994: 127). The Commission extended its role to broader judgement of performance in using resources, captured in the phrase 'value for money', thus moving beyond an emphasis on accounting. In pursuing value for money, it promoted the virtues of the three 'E's:

> *Economy* means ensuring that the assets of the authority, and the services purchased, are procured and maintained at the lowest possible cost consistent with a specified quality and quantity.
>
> *Efficiency* means providing a specified volume and quality of services with the lowest level of resources capable of meeting that specification.
>
> *Effectiveness* means providing the right services to enable the local authority to implement its policies and objectives.
>
> (Audit Commision 1983: 8)

In tandem, the Social Services Inspectorate replaced the Social Work Advisory Service in 1985 and took on the role of ensuring the implementation of central government's policies in relation to social work (Day and Klein 1990: 27). The Conservative government's monitoring of local authorities' compliance with central government policy and its constraints on local government expenditure constricted the freedom to pursue policies at local government level that were substantially different from those of central government:

> The more the balance of power shifted towards central government in the 1980s, the more it was able to insert its own values, methods and language into the new management practices and the more difficult it became for local institutions to shape new methods into their own image and for their own purposes.
>
> (Burns *et al.* 1994: 85)

After the Conservatives won the 1987 election, the attempts at shaping policy through financial control and monitoring policy implementation at the local level were augmented by a radical legislative programme to

- further limit expenditure;
- break up public provision;
- increase the scope of commercial sector operations;
- bring in business management principles to what remained of the public sector; and
- reduce the power of welfare state professionals (Jones 1994: 190, 205).

Jessop argues that this initiative by the third Thatcher government was a key aspect of the Conservative political project:

> [S]uccessive Conservative governments pursued a distinctive neo-liberal strategy intended to marketise social relations and create an enterprise culture so that individuals could operate in (and embrace) a market-oriented society. Such a strategy clearly cannot be confined to the (expanding) market economy alone; it must also be extended to the whole ensemble of social institutions, organisations, networks, and norms of conduct which regularise economic relations. This all-embracing tendency is especially clear from 1986 onwards when a near-fatally drifting Thatcher regime rescued itself with a wide-ranging radical programme to re-invigorate civil society as well as regenerate the economy and restructure the state. . . . This extended key elements of the neo-liberal accumulation strategy and also supplemented them by an ambitious hegemonic project for the wider society. What had pre-viously been hesitant and halting accompaniments of economic regeneration were accelerated and given a more coherent ideo-logical justfication. . . . For the public sector, it [involved] privati-sation, liberalisation, and an imposition of commercial criteria in any residual state sector.
>
> (Jessop 1994: 29–30)

This added twist to the Thatcherite programme encompassed funda-mental changes in the arrangements for local government services that were seen as revolutionary (Audit Commission 1988: 1). Shortly after-wards, as part of these wider arrangements, social work's future was set out. It was to take a different form and to be placed in a different context shaped by the Children Act (1989) and the National Health Service and Community Care Act (1990). Of these two Acts, it was the National Health Service and Community Care Act (1990) that became the primary vehicle for accomplishing the transformation of the culture of social work and the establishing of the social work busi-ness. The promotion of a new policy direction in community care, embodying a market framework, was integral to the Conservative government's radical reform of the welfare state and the reduction of Social Services Departments' role in service provision (Baldock and Evers 1991, 1992). As the social work business was established, the role of the state as a direct provider of services was to diminish, to be replaced by the roles of enabler, subsidiser and regulator. Thus an over-arching concern of the Conservative government as it set up the social work business in the late 1980s and early 1990s, was to move social work as close to market conditions as possible. Although the business initiative was seized originally in the sphere of community care, the restructuring of social work that ensued had ramifications across the board.

The business of community care

Although community care was ostensibly a policy direction adopted by successive governments from the 1950s onwards, it was only when the policy was interlinked with establishing the social work business, and was jolted into a change of direction in favour of the market from the mid-1980s onwards, that it received new impetus. In this period, a number of influential reports were published (for example, House of Commons Social Services Select Committee 1985; Audit Commission 1986; Griffiths Report 1988; Wagner Report 1988; Cm. 849 1989), culminating in the National Health Service and Community Care Act (1990). At a general level, the promotion of a new direction in community care, one which embodied a market framework, was integral to the radical project of establishing the social work business. Consistent with this business orientation, the immediate incentive was economic. It was only when community care policy development was linked to ways of containing public expenditure that far-reaching change was initiated.

A specific expenditure crisis had arisen from the public funding of commercially provided residential care, following a massive increase in social security payments to support residents in private sector residential and nursing homes (Audit Commission 1986: para. 90). Under arrangements introduced by the Conservative government in 1980, the social security system paid the board and lodging costs of people with assets of under £3,000. As a result, in many circumstances the easiest service provision to arrange for a person who needed day-to-day support was a place in a commercial residential home at central government's expense. The growth in the number of homes financed in this way was unprecedented. An influential report by the Audit Commission pointed out that, as a result, a 'perverse incentive' operated against the policy of community care: resources which could have been used for care in the community were locked up in costly residential provision, as central government stimulated the development of private sector residential care through this social security-funded arrangement for payment (Audit Commission 1986). From 1979 to 1990, as the number of places in private residential homes for older people increased from 37,000 to 98,000, central government expenditure increased from £10 million to £1.2 billion (Oldman 1991: 4–5).

As a result of the much-publicised 'perverse incentive' identified by the Audit Commission (1986), Sir Roy Griffiths, a supermarket executive and an advisor on health and welfare to the Conservative government, was invited to report on the financing of, and arrangements for, community care. The resultant Griffiths Report (1988)

> was essentially a single-handed effort characterised by speed, a lack of consultation and the need for a brief report. The process of reform in the community care proposals was an example of the new style adopted by the Thatcher government and a break with the long established tradition in British public policy of the use of committees in formulating and shaping policy.
>
> (Hallett 1991: 285)

Griffiths's terms of reference required him to focus on the business-like utilisation of resources rather than their adequacy, with the assumption that he would provide an appraisal stemming from ideas about generalist management which had shaped his earlier work on the National Health Service. He had been asked 'to review the way in which public funds are used to support community care policy and to advise the Secretary of State on the options for action which would improve the use of these funds as a contribution to more effective community care' (Griffiths Report 1988: 1).

Cutler and Waine's comment (1994: 5) on the Griffiths Report on the NHS could be as easily applied to Griffiths' Report on community care. In noting the previous report's abstract quality, they stated:

> The reader would learn much more about the views of the author on management, organisation, structure and control than on substantive issues arising from the services themselves. This is in fact a crucial feature of managerialism. The central issue is the form of management adopted; the activity being managed is at best a secondary matter.

The legislation which followed the Griffiths Report (1988) on community care demonstrated the government's determination to cease the open-ended social security commitment to funding residential care and promoted as an alternative a mixed market of care in which local authority Social Services Departments would be enablers rather than providers, co-ordinating and purchasing care rather than providing services directly. The NHS and Community Care Act (1990) gave this gate-keeping role to Social Services Departments in specifying that it was for the local authority to decide whether and how to meet need. Resources for this role were derived from the transfer to Social Services Departments of the funds for the care element in the social security support to residential homes, in the form of a special transitional grant to local government. (This was not new funding, and in addition many Social Services Departments found themselves implementing the NHS and Community Care Act [1990] in the context of wider local government budget cuts.) The implementation of the NHS and Community Care Act (1990) changed fundamentally the operation of Social Services Departments and the practice of social work. It spearheaded the establishment of the social work business through two inter-related developments: marketisation and managerialism.

Marketisation

The Conservative government's starting assumption for the introduction of market mechanisms into social work was that capitalist enterprise is more economical, efficient and effective than the public sector in providing services. This assumption stemmed from the belief that competition produces efficient services in which prices decrease while quality increases as a result of the market system requiring service providers to compete for contracts. The radical changes in social work were marked indelibly by the encapsulation of this belief in a 'quasi-market' arrangement (Le Grand 1993), with cash-limited budgets, purchaser–provider splits, contracting out, the use of independent agencies and more widespread use of charges. The welfare state became primarily a funder, with individual service-user budgets given to – or, more commonly, recommendations for expenditure from those budgets made by – a social worker (often redesignated a 'care manager') and the allocation of those budgets between competing suppliers.

Quasi-markets differ from 'pure' markets in a number of important respects. On the supply side, there is competition between service suppliers; but, in contrast with pure markets, suppliers are not necessarily privately owned, nor are they necessarily required to make profits. On the demand side, consumer purchasing power resides not in cash but in a budget confined to the purchase of a specific service, and the service user does not exercise the final choice concerning purchasing decisions; these are delegated to the social worker/care manager (Le Grand 1990). Despite such artificiality, the quasi-market is a key concept in the quasi-business discourse. Were social work to think of itself as though it were a business, then having a market with which it had to deal was crucial to the instillation of that thinking.

The degree of shift involved is indicated in the powerful political legitimation function the quasi-market performed for the Conservative government. Market outcomes are neither fair nor unfair. They are either the result of the operation of impersonal market forces or they stem from the body responsible for gatekeeping access to the market – in the case of social work, the local authority. As such, quasi-markets offered the possibility of central government holding at arm's length the responsibility for the outcomes of its social welfare policy (Taylor-Gooby and Lawson 1993b: 136; Jones 1994: 189–90).

The introduction of quasi-markets in social work, initially in the sphere of community care but later developing in a range of other services such as foster care and children's homes, made a significant contribution to establishing the social work business, for a number of reasons.

First, marketisation undermined the sense in which social services had represented a counterbalance to market values during the post-war consensus on welfare (see Ch. 2):

> Marketisation may be seen as one among many examples of the New Right's antagonism towards the decommodifying aspects of the welfare state. It is intended to challenge the, albeit limited, extent to which the social services intrude on market values and threaten their reproduction by promoting citizenship rights and needs-based priorities.
>
> (Walker 1989: 216)

Second, marketisation was intended to introduce competition among service providers. At first, the Thatcher government concentrated on extending market forces in health, education, pensions and housing (Le Grand and Robinson 1984; Papadakis and Taylor-Gooby 1987), with social work coming towards the end of the Conservative administration's strong commitment to a common policy of market-oriented reform across a range of services (Le Grand 1993). When it turned to social work, the Conservative government instigated market arrangements by stipulating that 85 per cent of the funds transferred to local authorities from central government's social security system for community care services had to be spent on the independent sector (Department of Health 1992: Annex C, para. 3). This was consistent with the concerns of the White Paper *Caring for People* (Cm. 849 1989), preceding the NHS and Community Care Act (1990), which stated that one of the key objectives of the reform of community care was to promote the development of a 'flourishing independent sector'

(Cm. 849 1989: para 1.11) and that Social Services Departments should 'make clear in their community care plans what steps they will be taking to make increased use of non-statutory providers, or where such providers are not currently available, how they propose to stimulate such activity' (Cm. 849 1989: para. 3.4.5). This point was reiterated in subsequent policy guidance (Department of Health 1990), with Social Services Departments being expected to make clear how they proposed to stimulate market activity where independent providers were not available. *Caring for People* set out ways in which Social Services Departments could promote a market by setting clear service specifications, stimulating the independent sector and floating off some of their own units (Cm. 849 1989: para. 3.4.6). Promoting such a market was seen by the Conservative government as essential to the development of competitive cost-effective services (Social Services Inspectorate 1991a: para. 1; 1991b: para. 1). Given that Social Services Departments were accorded a central role in promoting quasi-markets, any which were resistant to this role were encouraged to overcome their inhibitions by a government report commissioned from a firm of accounting consultants, while the commercial care industry, predominantly located in the residential sector, was encouraged to diversify (Department of Health–Price Waterhouse 1991).

The third contribution made by quasi-markets to establishing the social work business was the introduction of the purchaser–provider split, the theoretical origins of which lie in agency theory (Alford and O'Neill 1994). In the purchaser–provider split, control resides with the 'principal' (purchaser) who has the power to make decisions and see them carried through. The 'agent' (provider) has to implement the principal's decisions. This centralises strategic control while decentralising responsibility for service delivery (Muetzelfeldt 1992). The clear separation in the roles of principal and agent, required by the purchaser–provider split, was implemented through the use of service specifications and contracts. These provided a graphic indication of the cultural shift involved in establishing the social work business.

Fourth, the purchaser–provider split assumes that the principal and agent have clearly distinct interests and act on the basis of those distinct interests. The introduction of service specifications and contracts reinforced, indeed often generated, these different interests and provided strong incentives for acting in accordance with self-interest. Money began to be exchanged for the delivery of services – defined in terms of specific services for individual service users or for specified groups of service users – with little shared involvement with potential providers in determining the service specification on which the contracts were based. In other words, contracts assumed that purchaser and provider did not share common interests (Muetzelfeldt 1994). This was an intended consequence of establishing the social work business in this way and was seen as essential to the destruction of the cosy, self-serving collaboration which was alleged to characterise social work's bureau-professional regime in the pre-business era (see Ch. 2). With the introduction of contracts, the purchaser was to control the agenda in terms of who should receive a (tightly specified) service. The specification of outputs, usually expressed quantitatively, was to result in increased bureaucratic activity for the purchaser and the provider in terms of record keeping in relation to task completion and financial arrangements.

This consideration of the significant emphasis placed on marketisation in establishing the social work business has illustrated some of the new responsibilities allocated to social work in Social Services Departments at a time when those departments had little or no experience of operating in a market context. However, they had both to define their new role in the quasi-market and to engage in a corresponding process of substantial change in their internal organisational culture, shaped by managerialisation.

Managerialisation

As elsewhere in the restructuring of the welfare state, a key component in shifting social work in line with market forces was managerialism (Pollitt 1990; Clarke *et al.* 1994). Bureau-professional regimes (see Ch. 2) were regarded by the Conservatives as a barrier that had to be surmounted if the reconstruction of the state's role in welfare were to be achieved (Clarke and Newman 1993: 48–9; Clarke *et al.* 1994: 3; Newman and Clarke 1994: 23). Managerialism was regarded as a dynamic transformative process capable of demolishing the lingering welfare structures of the post-war consensus. It was the means through which the structure and culture of social work were to be recast (Clarke *et al.* 1994: 4) into the mould of the social work business. The generic model of management that was promoted regarded private sector practices as applicable to the public sector; it claimed to provide skills applicable in all circumstances, and it was seen as providing a management solution to any problem (Rees 1995: 15–17; Du Gay 2000: Ch. 4). This generic management model was represented as capable of rescuing the public sector from the dead-weight of the welfare state's social democratic faith in professionals (Pollitt 1990: 27). Pollitt argues that the importation of managerialism into the welfare state involved embracing an ideology with beliefs about the world which are systematically structured into a framework of ideas that justify particular actions by reference to the 'right to manage' and 'good management practice'. This framework of ideas, according to Pollitt (1990: 2–3), includes the following:

- Progress is achieved through economic productivity.
- Productivity increases come from the application of technology, including organisational technology.
- A disciplined labour force is needed.
- Management is the discrete and distinctive function which has the answers.

Given that the state would still be involved in social work, managerialism could be presented as a positive force for progress, distinct from the straightforward control of public expenditure which could fall prey to negative connotations. Nevertheless, the end result was the same: managerialism promised that state goals could be attained with the use of fewer resources (Cutler and Waine 1994: 26).

The revitalising of managers was seen as the key to achieving this ambitious 'more for less'/'value for money' agenda. Ironically, the Conservatives had regarded these same managers as deeply implicated in the alleged failings of the bureau-professional regimes (see Ch. 2) and had derided them as self-interested bumbling bureaucrats. Now they were offered the prospect of redemption through their participation in the dismantling of the bureau-professional regime and its reconstruction into a very different role in the social services market. Managers' alleged under-performance was to be addressed through the incorporation into social work of management practices from the private sector in order to revitalise and equip it for new challenges (Local Government Training Board 1985; Audit Commission 1988); by such means, those seen previously as professionally tainted were to be turned into uncontaminated activist managers (Hoggett 1991: 254). In this context the Audit Commission (1992) depicted managers as the 'Bolsheviks' of a managerial revolution. Following the revolution, management in social work was widely regarded as having a number of elements, among which were:

- strategic vision (clear sense of direction usually embodied in a mission statement);

- common values (ownership of values, throughout the social work organisation, which are consistent with the organisation's *raison d'être*);
- orientation to customer care (emphasis on complaints procedures);
- performance review (by inspectorates);
- budgetary procedures (which reflect strategic priorities);
- clear leadership (from top managers).

These facets of managerialism would be played out within the parameters of economy, efficiency and effectiveness.

As the social work business developed, four interlocking control strategies of managerialism (Hood 1991b, 1995; Hoggett 1996) came into play. First, the disaggregation of organisations into decentralised, clearly managed, operational units, concurrent with achieving a greater degree of centralised remote control over strategy and policy. This disaggregation combined with central control allowed a more rapid adoption of private sector techniques than would have been possible by seeking to work through organisations as they were previously constituted (see Ch. 2). Second, the disciplined use of resources was emphasised. Third, an enhanced level of (managed) competition was established. Fourth, the use of private sector performance management techniques was introduced through measurable standards and pre-set output measures, and monitoring against those standards and measures (audits, inspections, quality assessments, reviews), directed largely towards operationally decentralised units. Hoggett (1994: 45) describes the combination of some of these control strategies in the following way:

> Give managers and staff control over resources, make them accountable for balancing the books, add a framework of performance targets, and perhaps a few core values and mission statements, finally add a dash of competition and there you have it – a disaggregated, self-regulating form of public service production.

The earlier discussion (pp. 41–46) of the implementation of the NHS and Community Care Act (1990) showed that it involved the development of all of these control strategies simultaneously. The implementation of the Children Act (1989) witnessed a minimal amount of managed competition in the early days, but the other control strategies were used extensively and intensively (Packman and Jordan 1991; Parton 1996b). Managed competition has since spread across the whole range of social services, as a glance at the service provider advertisements in the back pages of any issue of *Community Care* magazine will confirm. Underpinning these control strategies is the assumption that professionals should be fully accountable to managers (see Ch. 4).

The social work business

Are the developments which have been outlined in relation to marketisation and managerialism sufficiently pronounced to warrant the use of the term 'the social work business'? Is there any justification in seeking to collapse the analytical distinction made by social democratic and neo-Marxist commentators between the public sector and the private market (see Ch. 2), with regard to differences in their characteristic logics, conditions and principles?

The analytical distinction between the public sector and the private market, in the Fordist era of the post-war consensus, rested on the proposition that state activities such as social work could be divorced from the conditions and dynamics operating in markets in a capitalist society. Capitalism was clearly represented in Marshall's formulation of the hyphenated society of democratic-welfare-capitalism, but it was seen as operating in a domain different from that of social welfare (see Ch. 2). As was demonstrated earlier in this chapter, the relative autonomy from capitalist conditions and dynamics that the hyphenated society's formulation implied for services like social work has been greatly eroded, with market incursions into social welfare's former fiefdom.

A similar point can be made about Carchedi's neo-Marxist distinction between capitalist activities and non-capitalist state activities (Carchedi 1977: Ch. 2). The basis for this sectoral classification, Carchedi argued, was that some aspects of society, such as social work, were focused on the meeting of needs through political processes and structures rather than via the market. The state was seen as 'polluting' capitalist relations – advancing capitalist development overall (by furthering the stability and reproduction of the capitalist system as a whole), but threatening it at the same time by its partial negation of market relations (Fabricant and Burghardt 1992: Ch. 2). What Carchedi, and other neo-Marxist writers, did not envisage was the possibility of the process being reversed: the political mediation of non-capitalist state activities being 'polluted' by market relations. As we have seen, the outcome of the political mediation of social work by the Conservative government was the very opposite of a constraint on the incursion of market relations. First, that government's overwhelming priority was the creation of conditions attractive to capitalist profitability in the face of global market pressures in the post-Fordist era. Second, it forced previously non-capitalist state activities, like social work, to function as if they were operating in a situation analogous to that of a private market. The net effect of the Conservative governments' interventions rendered almost meaningless Carchedi's distinction between capitalist activities and non-capitalist state activities, as capitalist mechanisms and systems were introduced into the management of the public sector (Salamon 1998: 17) and market mechanisms were introduced into the operating conditions of what had been non-capitalist state activities.

There was some potential political risk for Conservative governments in their embrace of the quasi-business discourse and their major revision of the state's *modus operandi*. In trading the social democratic welfare state's legitimation strategy (services for citizens, outside capitalist relations) for a market framework, a new legitimation strategy was derived from the market. It rested on the mantra of the three 'E's of economy, efficiency and effectiveness, discussed earlier (pp. 38–41), and on consumerism, which is considered in Chapter 7. Of course, this is not to suggest that everything was constrained within the market framework. Political decisions were still required about whether services should be provided and, if so, what their overall scope and purpose should be. Such political decisions were (semi-)detached from market criteria, albeit while still concerned with the implications of such decisions for overall capitalist profitability in the global context. The direct discipline of the market was exerted strongly not so much in relation to *whether* services were to continue to be provided but with regard to *how* services were provided. In other words, the market framework for exchange and the managerial framework for cost control established business-like market constraints and managerial mechanisms in state organisations, whose existence depended ultimately on non-market criteria. The context of the newly established social work business was this marketised state.

Although market mechanisms and criteria were introduced into the production of, access to and delivery of social services, the market, like all markets, was structured:

> [T]here is and can be no truly free or unstructured market: even the minimum regulation via the law of contracts and credit, without which there would be no market, imposes structure that favours some transactions over others, some market participants over others, some practices over others, and in the end some outcomes over others. In practice all markets, private as well as public, are

structured by the state, and in being so structured they position participants in ways that result in them contributing to outcomes not of their own choosing.

(Muetzelfeldt 1992: 195–6)

Such a formulation of the market conditions and dynamics of the social work business is very different from the rhetoric that accompanied its establishment by the Conservative government. While a 'pure' post-Fordist model might not have been recognisable in the social work business, that model was held up by Conservative governments as a symbol to which social work managers should aspire, with features such as decentralised management, devolved budgets, contracts and individually tailored services existing in the new mode of 'marketised state' provision (Edgell and Hetherington 1996: 4). An image was purveyed of the market rationale required by 'a type of consumer who cannot possibly derive satisfaction from universally provided, collectively financed and state-allocated services' (Warde 1994: 223). This rhetoric was steeped in individualistic consumerism (see Ch. 7) and was expressed in a series of slogans:

- 'Needs-led services'
- 'Tailor-made individual services'
- 'Freedom to purchase services wherever'
- 'Individual choice over the style of service'.

Such slogans presented marketisation as the route out of bureaucracy and insensitivity and towards freedom and choice. By breaking the alleged monopoly of public services, the Conservatives argued, service users would have a greater degree of control over the services they received. Thus, the political reconstruction and re-presentation of social work included moving the focus away from the relation with employers, associated with the bureau-professional regime (see Ch. 2), to the relation with service users and how they were treated. (This may explain why a Conservative government countenanced a reform of social work education which included the notion of anti-oppressive practice – see Ch. 6.)

However, in a marketised state concerned with value-for-money there are other imperatives involved in the production of services, among them:

- limited budgets;
- ensuring services are in place for large numbers of service users;

- set lists of contracted services to ensure value-for-money; and
- specifications laid down for service operation.

The outworking of this set of imperatives resulted in a shift away from the proclaimed aspiration to universalism and comprehensiveness in service provision of the Seebohm Report (Cmnd. 3703 1968) to the targeting of services on those unable to provide for themselves (Alcock 1989; Baldock 1994).

These two rationales – a market rationale, which stressed consumer choice, and a managerial rationale, which stressed control over the supply of services – produced contrary pressures and processes that are reflected in the formulation of the operating conditions and dynamics of the social work business. The juxtapositions are illustrated in figure 3.1.

These juxtapositions reveal the contradictory pressures and processes at work in the social work business, and illustrate the way in which marketisation and managerialism attacked the previous bureau-professional regime (see Ch. 2). The market rationale provided, at least rhetorically, a consumerist ideology that embodied a critique of professional discretion and the state rationale installed managerialist measures that curbed social workers' discretion in practice. While social work came under pressure from both the demand side and the supply side, in being subjected to market and managerial influences, the two sides were not equally felt. The running of the social work busi-

MARKETISATION (Demand side/consumption) *Market rationale > consumer choice*	MANAGERIALISM (Supply side/production) *State rationale > control of services*
Needs-led services	Limited budgets
Tailor-made individual services	Ensuring services are in place for large numbers of service users
Freedom to purchase services wherever	Set list of contracted services to ensure value for money
Individual choice over the style of service	Specifications laid down for service operation

Figure 3.1 Pressures and processes associated with market and managerial rationales

ness became managerial, making the supply side dominant, despite the rhetoric to the contrary. As the social work business was established, that rhetoric kept the focus of the argument on the market rationale for social work's restructuring. Yet there was little evidence of social work having become subject to the whims of the 'customer'. Central government monitoring moved rapidly from a concern with the development of 'seamless care' for users to managing the market (Lewis and Glennerster 1996: 208). By 1993, Wistow *et al.*'s research (1996) concluded that the social services market was not working, but two-thirds of directors of social services could see advantages in terms of cost awareness and cost control. Deakin (1996: 32) identified important variations in individual markets, with some characterised by provider monopolies. Lewis *et al.* (1996) concluded that their research evidence was at best equivocal as to whether market competition had been secured. The combined research evidence suggests that if social workers/care managers had taken seriously the rhetoric and rationale of the market and consumerism, and ignored the state rationale of managerial control, they would have been guilty of raising false expectations for service users of how the system operated.

Perhaps it is significant that while the terminology used in establishing the social work business referred to quasi-markets, it did not refer to quasi-management or quasi-managers. This points us to the possibility that the management dimension of the social work business, driven by the objectives of increasing efficiency and lowering costs, was more significant than the quasi-market arrangements. The market reforms were framed and managed into an existing set of powers and a historically accumulated set of understandings (Light 2001) about what social work was and how social work was to be delivered. The social services market was created and steered by the state, which managed the market structure and the terms of competition. Such markets can shape the decisions and actions of organisations and service users just as much as can bureaucratic regulation in public services. They can guide service providers to do, or insist that they do, more at less cost and in that sense are more about giving managers the power to set the terms of payment than they are about competition. Therefore, the wholesale transfer of social services into private hands, in order to create a market, was never an issue; private services can produce inefficient and expensive services in monopoly conditions (Flynn 1993: 107), and in any case there were gaps in the range of provision in the independent sector. Rather, marketisation was the key to introducing business management thinking across the public, private and voluntary sectors. Holding down public expenditure, took precedence over shifting ownership, although that was a feature as well in residential and domiciliary care because of the '85 per cent rule' referred to earlier (p. 64). Even if 'proper' competition within a market was not possible, competition for a market itself, through tenders for contracted-out services (Drakeford 2000: 32), still produced efficiency gains by driving down costs such as wages. In addition, the introduction of quasi-markets weakened the position of local authorities in Labour strongholds, while still making them responsible for services.

Conclusion

The chapter began by noting the pressures on nation states to reform their welfare regimes in response to the demands for competitiveness in the global economy. With regard to the trajectory of reform, Hood (1991a) points out the significance of variation in the organisa-tional arrangements of the welfare state in different countries. He argues that countries with a 'big government' profile in welfare state spending and staffing are likely to provide more *motive* for politicians to attempt reforms, while countries where the system is capable of being changed from a single point are likely to produce greater *oppor-tunity* to carry through reform (Hood 1991a: 104–5). In these terms, the Thatcher government had both the motive and the opportunity for reform, an opportunity enhanced initially by a sense of crisis.

In relation to social work, the Conservative government launched an attack on the bureau-professional regime, which was the subject of Chapter 2. The attack was two-pronged and brought together market-isation and managerialism. The Conservative reforms were crucially important in establishing the social work business. Whilst previously different operating conditions and dynamics had been considered to exist in non-capitalist state services and capitalist enterprises, the 'common sense' of the market was now pervasive, making quasi-capitalist rationality more extensive and more dominant than previously:

> [P]rovision through the public sector has been incorporated into an understanding of consumption. . . . [Previously welfare] was not to be understood as belonging to the same genus as the purchase of an ice cream or a new item of clothing. Today the dividing line between the two is not so clear-cut. . . . [Consumption theory has merged] the public and private forms of provision as potentially equivalent forms of (private) consumption. Such developments in the understanding of consumption reflect a reaction to the shifting boundaries between the social and the private, and between the

collective and the individual. . . . For, just as the rise of the welfare state in the post-war boom appeared to have set public provision aside from the ethos and practices of private consumption, so the economic crisis of the mid-1970s has brought the two into collision with one another; and where the restructuring of private and public provision has occurred, treating [the two] as alternative modes of consumption has (conceptually) eased the adjustments involved, whether these be cuts in levels of provision and/or redivisions between public and private provision.

(Fine and Leopold 1993: 17)

If people's lives are spent in one ('pure' or 'quasi-') market system or another, within overarching business or quasi-business discourses, then the previous challenge of public services to capitalist rationality is much reduced, as those services take on a quasi-capitalist rationality. If markets and businesses are everywhere, it is much harder to think outside of them. As a result, much of the debate that has taken place about social work has been confined within this rationality and has been concerned with seeking to influence the direction and mode of operation of the social work business: it has been preoccupied with the running of the business, the subject of Chapter 4.

4 Running the business

As was seen in Chapter 3, the attack by Conservative governments on the social democratic welfare state was two-pronged: first, the state's social spending was presented as a drain on the generation of profits by capitalist companies; and, second, the state was castigated as an inefficient producer of services because of its protection from market exchange relations. The establishing of the social work business took place in this context. It involved the deployment of managerialism to focus attention on economy, efficiency and effectiveness; and this, in turn, meant making managerial inroads into professional autonomy and power, with wide-ranging ramifications for the day-to-day running of the business. As a consequence, Thatcherism broke through the fledgling claims of social work to define itself according to the internal criteria of practice (Keat 1991) developed within its parochial professional culture (see Ch. 2), insulated from the market and from political interference, and with concerns distinguished from those of the manager or the politician:

> The Seebohm departments relied above all on professionalism which provided an intuitive feel for the kind of services that were needed. Many of the new processes, for example assessment, were carried out but were not formalised in the same way. Rather, departments relied on professional discretion and much was carried round in social workers' heads rather than being made explicit. The new structures [i.e. the reforms considered in Ch. 3 this volume], based on purchasing and providing, and the new processes associated with them . . . have required new systems to be put in place which in turn require managerial skills. Departments have thus been pushed into achieving a new balance between professionalism and managerialism.
>
> (Lewis and Glennerster 1996: 71)

This push for a new balance between professionalism and managerialism was premissed on the development of management as a separate profession, leading to the suggestion that managers in social services did not need a qualification in social work (Pahl 1994: 206). The embrace of managerialism in this context was an aspect of Thatcherism's diffusion of quasi-capitalist rationality into the void left by the demise of social democratic ideology (see Ch. 2) and was geared to achieving a shift in organisational power relations in Social Services Departments through substantial changes in their internal organisational structures and cultures (see Ch. 3).

This chapter turns the spotlight on some of the implications of the latter for the running of the social work business. After considering the similarities that developed between private sector business management and the management of the social work business, guided by quasi-capitalist rationality and constrained by cash limits and the intensification of competitive forces through quasi-markets, the management of professional work is explored. Measures installed to curb the activities of social workers are then specified and are seen as curtailing social workers' discretion in a new workplace culture of control.

Managerialising social work

The process of managerialising the social work business introduced social work to a key aspect of the quasi-business discourse, what is termed here 'quasi-capitalist rationality' – a way of thinking grounded in managerialism's capitalist origins. It is designated 'quasi-capitalist', rather than 'capitalist' or 'pure capitalist', because state funding, a regulatory framework and (ultimately) political accountability underpin managerialised quasi-market arrangements for social work. Notwithstanding these distinguishing facets, managerialism has been critical in pushing forward a way of thinking about the social work business that stems from capitalist rationality. The assumption made has been that the social work business should be run as far as possible as though it were a private sector company pursuing profits.

As it squeezed the running of the social work business into the mould of quasi-capitalist rationality, the main object of managerialism's attack was the bureau-professional approach to social work associated with the social democratic rationality of the pre-business era (see Ch. 2). The Conservative governments sought to displace the power of bureau-professionalism, which accepted professional discretion as necessary in order to tailor the state's overall framework of rules and resources for social services to individuals' particular circumstances. Being like management in the private sector involved being 'free to manage', including being free to manage professionals (Pollitt 1990: Ch. 1). As part of this newly vaunted management freedom, one of the goals was to exert greater control over the 'professional space' represented by the relationship between the social worker and the service user. If social work's aspirations to deal with 'the whole person' were to be restricted to assessing needs, commissioning other service providers and managing the market, the variability and unpredictability of professionals' discretion to respond differentially to the range of life situations presented by different service users had to be curbed, despite official rhetoric to the contrary. The managerial confidence displayed in tipping the balance away from the exercise of professional discretion stemmed from the assumption that management was a generic skill that could be applied in all circumstances (Ife 1997: 16, 62). This assumption was translated into the firmly held managerial belief that the life situations of service users could be classified into discrete problem categories susceptible to the strictures of management in terms of setting criteria for initial decisions about access to assessment for services, the service options made available following assessment and the quantifying and costing of service outputs. This managerialist approach to running the social work business was reductionist: it disregarded the potential complexity of service users' lives and circumstances that contributes to the 'causes' of the problems they present. Hence the preoccupation with driving out as far as possible the indeterminacy associated with the bureau-professional regime of the pre-business era (see Ch. 2) because of the scope it afforded professionals to stress the complexity of service users' lives and the difficulties they experienced. Thus, one of the consequences of the application of quasi-capitalist rationality, as part of the all-enveloping quasi-business discourse, has been the obscuring from view of broad individual and social issues arising from social work.

In promulgating quasi-capitalist rationality through the establishment of the social work business (see Ch. 3), Conservative governments did not simply rely on persuading managers ideologically about what they had to deliver, although that was an important aspect of the quasi-business discourse which changed the balance between managerialism and professionalism. Powerful material constraints also were introduced, and these reinforced the ideological direction. Two sets of measures were particularly relevant here.

The first was the setting of cash limits on the budgets available to local authorities responsible for providing social services. These ceilings on central government income streams to local government contained assumptions about efficiency gains in percentage terms. This measure exerted general downward pressure on costs, in services such as social work, by imitating the pressures towards falling profits in the capitalist market. The second measure has already been considered, in Chapter 3 – the establishment of a quasi-market – but its implications for instilling quasi-capitalist rationality into the running of the social work business can be developed here. If social work managers were to be required to behave as if they were managing a capitalist business seeking to maximise profits, then they had to be subjected to imperatives that were similar to those that drive the actions of managers of such businesses. The introduction of competitive markets pushed management practice in the social work business into line with management practice associated with capitalist enterprises. In part this came about through the role managers had in managing the quasi-market, as a consequence of which they had to get up to speed on market operations and the forms of managerialism associated with them. In addition, some of the services for which social work managers were responsible were floated off into the independent sector (for example, domiciliary services and residential care), as local authorities were required to promote a mixed economy of providers by spending 85 per cent of their community care allocation outside of the public sector. The services that remained in the public sector were then competing in the quasi-market. These developments simulated the effects of market competition on capitalist businesses, in particular through the central emphasis on costs. Services had to be cost-efficient in order to survive in the context of the purchaser–provider split and the ensuing service provider proliferation. In addition, the quasi-market turned the purchase of services and the assessments leading to purchase – in other words, the activities of social workers – into the equivalent of a business overhead. Unsurprisingly, this overhead was made explicit and monitored by breaking down purchasing units (social work teams) into distinct decentralised accounting entities (cost centres).

The combination of these two measures – cash limits and market-like mechanisms – resulted in public social work services which were more akin to commercial, profit-making, private sector businesses in their characteristic logic, conditions and principles. They retained their formal designation as public sector services because social policy decisions concerning the overall scope and purpose of social work were still (semi-)detached from market criteria (although always taken within the wider context of the effect of such decisions on the degree of capitalist confidence about the conditions for profitability). Nevertheless, the quasi-market framework and managerialism imbued with quasi-capitalist rationality instilled new considerations and disciplines into the running of Social Services Departments that were strengthened by changes in legislation (see Ch. 3). These changes were so radical and far-reaching that they could be achieved only by the exercise of firm direction by senior managers (Lewis and Glennerster 1996: 69). In addition to the impetus coming from the New Right, managers also had the potential to use the quasi-business discourse to pursue their own agendas, status and power (Clarke 1998), which may explain in part why managers were more enthusiastic than social workers in accommodating to the changes (Pahl 1994; Farnham and Horton 1996; Lewis and Glennerster 1996: 143), shedding their professional association with social work as they did so (Nixon 1993).

Managing professional work

Having set out the general tendency towards managerialisation in the running of the social work business, models of intensified managerial control are now considered in order to approach the management of professional work in general and of social work in particular. The most celebrated critique of trends towards increasing control is Braverman's analysis (1974) of the spread of scientific management from its origins in industry.

Braverman sought to counter the apparent neutrality of management techniques. His thesis was that the management of work is moulded in a direct way by the demands of capitalism through the deliberate control and de-skilling of labour (Braverman 1974: 121). He emphasised the need to take into account the nature and purpose of production under capitalism when analysing the conditions of work. He saw the design of jobs, the division of labour and the forms of work organisation all as underpinned by the motive of accumulating profit. The employers' need to maximise profits dictated the necessity for a management-initiated strategy to gain control over work processes. As part of this strategy the scope for workers' control of and discretion in undertaking work had to be severely limited. In specifying the nature of this management-initiated strategy, Braverman argued that the detailed design of work processes results in fragmentation of those processes into smaller, less skilled, tasks that are more susceptible to managerial co-ordination and control. As a result, only managers have a grasp of the overall business:

Workers who are controlled only by general orders and discipline are not adequately controlled, because they retain their grip on the actual processes of labour. . . . To change this situation control over the labour process must pass into the hands of management . . . by the control and dictation of each step of the process, including its performance.

(Braverman 1974: 100)

Braverman described this process as the separation of the processes of conception and execution, of thinking and doing. The essence of scientific management – or 'Taylorism' (named after its originator) is the separation of planning how to do a job from the doing of it. As execution becomes increasingly separated from conception, the bulk of employees are involved in simple mundane tasks. For Braverman scientific management was the pervasive driving force, the means by which capitalist production had been, and continues to be, systematised. Braverman summed up scientific management as follows:

[T]he first principle is the gathering together and development of knowledge of the labour process, and the second is the concentration of this knowledge as the exclusive preserve of management – together with its converse, the absence of such knowledge among workers – then the third step is the use of this monopoly of knowledge to control each step of the labour process and its mode of execution.

(Braverman 1974: 119)

To what extent can Braverman's account, primarily geared to explaining developments in capitalist production, be used to understand aspects of running the social work business, for which the generation of profit is not the objective and where the political and ideological context is therefore significant? Braverman himself made no distinction between workers in the private, profit-producing, sector and those in the public sector. By implication, Braverman assumed that the encroachment of managerial control he had identified was universally applicable and the state was a 'shadowy background factor' (Thompson and McHugh 1990: 11).

In contrast, in neo-Marxist theories, the distinctiveness of working in the state is seen to consist in its political location and its being subject to political contingencies. For example, Offe (1975) argued that specific areas of state employment are organised in different ways, ranging from the bureaucratic mode, involved in state activities such as making social security payments, through to dependence on professional workers in those state occupations that have retained some autonomy on the basis of expertise. Such an account emphasises the importance of the state as the political domain in which certain professional work is located. Johnson (1972) included this location in his analysis of professions as structures of power. He identified three types of professional power structure: collegiate; patronage; and mediated. In the case of mediated professions, an agency, usually a state organisation, acts as mediator between the profession and its clientele in deciding who the profession's clientele will be and in broad terms what should be provided for that clientele through a legal framework and the overall allocation of resources. The state acts as the corporate patron of agencies that provide services on its behalf (Johnson 1972: 77). While Johnson marked out the distinctiveness of mediated professional work as one organisational variant, he did not move on to an analysis of professional work itself. That concern was addressed by Derber (1982, 1983).

Derber argued that professional work has distinctive features. In order to demonstrate this distinctiveness, he posed a central question: what does lack of control over work mean? Braverman had suggested that it had two components: lack of control over the *process of labour* and lack of control over the *uses of the product*. The first component (technical control) highlights the tendency for managers to impose their own conception of how to organise and execute the job. The second component (ideological control) points to managers' control over what is produced, the purpose for which it is used and how and when it is sold (Derber 1983: 312). In other words, Derber argued, technical control is about the *means* and ideological control is about the *ends* of work (Derber 1983: 313). Derber argued that the emphasis in Braverman's work had been on the first component – lack of control over the process of work (Derber 1983: 315). As a result, the second component – lack of control over the ends (goals and purposes) of work – had been ignored. This, as Derber emphasised, is understandable because most industrial workers experience both the technical and ideological components of control simultaneously (Derber 1983: 313).

Having disaggregated technical and ideological control, Derber suggested that in the case of professional work, ideological control 'creates a type of worker whose integrity is threatened less by the expropriation of his [*sic*] skill than his values or sense of purpose. It reduces the domain of freedom and creativity to problems of technique. . . . It is the lack of control over the ends to which work is put' (Derber 1983: 316).

Professional workers, Derber argued, can maintain a considerable degree of technical autonomy by adapting to ideological control through 'co-optation', a process of redefining the goals of their work so that the disparities between professional and organisational interests are minimised and their employing organisations are perceived as committed to professional workers' underlying values and purposes: 'Ideological co-optation reflects the new hybrid identity in which professionals take their moral values and objectives from their new institutional employers, but sustain an identity separate from other employees by their investment in technical expertise' (Derber 1983: 330–1). As far as social work was concerned, Derber argued:

> The therapeutic approach formed the basis for a highly sophisticated ideological co-optation, where social workers' moral concerns for the well-being of their clients could be accommodated in a form of practice that served institutional ends.
>
> (Derber 1983: 333)

Derber's distinction between ideological and technical control and his emphasis on the possibility of co-option of professional workers are a fruitful line of analysis. In the pre-business era, social work can be regarded as not being subjected to technical control (see Ch. 2). It was subjected to ideological control in working to the goals and purposes defined for it by the state and expressed in legislative mandates and statutory duties. However, even here there was apparently some room for manoeuvre, otherwise it is difficult to account for the emergence of radical social work, feminist social work and anti-racist social work as perspectives overtly concerned with the goals and purposes of social work. This suggests that social work's location in the legislative, fiscal and organisational base of the welfare state was compatible with considerable professional discretion and that the existence of a bureaucratic hierarchy was not necessarily synonymous with rigidity (Webb and Wistow 1987: 107–8). In similar vein, Hugman (1991a: 78) identified the possibility that bureaucracy would allow professional work to develop, rather than constrain it as is conventionally assumed. The implementation of the Seebohm Report, for example, delivered resources that consolidated social work's control over its area of work, as we saw in Chapter 2. Accordingly, bureaucratic hierarchies could be seen to be as much a basis for the power exercised by professionals as the basis for the exercise of power over professionals (Hugman 1991a: 62). The establishing of the social work business changed all this, for it resulted not only in the tightening of ideological control (see Ch. 3) but in the imposition of technical control over social work.

Technical control and quasi-capitalist rationality

With the adoption of quasi-capitalist rationality as part of the quasi-business discourse, the parochial–professional 'craft' of social work (see Ch. 2) was subjected to a sweeping wave of inter-related changes, leading in the direction of technical control. These changes are now considered.

Managers with a business orientation

Managers were seen by the Conservative governments as deeply implicated in the failings of the welfare state but were seen also as central to its dismantling and subsequent reconstruction into a quasi-market economy of social services. Senior managers became responsible for securing commitment to Conservative policies and were expected to take the lead in challenging power structures and vested interests left over from the regime of the pre-business era (Audit Commission 1992: 27). Overall guidelines on organisational and managerial issues were provided for senior managers in local government (Local Government Management Board 1993, 1995; Audit Commission 1995). Such managers were seen as in need of continual reassessment in terms of meeting targets and the achievement of strategic objectives. In order to achieve objectives, it was seen as important to remove intermediaries between those responsible for strategy and planning and those responsible for providing services (O'Higgins 1992: 48), so that senior management could take the lead in establishing strategy, planning change, defining and measuring needs, and establishing priorities and targets. The managerial objective was to create a tier of senior management with a strategic role, able to survey the 'business environment', make choices and deploy resources in pursuit of value-for-money services. This variant of managerialism was fastened to the establishment and running of the social work business, as it extended to the public sector the centralisation of management command that characterised capitalist enterprises (Hoggett 1991).

Lower down in Social Services Departments, operational managers, usually at team manager level, occupied a key position in running social work within the strictures of a quasi-business orientation. Although, in many respects, they could still be seen as senior manager–social worker go-betweens, they were now collecting information on team performance for senior management and were made responsible for improving overall achievement. Many of them still wanted to see themselves as carriers of the parochial–professional culture of social work (see Ch. 2) but were simultaneously made responsible for transforming that culture and giving it a quasi-business orientation:

> I am supervised by my manager but the person who I need to see the most, and this is no reflection on my manager, is the Finance Officer. As the culture and nature of my work has changed so my speak has changed and my attitude has changed. At the end of the day, the last thing I want on my epitaph is 'he filed the last invoice', because that is what it feels like, you know. Prior to 1993, you could measure someone's worth as a team leader – that is another thing, we're not team leaders any more, we're managers of small business units – you could measure your outcomes by the quality of your supervision and things like that which we had and would talk about. Now you feel that you are your own kind of business unit, your own enterprise.
>
> (Front-line manager[1])

These sentiments echo the findings of the study by Lewis and Glennerster (1996: 143) which concluded that 'there has been a fundamental shift away from the dominance of the professional culture. The team leader is now less a professional supervisor and more a manager with financial responsibility'. The 'business orientation' at operational management level was accompanied and reinforced by such devolved budgetary responsibility: 'We wanted the budget decentralised to as low a level as possible for the care managers. The chain of command for access to budgets had to be no more than one person up in the hierarchy' (senior manager).

Turning professionals into managers

The managerialisation of the running of the social work business was significant not just for managers: it required a shift in orientation also from social workers. The scale of change is indicated in this comment by Sir Roy Griffiths, who, as noted in Chapter 3, was the originator of many of the changes that were implemented:

---

1 All unattributed quotations are from a study reported in Harris 1996.

Many social services staff already have a managerial function, but my approach will give this added emphasis, for example in the development of skills needed to buy in services. Other new skills, particularly in the design of successful management accounting systems and the effective use of the information produced by them, will be needed. The changing role of social services authorities might also allow them to make more productive use of the management abilities and experience of all their staff.

(Griffiths Report 1988: 25)

As this extract from the Griffiths Report anticipated, the direction in which managerialism took social work after the establishment of the social work business was away from approaches that were therapeutic or which stressed the importance of casework, let alone anything more radical or progressive. Turning professionals into managers involved making them responsible for running the business. It meant that the quasi-capitalist rationality of social work's quasi-business discourse was to become their business. They were to be different people, with the capacities and dispositions the social work business required:

This involves 'offering' individuals involvement in activities – such as managing budgets . . . previously held to be the responsibility of other agents. . . . However, the price of this involvement is that individuals themselves must assume responsibility for carrying out those activities and for their outcomes . . . forms of 'responsibilisation' . . . are held to be both economically desirable and personally 'empowering'. This requirement that individuals become more personally exposed to the risks and costs of engaging in a particular activity is represented as a means to their empowerment because it is held to encourage them to build resources in themselves rather than simply rely on others to take risks and endure uncertainties on their behalf.

(Du Gay 2000: 66)

This crucial aspect of the transformation of professionals into managers – the inculcation of a responsible managerialised orientation to the social work business – emphasised the need for scrupulous gate-keeping and strict rationing of scant resources:

Well if you want to become a counsellor, don't come into social services. If you want to be an assessor and a purchaser of services and a care manager, which is a more managerial, monitoring, reviewing type of role then those are the sorts of skills that are going to be needed for today's social worker and social workers into the next century or how ever long we last. So, in a way, you're becoming a different kind of animal. You've got to be skilled at using modern technology, you've got to be skilled at managing funds, money and that's all a new skill for me – in terms of costing. You've got to be, as a care manager, good at liaison, communicating, care planning.

(social worker)

Decisions, based on managerial criteria, now had to be matched with financial data:

In fact, to access any service for a client now, it's got to be on the [computer] screen because you also as a social worker are responsible for loading the costing of that service onto the screen. So any agency that you are using, any service, won't get paid for offering the service to the client if it's not on the screen. Because not only are we doing assessments on the screen but also putting the service package on the screen, which is the costings, and we're also putting the care plan on the screen. So to ensure that the client is getting what's identified as their needs in any service, whether it's domiciliary agency or whatever or residential care, the care plan has got to be on the screen and you can't access the service package screens without having done the care plan screen.

(social worker)

These statements indicate the depth of the trend, within the running of the social work business, towards complex procedures for regulating social workers in their dispersal of goods and services, based primarily on budgetary considerations (Jones and Novak 1993: 202). In this context, social workers were to see themselves not as professionals but as care *managers*, putting together *packages* of care from the quasi-*market* for individual consumers, or *customers*, on the basis of assessments of needs and identifying others to meet those needs. Accordingly, the national body then responsible for social work education, the Central Council for Education and Training in Social Work (CCETSW), produced training materials for social workers on topics such as purchasing and contracting (CCETSW 1992, 1994a). Social workers and care managers were expected to have skills in assessing services required by individual service users, making judgements about how and by whom those services would be delivered and managing budgets in ways which ensured that value-for-money services were provided (CCETSW 1991a). Any specific skills traditionally associated with social work seemed no longer to be highly valued. The highly valued skills that contributed to the efficient running of the business were managing budgets, managing collaboration and understanding management information systems. New skills were required in setting standards, specifying services, awarding contracts, monitoring performance and taking action if performance fell short of specifications (Wistow *et al.* 1994: 17). Social workers were encouraged to see themselves not only as fully accountable to managers, who were portrayed as representing service users' interests, but as needing to act responsibly in developing their own increasingly managerial orientation to their day-to-day work (see Ch. 9).

Work organisation

Under the pressure of cash limits and quasi-market conditions (see pp. 58–59), managers responsible for running the social work business took a much more active interest in the way day-to-day work was organised and controlled as part of the effort to drive down costs. One way of holding down costs is to employ fewer staff, but that is rarely an option in people-intensive work like the provision of social services. (The reduction in number of middle managers, and their replacement by information technology, is a notable exception.) Another way of holding down costs is to cut pay. Given that pay determination in Social Services Departments continued to occur at a national level, for the most part cuts could not be made in social workers' scales of pay, although the introduction of 'single status' pay schemes has reduced the income of some social workers and cuts have been made to remuneration for other staff such as care assistants with regard to sickness pay and additional payments for working unsocial hours. (In addition, one of the continuing motivations for floating off provider units is that private sector providers are seen as unshackled by public sector pay arrangements and are thus able to cut wage costs.) Social work managers were boxed in by such constraints, and in order to keep a grip on running costs had to rely on various combinations of measures derived from the options of increasing the amount of work done by each social worker, redistributing work to lower paid staff, raising charges to service users and raising the threshold for entrance to service provision through the modification of eligibility criteria. The latter option has the advantage of obscuring cuts in the number of service users, which are nevertheless revealed in official statistics (see, for example, Department of Health 2000b).

In implementing combinations of these measures, two main trends were evident: the intensification of work; and an increase in the scrutiny of work. The underlying message, rarely explicitly articulated, was that social workers should work harder. They began to be managed as if they were employees in capitalist enterprises, with the pressure exerted on managers to extract the maximum amount of work from them for the overhead costs they represented (see p. 59). As work intensified, it was no longer assumed, as it had been in the pre-business era (see Ch. 2), that social workers would simply get on with the job. Measures were introduced to scrutinise and control their performance. One of these measures was stricter control over absence from work, with the introduction in some Social Services Departments of Japanese enterprise-style interviews upon return to work after sickness. The most significant measure was the introduction of information technology. Earlier in the chapter it was noted that information technology was used to monitor social workers' rationing of resources in prioritising budgetary considerations in the allocation of services. In the process, computerisation subjected social workers' recordings to standardised procedures for information processing, codifying professional knowledge and giving it to managers. Campbell, in the Canadian context, describes how developmental work in preparation for the introduction of a computer system into the running of a social work agency included 'informed and careful description and categorisation of work practices, as a preliminary step to computer programming' (Campbell 1990: 85). Such processes were also in evidence in Britain as care management was codified on computer systems:

> The use of computers therefore reduces the scope for interpretation of data and, in so doing, is transforming organisations from professionalised bureaucracies to centrally controlled administrative activities. While the rules and regulations of agencies will increase, adding controlling bureaucratic features, their flexibility and responsiveness to individuals in need will decrease. The primary task of the organisation may also be changed . . . from one of welfare provision to the collection of data to regulate and determine eligibility for such provision. . . . Social workers will find themselves . . . part of a machine that has achieved an objective reality. . . . Such systems will inevitably result in greater control

over the interpretation of data and consequently over the activities of practitioners.

(Sapey 1997: 809)

With the computerisation of care management, it became *the* way to do social work. The model was welded inseparably to the technology through which it was codified and turned into a set of practice requirements. Earlier debates about social work methods and theoretical perspectives were replaced by computer systems controlled by managers, with staff following through the actions required by the information technology system, in the space previously largely controlled by practitioners: 'The rise of care management can be seen as a means of undermining social work as a profession by constructing an alternative professional discourse' (Cochrane 1994: 128). Fabricant and Burghardt (1992: 86) captured the nature of such developments in their research into parallel trends in the American context:

> [T]he structure or conception of work is redefined, breaking it down into ever more discrete and measurable elements. Then, this structure limits the worker's capacity to exercise independent judgement or discretion by mandating what can or cannot be done at each stage of the process.

By such means, computerisation led to the reification of control in the running of the business. When a supervisor and a social worker encountered some aspect of the control of practice, they were likely to see it as simply a computer requirement, as part of the assembly-line character of computer systems, with social workers having to do certain tasks at specific points in the programme. Rather than experiencing this in straightforward managerial terms – as a superior coercing a subordinate to undertake work in a particular way – the computer system could be portrayed as identifying workers who had failed to perform *neutral* 'technical' tasks at the required stage in the care management process. Of course, the codification of care management in information technology systems was a managerial process that provided a crucial opportunity for rationalising, routinising and controlling social work, as one senior manager made clear with reference to the introduction of a computer system:

> You get to a point where you have to say 'we can develop a system, that's not a problem', but it's actually your business you've got to sort out first, the business requirements. And I think in the past . . .

we've not taken full enough account of the business. Partly because people didn't want to define the business. Yet when you're defining mega-systems like this, you've got to, it forces you to . . .
(Quoted in Lewis and Glennerster 1996: 95)

Contrary to how they are often presented, the facilities such systems provide are, therefore, not concerned simply with the automation of routine administration in the social work business; they also 'informate' (Zuboff 1988), tracking by computer what social workers do, all the way through the care management process, opening them up to closer scrutiny, through more continuous, more intense, surveillance information. Social workers do not know when surveillance will take place, but have to comply with the computerised requirements on the basis that surveillance could take place at anytime. In addition to any meetings for 'live' supervision, a form of surrogate 'continuous' surveillance is introduced by information technology, as effective and detailed as the surveillance previously possible only in the running of factories. Information technology systems are capable of generating information on a large amount of what social workers do, such as the number of assessments undertaken over a given period, the number of activities carried out on a particular case and the number still outstanding, the time taken to follow-up cases picked up on duty and so on. Of course, such data shed no light on the qualitative nature of social workers' interactions with service users or on the actual outcomes, rather than the outputs, of the work undertaken. To address this shortcoming, a common practice is to draw on proxy measures of outcomes in the form of outputs or 'core quality standards'. For example, in one Social Services Department, four core quality standards were adopted for work in adults and children and families teams:

1 All people who receive a formal assessment of their needs will be offered a copy of their assessment.
2 For all people who receive a service provided or arranged by the Department, a written statement or care plan, describing the service they are to get, will be produced and they will be given a copy of it.
3 All written statements (care plans) will indicate when and how the plan is to be monitored and/or reviewed.
4 All written care plans will show in measurable terms the outcomes which the service is designed to achieve.

Ten pages of guidance are provided on how these four standards are to be recorded on the computer software. If social workers indicate on the computer software that they have given service users copies of assessments and/or care plans, that will be taken as a measure of the quality of the service encounter, a 'core quality standard'. Therefore, a service user could have had the worst possible assessment, but, provided this output requirement could be demonstrated as having occurred, a quality outcome would be assumed to have taken place. The assumption is that if such proxy output standards are being met, beneficial outcomes are being achieved.

Such managerial scrutiny and control in the running of the social work business stands in stark contrast to the need for retrospective accounts of work that characterised the reliance on permissive supervision sessions in the pre-business era (see Ch. 2):

> Now really I think you're only as good as the work you can get on the computer because that's where it's shown what you're doing. On our computer screens now a duty senior will focus the structure of the supervision with the workers they supervise by raising up on the screen a worker-to-do list because every client that we're working with is on the screen. For every client, rather than having written recordings, every task, every telephone contact, every home visit is on the activities screen for each client as an activity that we're doing. Listings of phone calls you make and letters you send out, that's all on the activities screen under a particular client's ID number and on the activities screen it goes in as a new task. Say you did a home visit, that would go in as a new task. When you've done that home visit, you then go back to that activity on screen and you put in that you've completed the task. When your supervisor is supervising you, they will know at which point your workload is with each particular client by the amount of tasks that are outstanding on the screen. And that's your worker-to-do list so they will know where you're at with each client and with each task that you're doing with that client. By the press of a button, it's traced back to you. Any phonecall, any response, it's on screen. Now they can actually tune into the screen without you being in the room and look for what is being done on this client.
>
> (social worker)

This process of detailed specification of tasks, and checking on their completion using information technology, can be augmented in many social work settings by other means as a result of the proximity and openness of workplaces, with strong peer norms that have traditionally encouraged sharing information concerning interactions with service users. Such visibility allows the possibility of supervisors acting more like progress chasers than the peer-consultants associated with the permissive supervisory relationships of the pre-business era (see Ch. 2):

> We did have a situation a year ago where I appointed a member of staff who I called a floor manager. That's interesting isn't it? The terminology goes back to the car factory: the floor manager. All they did every day was to prioritise work, to ensure that the work was done and was allocated. Now with the computer system that we work, the duty senior's role is to go through, assign or allocate all the work as it comes in. The duty officer will deal with it, put it on screen, and then it all has to go through to the duty senior for the next phase on the computer to be completed.
>
> (Front-line manager)

This managerial concern with scrutinising the quantity of work being undertaken through human and information technology surveillance can be combined with workload measurement integrated into social workers' routine online recordings, as was seen earlier (p. 72). The amount of time needed to manage a caseload an then be determined, and managerial attention cand be given to 'slow workers' with supervision sessions concentrating on 'productivity'. This raises questions about the quality of the work that it is possible to perform in the working conditions of the social work business – an issue crucial in a service like social work, which has interpersonal encounters at its core:

> Social workers can also be rated as to how much work they can manage and how good they are at moving things through. If seniors haven't got workers that are moving work through, seniors can end up with waiting lists and then they're answerable for the waiting lists. So there is the culture now of moving work through and it's seen as good if you can be closing cases. The fact that you might close them this month and the same client might need you in three months' time doesn't seem material. If possible, close cases and move work through, and there is the pressure to be seen to be moving work through, so therefore it's not in your interests as a worker really to get bogged down in clients, to be working with people who need long-term emotional help. If you only had 10 to 15 clients that you were doing really good thorough

work with, it's really not so important to be doing that sort of work any more.

(social worker)

This battery of changes to the organisation of work within the running of the social work business obviously had implications for the use of discretion by social workers.

Reducing social workers' discretion

Prior to the Conservative governments' reforms, social workers had a considerable degree of discretion (see Ch. 2). They would undertake work with 'the aim of easing or ending some existing social problem for a specific . . . individual, family or group', which included tasks such as 'assessment, giving practical services and advice, surveillance and taking control, acting as intermediary and counselling' (Barclay Report 1982: 12), usually tackled on the basis of casework. The social worker assessed the service user's needs, arranged any services that were needed and, when necessary, maintained a continuing relationship with the service user as part of her caseload. Social workers were directly involved with service users and acted as their advocate to a variety of agencies. In contrast, the establishment of the social work business brought about a new division of social work labour in which most social workers ended up on the purchaser/assessor side, with a consequent weakening of their practitioner role. As we have already seen, this resulted in their becoming part of the overheads carried by Social Services Departments and that this led in turn to managers focusing on their compliance with agency policies in processing as many service users as possible.

There was a marked impact on social workers' use of discretion, as has already become clear in the previous section. Constraints on expenditure were achieved either in spite of social workers' assessments or by constraining their assessment decisions. Either way, the role of the social worker in allocating resources was undermined. In tandem, other external forces operated to impose constraints on social worker decisions, often in the form of public inquiries and the legislation and/or guidelines that arose from them. High-profile cases of child abuse, for example, frequently resulted in official inquiry reports that detailed the 'failures' of social work and made procedural recommendations without considering the implications for social work practice (Howe 1992). More routinely, the Audit Commission and the Social Services Inspectorate reported on a range of issues, with a major focus on the increasingly close management of social workers. The implications of these developments were increased control and oversight of the running of the business, of the sort considered above, and decreased discretion for social workers. This control was to enable scarce resources to be directed at 'core business' and to increase efficiency. Much of this control is expressed in manuals, directions and guidelines that limit professional discretion and set up standardised and repetitive systems: tightly defined criteria for eligibility for services; standardised assessment tools; interventions which are often determined in advance from a limited list; minimisation of contact time; micro-case management and pressure for throughput. Key decisions about social work provision are made by managers, rather than by social workers. The fragmentation of social work tasks and their re-division between qualified and less-qualified staff mean both de-skilling and a loss of social worker control over the process (Simiç 1995; Dominelli 1996), turning the social worker 'from semi-professional to state technician' (Jones and Novak 1993: 204).

Conclusion

It was seen in Chapter 3 that the reconstruction of the state and its role in welfare by the Conservative governments led to the establishment of the social work business. The way the social work business was run thereafter was premised on a generic model of management, which minimised the differences between the management of capitalist enterprises and the management of public services in a new mode of 'marketised state' provision. One major emphasis in commentary on and analysis of these developments has been to consider in what ways quasi-markets differ from pure markets (Le Grand 1993). Another has been to analyse how the quasi-market has operated in practice (Lewis and Glennerster 1996). The diffusion of quasi-capitalist rationality, as part of a quasi-business discourse, and the consequent similarities that have developed between running private sector businesses and the social work business have tended to be ignored, even though the achievement of such similarities was one of the main goals of the Conservatives' reforms.

The adoption of quasi-capitalist rationality represented a fundamental shift in the basis on which social work was undertaken. In the pre-business era, the state set out the broad ends and purposes of social work (see Ch. 2), leaving social workers to determine the means by which those ends and purposes were achieved. The establishing and running of the social work business resulted in managerial incursions into the means of achieving the state's ends, guided by quasi-capitalist rationality and constrained by cash limits and the intensification of competitive forces through quasi-markets. The process of managerialisation installed measures for controlling the activities of social workers, displacing the parochial–professional culture of the pre-business era, within which social workers exercised wide areas of discretion, with a new workplace culture of control. These developments could be depicted as the beginning of the 'McDonaldisation' of the social work business, involving the managerial application of the four guiding principles that Ritzer (2000: 11–15) derives from the running of the fast-food restaurant: efficiency, predictability, calculability and control through non-human technology.

5 Modernising the business

By the time New Labour came to power in 1997, the context within which social work operated and the content of social work itself had changed fundamentally as a result of the establishment of the social work business and the embrace of quasi-capitalist rationality in the way it was run (see Chs 3 and 4). New Labour accepted the business legacy it inherited from the Conservatives and set about its modernisation. This chapter identifies the origins of the modernisation programme in 'Third Way' thinking, and the substantial areas of overlap between the New Right and New Labour, before considering the distinctive communitarian twist New Labour has supplied. The modern business model, represented by 'Best Value', is outlined as a precursor to charting the modernisation of the social work business through the activities of four new institutions. The central significance of regulation and audit is then discussed as part of the framework that has been reconstructing social work's practice and controlling professional discretion.

Enter New Labour

After eighteen years of Conservative administration, influenced by New Right thinking, New Labour was at pains to distance itself from the 'Old Left' and from the New Right. It did so by depicting itself as the 'Third Way' (Blair 1998). This label was meant to capture the ideological indifference of New Labour, as it steadied itself to steer a middle course through whatever issues it had to confront. However, there were substantial areas of overlap between the Conservative governments and New Labour in terms of the primacy accorded to globalisation, the restructuring of the economy and of society required in response to its impact and the changes required to established practices and ways of working as a basis for capitalism's future prosperity, in particular the imperative towards low costs and highly flexible forms of working. Four shared themes can be identified: the primacy of economic competitiveness; the subordination of social policy to the needs of a competitive national economy; the limited or reduced scope envisaged for government intervention or direction; and a central concern with control over public expenditure (Clarke *et al.* 2000a: 13). New Labour put this more tersely in the cut and thrust of everyday politics by repeating its mantra that priority is accorded to economic performance, growth and low inflation. In this reading of New Labour, it represented a readjustment of the New Right's neo-liberalism, rather than its replacement. Hall (1998) fleshes out the key elements of continuity between the New Right and New Labour in the stress on:

- the representation of globalisation as an uncontradictory, uncontrollable, unitary phenomenon to which British society must adapt in ways required by global capital;
- market deregulation and flexibility, including privatising public assets;
- low taxation;
- private provision for personal risk;
- residual public sector (this began to change with the renewed emphasis on the public sector as the project for the second Blair government from 2001 onwards);
- new managerialism in the public sector;
- individual values not vested interests;
- moral discourse of self-sufficiency and competitiveness.

The role this neo-liberal continuity carved out for social policy can be summarised (Jessop 1994) as follows:

- Social policy functions for capital. The state promotes permanent innovation and flexibility in a relatively open economy and seeks to use social policy to strengthen economic competitiveness.
- Social policy is itself subordinated to the demands of labour market flexibility and economic competitiveness.
- Increasing importance is attached in social policy to non-state mechanisms compensating for market failures and delivering state-sponsored policies.

In its particular representation of the new neo-liberal consensus and its approach to social policy, New Labour's 'Third Way' was strongly influenced by the reflexive modernisation thesis of Beck (1992) and, especially, of Giddens (1991, 1994). This thesis suggested that new political responses were needed to meet the challenges posed not only by globalisation but by social reflexivity, detraditionalisation and a heightened sense of risk in the late-modern world. The thesis asserted that these forces undermined the social democratic welfare state, as traditional class identities dissolved and there were changes in the labour market, gender relations and household forms (Benton 2000). In the politics of New Labour, which emerged from the influence of this thesis, self-conscious citizens were emphasised, rather than the more narrowly focused 'customers' of the Conservative era (see Ch. 7), but they are, nevertheless, citizens concerned with consumerism and the market, with identity and 'life politics' (Giddens 1994). New Labour's overall direction was thus conducive to the maintenance of quasi-capitalist rationality in the public sector, but its emphasis on modernisation replaced the rampant market rhetoric associated with its predecessor Conservative governments. As a result, the continuation of quasi-capitalist rationality, within a quasi-business discourse, is conducted in a more 'civic'-oriented language.

The particular 'civic' twist offered by New Labour is its emphasis on its ability to represent the whole of society in encompassing everybody's interests. This claim rests on New Labour continuing to change the relationship between the state and citizens begun by the Conservatives (see Ch. 3). The key principles underpinning that relationship are *agency* and *interdependence*. New Labour expects individuals to be active in meeting their needs in ways that depend on and contribute to the maintenance of networks of economic, social and cultural relations between people, with the state's primary role seen as the strengthening of the capacity of individuals to act on their own behalf in supportive communities (Barnes and Prior 2000: 20). As 'community' achieved a new prominence in this 'civic' thinking, a key aspect of New Labour's political project was a stress on communitarianism (Frazer 2000: 178–81). Communitarianism contributed to New Labour's presentation of itself as the 'Third Way', moving beyond the market and bureaucracy and on to new configurations of the state, the market and civil society. In other words, communitarianism was used to mark out New Labour's difference from the Conservative governments in its commitment to a set of social values that promotes togetherness and trust or, in the term New Labour usually prefers to adopt, 'social inclusion'. Thus New Labour used communitarianism to express its notion of a 'stakeholder society' (Finer Jones 1997). However, its version of communitarianism is morally prescriptive, economically liberal and socially conservative (Fitzpatrick 1998). It is top–down and authoritarian, rather than bottom–up and solidaristic, and it is driven by central government and statute, with 'the community' often functioning as a code word for the state (Driver and Martell 1997: 39–40). The relevance for social work of New Labour's communitarianism is that it involves strict regulation of public services and a re-visioning of government as the guardian (but not the direct implementer) of the social interest (Freeden 1999: 49). As will be seen later in the chapter, this is reflected in the top–down policing of professional performance in a way that powerfully reinforces and develops the Conservative governments' message that professionals cannot be trusted.

The stress on communitarianism does not imply indifference on the part of New Labour to the importation of quasi-capitalist rationality and the implementation of managerialism, as part of the incorporation of a quasi-business discourse in the public sector. On the contrary, New Labour has stressed the need for 'modernisation' as a shorthand term for bringing the public sector into line with the modern practices of capitalist enterprises. It is to that aspect of New Labour that the discussion now turns.

New Labour's modern business model

New Labour's drive for modernisation has intensified pressure on the public sector generally and has placed particular pressures on social work, which for some years has been treated as though it were not just a business, but one that was failing. The requirement for price competition in some areas of the public sector, introduced by the Conservatives through compulsory competitive tendering, was replaced by a much more thoroughgoing quasi-business regime: 'Best Value'. The demands of New Labour's 'Best Value' are far more comprehensive than anything attempted by the Conservative governments.

'Best Value': the quasi-business regime

'Best Value' was flagged up in a New Labour White Paper on local government, *Modern Local Government: In Touch With the People* (Department of the Environment, Transport and the Regions 1998). The White Paper indicated that continuous improvements in both quality and cost would be the hallmarks of modern local government and the test of 'Best Value' which became a statutory duty from 1 April 2000: 'This is a statutory duty to deliver services taking into account quality and cost by the most effective, economic and efficient means possible' (Local Government Act 1999: Annex A). The expectation was that, over a five-year period, all local authority services would be reviewed and best value performance plans would be produced, with user satisfaction indicators for all services. As well as social work being swept up in this general flurry of activity, it was explicitly linked to 'Best Value', with requirements to deliver services to clear standards, paying attention to quality and cost and demonstrating a commitment to continuous improvement in the efficiency and effectiveness of its performance (Department of Health 1998b). The most tangible expression of the arrangements for 'modern' social work being based on the 'Best Value' regime was the implementation of national performance standards and targets.

Four principles (according to the Department of the Environment, Transport and the Regions 1998) underpin 'Best Value':

- *challenge* (why and how a service is provided)
- *compare* (with others' performance, including the use of performance indicators in benchmarking exercises)
- *consult* (local taxpayers, service users and the business community in setting performance targets)
- *competition* (as the means to efficient and effective services).

These four principles emphasised the ethos of 'Best Value' as placing 'everything up for grabs'. There was no guarantee that a particular service should be provided; there were no assumptions that services that are provided have to continue to be provided in the same way as previously; and there was a driving dynamic of saving money. As well as absorbing the cost of the 'baseline assessment' and review processes required by the 'Best Value' regime, local authorities were expected to make efficiency savings (*Community Care* 2000: 20–1). In Social Services Departments, for example, 'Best Value' reinforced existing pressures to dispose of residential care to other providers because of assessments of local authority labour costs that were considered too high for such services to function 'efficiently' (Newman 2000: 55) and thus failing to provide 'Best Value'. This was confirmed by the 'Best Value' pilot programmes, in which 'there was increasing interest in alternatives to in-house provision . . . It seemed likely that a number of authorities would be out-sourcing aspects of residential care' (University of Warwick 2001: 15). When transfers to the private sector have taken place, many staff working in residential settings have found that their wages are driven *down* to the much-vaunted minimum wage introduced by New Labour. In the 'Best Value' regime, efficiency savings are both enabled by the transfer of services to alternative providers and anticipated from the stimulation of new markets by creating 'the conditions in which new suppliers might take root where the current market is demonstrably weak, poorly developed and offers no credible alternative to the current supplier' (Department of the Environment, Transport and the Regions 1999).

Thus, under 'Best Value' the drive for efficiency continued and intensified the quasi-capitalist rationality initiated by the Conservatives. This drive was supported by the way in which 'Best Value' forced public services into a 'business performance' mould, with an emphasis on quasi-business results, increasingly defined by government performance targets. In keeping with the quasi-capitalist rationality of a business performance approach, there was a parallel emphasis on customers as the focus of the drive for high quality and efficient public services (Cabinet Office 1999). Modernising was presented as a process that involved this dual emphasis on matching the expectations of modern customers and meeting the business requirements of the modern world (Newman 2000: 46). The emphasis served to obscure and neutralise questions of any wider values and objectives and has permeated into the 'best value plans' produced by local authorities, as in this example:

> The whole organisation becomes a place with a Best Value culture of listening to its customers, the citizens of ['X'], and constantly striving to better its service. . . . The Council will achieve this through . . . promoting the values of Best Value, for example by ensuring that any training . . . will reinforce the need to focus on the . . . customer's priorities.

In another example, a local authority has used 'mystery shoppers' as part of its 'Best Value' strategy:

> To encourage continuous improvement in the way we treat our customers the Council has employed external consultants to carry out a mystery shopping exercise (an exercise involving anonymous callers posing as customers). . . . It is our intention to use this data to assess and improve our performance against the performance of private sector companies.

In Chapter 7 there is a full discussion of the status and experience of the 'customer', but suffice it to note here that in these extracts, and more generally, 'Best Value' has been seen as a self-referential process. It is regarded as embodying quasi-business values of its own to which local authorities, including their Social Services Departments, should aspire, rather than serving as a means to achieve values defined by the local authority in general or its Social Services Department in particular. That view is captured succinctly in this third example: 'This [performance] plan tells you how the Council is aiming to deliver Best Value – in other words how we are striving to provide the best possible service, for the people we serve, at an affordable price.'

'Best value' had an inauspicious introduction. As a result of the experience of the pilot programme, less than half of 'corporate best value officers' believed that the costs of implementing 'Best Value' would be outweighed by service improvements and efficiency gains. This pessimism was likely to have been unrelieved by the statutory regime that followed because that involved additional costs, 'including an on-going programme of implementation of review findings, preparation of performance plans and demonstration of compliance to auditors and inspectors' (University of Warwick 2001: 16). Undaunted, New Labour introduced 'Best Value' as a statutory duty. At the end of the first year of the statutory operation of 'Best Value' (in March 2001), the Best Value Inspectorate (within the Audit Commission) reported on how the local (authority) businesses were doing. It concluded that local authorities had not been sufficiently ambitious or urgent in what they had sought to achieve since April 2000, and concluded that a 'sea-change in performance' was needed in the second year of 'Best Value's' operation (Best Value Inspectorate 2001). The introduction of 'Best Value' suggests that New Labour had clear ideas about how it wanted to do business.

Doing business New Labour's way

As we have seen, New Labour extracted its emphasis on social inclusion from communitarianism and this was combined with the drive for modernisation, through the quasi-business regime provided by 'Best Value'. Modernisation is a much bigger project than 'Best Value', however. In essence, modernisation is a revamped version of managerialism (see Ch. 3), linked to a different political agenda. This potent combination of ends and means enables New Labour to present its quasi-capitalist rationality, within a quasi-business discourse characterised by top–down managerialism, as both empowering and requiring identification with the organisation.

In New Labour's view of the world, the organisational context embodies and represents its attempts to secure social inclusion. Organisations, as the delivery mechanisms for New Labour's political agenda, are the carriers of corporate values that symbolise a common purpose and way of working (Corrigan 1999). Managers are, therefore, not simply to be concerned with managerial control, but are seen as guardians of New Labour's political agenda. In contrast to the Conservative variant (see Ch. 3), this version of managerialism is presented as 'empowering' everyone; and it is represented as an apolitical and self-evidently 'good thing'. In particular, this empowering managerialism purports to speak for service users, and any resistance to managerialism by social workers is attacked as simply élitist professional attempts to avoid accountability to customers. This enables New Labour to present the Conservatives as having been misguidedly concerned with management and the power of managers as ends in themselves, as contrasted with New Labour's use of managerialist approaches in order to achieve 'higher' purposes. Newman (2000) argues that key aspects of modernising management's higher purposes were presented as the updating of services to match the expectations of modern consumers (see Ch. 7), empowering citizens and communities and including the socially excluded. However modernising management is concerned also with meeting the business requirements of the modern world and finding business solutions for the operation of public sector services. The public sector is enjoined to deliver services within the discourses of quality management, customer service and user involvement – all of which require continual improvements to services – and to break traditional models of service provision and become more like the private sector. Business entrepreneurialism and modern commercial practice are seen as core components in challenging and transforming the shape and role of the public sector (Newman 2000).

This New Labour vision of how modernisation translates into local (authority) businesses emanated from strong central government control of the agenda to be implemented. Like the corporate headquarters of a modern business, New Labour has defined social work's objectives at national level, set outcomes to be achieved locally and monitored the results (Malin 2000: 18). The emphasis on local leadership, entrepreneurialism and a strong performance culture with regard to standards and quality has been pinned to the achievement of targets set by central government (Waine 2000: 247). This is close to a public sector model of franchising – 'franchise holders, although legally independent, must conform to detailed standards of operation designed and enforced by the parent company' (Dicke quoted in Ritzer 2000:

36) – with central government requiring local government, including Social Services Departments, to carry out its policies according to its regulations and systems guidance. In this franchising arrangement, there is limited operational autonomy and the threat of having the franchise taken away, if performance is not up to scratch. This is very different from the Conservative governments' faith in managers to design the process of delivering a service: 'If managers are simply operating a pre-set process whose elements are fixed by someone else, then they have a very limited management role' (Flynn 1993: 111). The limited management role in this franchising model can be illustrated by New Labour's approach to the social work business in its *Quality Strategy for Social Care* (Department of Health 2000a).

The *Quality Strategy* exemplifies local delivery of a central government agenda: 'Delivering high-quality social care services is essentially a local responsibility. The *Quality Strategy* will set a national framework to help raise local standards, but this will only be achieved through local policy and implementation' (Department of Health 2000a: para. 18). This encapsulates the franchising relationship: central government designs, local (authority) franchised businesses deliver. The approach to the design and delivery of services is rooted in a quasi-business discourse in which the buck stops with the franchisees: 'An inadequate framework for quality improvement has meant that local authorities have been unable to drive up the quality of social care' (Department of Health 2000a: para. 17). Again:

> The new quality framework will be the mechanism through which local councils will drive up the quality of social care and be fully accountable for its delivery. Instituting a new quality framework will mean the creation of a coherent structure and processes – both across local councils and within social services – and clearly defined lines of accountability.
>
> (Department of Health 2000a: para. 22)

Elements of the design of the quality system were set out in the *Quality Strategy* and included national service frameworks, national standards, service models and local performance measures against which progress within an agreed timescale could be monitored (Department of Health 2000a: para. 26). The *Quality Strategy* charged the Social Services Inspectorate with setting and monitoring standards for how each local (authority) business carries out its social services functions. These are attuned to each franchisee in being specific to each inspection and can be used by local authorities in their own audit and review processes (Department of Health 2000a: para. 27). Finally, the *Quality Strategy for Social Care* is keyed into the surrounding quasi-business regime: 'This will support the implementation of Best Value' (Department of Health 2000a: para. 31).

This quasi-business discourse had already appeared in the *Modernising Social Services* White Paper (Department of Health 1998b) which, for example, required local authorities to carry out surveys to gauge levels of satisfaction among service users and carers. One Social Services Department, which has embraced the 'business excellence model', quotes that model's guide in declaring: 'Customer satisfaction, people satisfaction and impact on society are achieved through leadership driving policy and strategy, people management, resources and processes, leading ultimately to excellence in business results.' Another Social Services Department has reconfigured around two 'clusters of functions': 'business performance' and 'business improvement'. (Note that even the word 'service' has been replaced by 'business'.) These are just two examples of what it looks like to do business New Labour's way. They are part of a wider modernisation programme for the franchised social work businesses, emerging from New Labour's corporate headquarters.

Modernising the social work business

The implication of the discussion thus far is that when New Labour came to power there could have been no question of any return to the bureau-professional regime that characterised the social democratic welfare state (Clarke *et al.* 2000a: 15; and see Ch. 2, this volume). The neo-liberal consensus (see pp. 77–78), had begun to emerge from the late 1980s onwards, as the range of language used in debates about the future of the social services narrowed. On the Right, as we saw in Chapter 3, a strategy was implemented of transferring services and resources outside the public sector and setting in place quasi-market arrangements. In parallel, the Labour Party was at pains to present itself as hostile to a bureaucratic and domineering welfare state (Taylor-Gooby 1987: 199–201) and a Right–Left consensus was evident on markets and managerialism as the way forward (Labour Party 1991; Prime Minister 1991). In fact, the three main political parties endorsed the key themes of the Conservative reforms considered in Chapter 3 (Taylor-Gooby and Lawson 1993a: 2; Butcher 1995: 161), leading commentators to the view that, regardless of the political party in power, the new managerialism associated with a quasi-business discourse would be likely to endure (Wilding 1992:

204; Pierson 1994: 109). The commentators were vindicated; as I noted earlier, New Labour maintained this consensus on coming to office, and markets and managerialism remained as key components in New Labour's continuation of the Conservatives' transformation of the public sector.

One of the themes which settled around the consensus was the focusing of organisational attention on sharpening up service delivery (Clarke and Newman 1997: 111). As we have seen, New Labour maintained the organisational structures of the social work business, established by the Conservatives, and intensified the elements of discipline and scrutiny in its concern with pragmatic performance. In this respect, New Labour was not as overtly ideologically driven as the Conservatives (Bartlett *et al.* 1998: 1). Its ideological indifference emerged in the willingness to accept the architecture of services left by the Conservatives. For example, *Modernising Social Services* acknowledged difficulties in relation to eligibility and equity in market-based social services but stressed that New Labour did not take an 'ideological approach' to service provision (Department of Health 1998b: Ch. 7). Notwithstanding New Labour's maintenance of its Conservative legacy, the renovations made to it have been extensive.

The basis from which the renovations proceeded has been a discourse of failure, directed at both the Conservatives and at social services departments (Langan 2000: 157–8; Jones 2001: 555). *Modernising Social Services* (Department of Health 1998b) counterposed against this discourse of failure the principles that underpinned New Labour's 'Third Way' renovation of social work and raised expectations of what it would achieve:

- supporting independence and respecting dignity;
- meeting individuals' specific needs;
- giving people a say in the services they get and how they are delivered;
- fairness, openness and consistency in organising, accessing, providing and financing services;
- giving children looked after by local authorities a decent start in life;
- children and adults should be safeguarded against abuse and neglect;
- staff should be sufficiently trained;
- social services should work to clear standards and action can be taken if they are not met.

(Department of Health 1998b: para. 1.8)

Although some of these principles imply the need for skills and expertise if they are to be achieved, those skills and expertise are difficult to locate in the New Labour agenda:

> Built into everything that New Labour's policy documents say . . . is a view of local authority personal social services as concerned with policing the community to forestall breakdowns in informal caring functions and with stepping into the breach to provide care of various kinds when such breaches occur or shortcomings are identified. . . . Practice itself remains entirely shadowy, portrayed either as anxious monitoring or decisive protection or even as tough enforcement, but never as sensitive, aware, dialogical and flexible negotiation about the kinds of complex messes that constitute ordinary crises in ordinary lives.
>
> (Jordan and Jordan 2000: 125)

In contrast, as might be expected given the quasi-business discourse of New Labour, there has been considerable emphasis on 'quality management' tools and techniques applied to the tasks and content of social work and linked into the 'Best Value' framework (Department of Health 2000a: para. 71). Decisions about strategies for improving quality were to be made (Cabinet Office *et al.* 2000), within a new quality framework which 'guarantees the quality of local social care services' for users and carers (Department of Health 2000a: para. 72, Box 10). This framework 'will drive change at all levels in social care organisations through a shift to a culture of continuous improvement' (Department of Health 2000a: para 73). All of this drive for change is located within the wider quasi-business regime of 'Best Value':

> Best Value sets a challenging new performance framework for the whole of local government. The government has defined Best Value as the duty to deliver services to clear standards – covering both quality and cost – by the most economic, efficient and effective means available.
>
> The quality of social services will be subject to internal and external scrutiny . . . the duty of Best Value will drive continuous improvement. . . . The delivery of this quality strategy will form an integral part of the Department of Health performance assessment arrangements.
>
> (Department of Health 2000a: paras 93, 95)

In addition to raising expectations about transformation through grounding social work in the quasi-business regime of 'Best Value', four dedicated modernising organisations have been established to carry through the renovation of the local (authority) social work businesses.

The modernising organisations

New organisations have been established by New Labour to modernise social work (Department of Health 1998b; Scottish Office 1999; Welsh Office 1999). The new organisations join existing outfits with a modernisation mandate, such as (in England) the Best Value Inspectorate in the Audit Commission (Audit Commission 1999), mentioned earlier in the chapter, the Social Services Inspectorate (Department of Health 1999) and the combined forces of the Audit Commission and the Social Services Inspectorate in Joint Reviews (Joint Reviews 1999). In addition to this activity of organisations initiated directly by central government, the Local Government Association set up the Improvement and Development Agency in April 1999 to support local councils in responding to the activities of these existing outfits charged with the carrying through of the modernising agenda (McCurry 1999; Caporn 2001). The Performance Support Unit is also on hand to co-ordinate teams of troubleshooters: 'The teams will be a resource for local authorities wanting practical assistance to achieve performance improvement' (Local Government Minister B. Hughes, quoted in *Community Care*, 1 February 2001, p 2). The four organisations that are dedicated specifically to modernising the social work business (Department of Health 1998b) join this existing plethora of modernising activity.

The Commission for Care Standards

The Commission for Care Standards sets standards for agency practice in the public, private and voluntary sectors and regulates service quality through inspections – it has taken over the responsibilities of local government in this regard. Most field social work is excluded from the Commission's remit at present, but that is likely to change.

The General Social Care Council

The GSCC oversees the regulation of training and of the conduct and practice of social workers. It regulates the workforce through a statutory code of conduct for staff and a code of practice for employers. It is briefed

> to strengthen public protection by relevant and appropriate regu-
> lation of personnel which has the interest of service users and the
> public at its heart; to ensure through a coherent, well-developed
> and regulated training system that more staff are equipped to
> provide social care which allows and assists individuals to live
> their own lives, and offers practical help, based on research and
> other evidence of what works, and free of unnecessary ideological
> influences.
>
> (Department of Health 1998b: para. 5.15)

The Conservative governments had been dubious about setting up a regulatory body (Department of Health 1996). However the Labour Party, shortly before the 1997 election, announced its commitment to the establishment of such a body. The specific functions and outline constitution of the GSCC were set out in *Modernising Social Services* (Department of Health 1998b): The 'paramount general duty is to secure the interests and the welfare of service users and the confidence of the public'. The Council regulates the conduct of staff and the prac- tice of social work through:

- registration of staff [linked to the holding of a recognised qualification];
- recognition of specific qualifications as a basis for registration;
- publication of codes of conduct for staff and codes of practice for employers;
- holding disciplinary hearings when allegations of breaches of the code of conduct have been made against one or more individuals;
- removal or suspension from the register of individuals who have been found to be in breach of the code of conduct and who are con- sidered unsafe to practice and the imposition of penalties or other measures in respect of those who are not struck off the register.

The Training Organisation for the Personal Social Services

New Labour has established a national training organisation in every sector of the economy to increase training and qualifications and improve the overall performance and competitiveness of the workforce. The Training Organisation for the Personal Social Services (TOPSS) is one of these NTOs, licensed by the Department for Education and

Employment. The remit of TOPSS is workforce planning (TOPSS 1999a), including national standards for qualifications and awards which are linked to particular job roles:

> This training strategy [supplied by *Modernising the Social Care Workforce* (TOPSS 1999a)] is designed to produce a fully skilled and qualified workforce suited to the performance culture in which we work and able to meet the national service standards for the work undertaken. The strategy must also provide a basis for individuals' registration with the forthcoming GSCC.
> (A. Keefe, quoted in a TOPSS news release, 17 September 1999b)

TOPSS has been made responsible for:

- developing a workforce strategy;
- · setting up workforce data and analysing future workforce needs;
- mapping qualifications against workforce requirements and agreeing priorities for future developments;
- providing guidance on getting 'Best Value' from training;
- drawing up national occupational standards as the basis for qualifications.

The Social Care Institute of Excellence

The Social Care Institute of Excellence (SCIE) is a not-for-profit company limited by guarantee. It is intended to be an operationally independent 'authoritative voice about what works in social care. SCIE will work closely with the Government . . . with the new regulatory bodies and with social care organisations to implement the Government's quality agenda for social care' (Department of Health 2000a). The central remit of SCIE is to ensure that 'knowledge about what works becomes an effective force for improving quality' (Department of Health 2000a: para. 30). Its responsibilities include:

- developing a rigorous knowledge base founded on the views and experiences of users, research evidence, Social Services Inspectorate and Audit Commission reports and the experiences of managers and practitioners;
- identifying, disseminating and promoting best practice; and
- producing authoritative and accessible guidelines on effective social care practice, models of service delivery and organisational arrangements.

The fulfilment of these responsibilities is seen as cruical to the modernisation of the social work business:

> SCIE will ensure greater consistency between services offered in local areas, and better quality of services. Users and carers can expect that the best possible decisions are made about service delivery and about individual care. SCIE will do this by pulling together the knowledge about what works in social care and producing authoritative guidelines. It will ensure that this reaches all parts of the social care workforce through new technology and good communication.
>
> (Department of Health 2000a: para. 52, Box 8)

> SCIE's development and dissemination of the knowledge base for social care will be crucial to the training of social care workers and to the monitoring and regulation of social care services. As knowledge about what works in social care develops this can be used to inform the standards against which services are inspected. These activities will be strengthened by the existence of sound evidence from which practice and services can be improved and evaluated.
>
> (Department of Health 2000a: para. 32)

The weight placed on SCIE's contribution to the modernisation of the social work business is indicated in

- local authorities being held to account for the implementation of SCIE's guidelines;
- the use of SCIE's work on best practice and cost-effective solutions in local (authority) businesses' 'Best Value' reviews;
- Social Services Inspectorate's and Joint Reviews' use of SCIE's guidelines (as well as their reports contributing to SCIE's knowledge base); and
- SCIE's guidelines informing the National Care Standards Commission's work in regulating and inspecting social care services.

(Department of Health 2000a: para. 37)

Underpinning the activities of these four organisations is the assumption that the local (authority) social work businesses are part of the problem, requiring additional monitoring bodies and enforcement agencies to be dispatched by corporate headquarters, in order that more standards and targets can be stipulated as the basis for improvement in the performance of workers employed by the franchisees:

'[Social workers] are to be changed – controlled, regulated and quality-assessed in ways which will tie them more closely to their statutory tasks and ministerial guidance, within a fairly circumscribed policy domain' (Jordan and Jordan 2000: 15). Whereas the Conservatives' agenda for the social work business tried to bypass social workers by placing faith in managers (see Ch. 3), New Labour's modernisation agenda confronts social workers much more directly (Davies 2000: 281). For example, the General Social Care Council is now charged with the statutory regulation of social work, replacing the previous quango (CCETSW). As already noted, this idea had been rejected by the Conservatives (Department of Health 1996). Far from acting as a traditional circumscribed professional registration body, concerned with standards of conduct and practice, the General Social Care Council is involved in creating consistency between its practice standards and the employer-led occupational standards of the Training Organisation for the Personal Social Services, the Social Care Institute of Excellence knowledge base and the government agendas being pursued through the activities of other bodies, such as the Social Services Inspectorate (Davies 2000: 286). The theme running through all of this activity is that the social work business needs high levels of regulation.

Regulating the social work business

It has already become apparent that New Labour has placed greater emphasis on direct regulation as one of the key strategies for undertaking its modernisation of the social work business. The implementation of specific initiatives in relation to social work is inextricably intertwined with and evaluated by external audit, inspection and review, for example, by the Best Value Inspectorate (Audit Commission 1999), by performance assessment framework reviews by the Social Services Inspectorate (Department of Health 1999), by quinquennial joint reviews (Joint Reviews 1999), by inspections by the Commission for Care Standards and by thematic inspections by the Social Services Inspectorate. This brief indication of the high level of regulatory activity suggests that while the Conservative governments placed their faith in local management having a constraining impact on professional judgement and discretion, New Labour has adopted a more hands-on approach in its dealings with its franchisees. In effect, civil servants and central government ministers are dictating priorities at the local level in order to ensure that social workers are delivering central government's agendas. The intertwining of policy and regulation results in detailed stipulations about the management of practice, with strong expectations that governmental agendas will be delivered by local (authority) businesses. This emphasis can be traced back to the Labour Party manifesto for the 1992 general election, which embraced the language and ideas of targets, monitoring and performance (Labour Party 1992). The proliferation of regulation since New Labour came to power has resulted in a high degree of uncertainty and instability as local (authority) businesses are judged by the different means and methods used by specific inspectorial agents. The pressures of being constantly accountable, measured and recorded are thus amplified by changing demands and indicators.

New Labour's surveillance and regulation of the public sector through audit and inspection are combined with competition through rating systems and league tables (Hood *et al.* 1999) which encourage local (authority) social work businesses to make themselves different and to stand out from the run-of-the-mill. There are performance assessment indicators and league table comparisons between social services departments (Department of Health 2000c). From such data, we learn that 122 out of 150 Social Services Departments have improved; we know the 'top three' of those most improved; and we are aware of which Social Services Departments have more than half of the thirty-seven indicators in bands 1 ('investigate urgently') or 2 ('ask questions about performance'). Yet we are told by the government minister John Hutton that these are 'not league tables' (quoted in White 2000: 3).

Such developments indicate that the processes of regulation and review have brought into being new 'jurisdictional claimants' – 'appraisers, auditors and monitors of expert services' (Johnson 1995: 22) – as the disciplinary agents of an increasingly authoritarian state (Jordan 1998). What were previously seen as questions of professional standards are now seen as management processes (Jones 1999: 4) which need to be subjected to the 'independent evaluative practice' of audit (Clarke *et al.* 2000b: 253). In that sense, regulation of the social work business results from mistrust of professionals and replaces the perceived untrustworthiness of the bureau-professional regime (see Ch. 2). In addition, it indicates a degree of mistrust of unfettered markets, with more emphasis on active supervision and direction by government of dispersed quasi-market services. As audit is associated with dysfunctions and pathologies it 'shrinks trust' (Power 1997), with a constant flow of naming and shaming reports and stories about untrustworthy services appearing and indicating the need for more audit. Assumptions of distrust become self-fulfilling as auditees adapt their behaviour to the audit process, distorting reality so that it conforms to an auditable reality and becoming less trustworthy as a result of a process designed to make them more trustworthy (Power 1997: 135–6). This adaptation to the process of audit on the part of auditees indicates that, in order to be regulated, organisations have to render themselves auditable. They have to produce and shape the information on which regulation relies (Clarke *et al.* 2000b: 255).

The regulators' perceptions of performance and quality are further influenced by the degree of compliance with the 'objective' reality of regulation on the part of managers and social workers. In other words, regulation requires 'performativity' (Lyotard 1984): the construction and delivery of what counts as performance. Performances by social work organisations to the audience of regulation serve as measures of productivity and output that represent the organisations' worth. Only when this fabrication of impression management has taken place can local (authority) businesses be evaluated according to their internal efficiency and their efficiency as compared to other local (authority) businesses. Results are published as comparative data in league tables, indicating relative success in reaching New Labour's requirements. The dominant image of the public in this process is as the tax-payer, anxious to see her/his interests met through audit revelation of efficient and cost-effective services with business-like practices (Clarke *et al.* 2000b: 260). As has been seen, there is an assumption that exposing performance in this way will stimulate continuous improvement. Of course, there are costs involved in making social work auditable that have an impact on their capacity to bring about improvements. Resources have to be diverted – from whatever else they could have enabled the local (authority) businesses to do – to accounting for what they do (Clarke *et al.* 2000b: 256).

The processes here outlined contribute to the sustenance of the quasi-business discourse in social work, through constant repetition of the imagery of capitalist businesses and the presentation of them as superior to the public sector. As regulatory mechanisms imbued with this imagery have become a powerful means of monitoring performance, through a fusing of financial and professional concerns, the form of regulation has been frequently anti-professional in tone and ostensibly consumerist.

Implications of New Labour's approach to the social work business

As far as the Social Care Institute for Excellence (New Labour's quasi-business intelligence unit) is concerned, the knowledge base on which it will draw for its practice guidance on 'what works' is diverse, comprising Social Services Inspectorate and Audit Commission reports, evidence from research, and the views and experiences of service users, managers and practitioners (Department of Health 1998b: para. 38). However, thanks to this postmodern embrace of a variety of narratives, SCIE is paradoxically presumably in a powerful position to produce the definitive metanarrative on any topic. The problem that these SCIE metanarratives are meant to address has been set out in simple terms:

> Establishing best practice and disseminating this effectively has been a stumbling block in social care. This has led to inconsistent levels of quality throughout the country. SCIE will determine what works best in social care, allowing us to improve consistency in the quality of practice and service delivery.
>
>   (Hutton, a government minister, quoted in *Community Care* 2001b)

One remedy to the problem is seen as relatively straightforward. In the same *Community Care* news article, Arthur Keefe, TOPSS (England) chairperson, stated that

> SCIE will provide much better information for people during training and if they develop the habit of using evidence-based good practice at that stage, they will use it during their life-long work. . . . If there is good information coming out that people can easily put into practice most workers will want to follow it.

Thus, the main difficulty facing the social work business is portrayed as that of getting social workers on board with 'what works': 'Give me evidence-based practice and policy any and every day rather than practice based on prejudice and arrogance, or practice which is just chaotic and unstructured' (R. Jones, chief executive of SCIE, quoted in *Care and Health* 2001–2: 4).

These somewhat simplistic analyses are at odds with the day-to-day realities of many social workers. For example, TOPSS calculates that 70,000 qualified social workers are needed and only 30,000 are available (Orme *et al.* 2001: 1). There is a national vacancy rate, according to Joint Reviews, of 16 per cent (Joint Reviews 2000a). In the fifteen Social Services Departments on 'special measures', the problems include social work vacancy rates of over 30 per cent, many vacant or 'acting' senior management posts, an unstable political environment and low morale (Social Services Inspectorate 2000). Even more significant are the straightened circumstances of the majority of the clientele social workers are dealing with in a society in which over 14 million people are living on less than half the average income (Gordan and Adelman 2000). Faced with these realities, regulation relies on the rhetoric of driving up standards and quality at a time of narrowed interpretations of need, reduction of access to services, rapid encounters between service users and social workers and circumscribed concrete definitions of outcome. In such circumstances, the pressure is on to process as many service users as possible, in part through a reduction in professionals' discretionary decision making and a consequent uniformity of service experiences (see Ch. 4), which flies in the face of the quasi-business discourse's emphasis on customers (see Ch. 7).

Against this background, we have little evidence of whether, and if so how, regulation promotes change. This is somewhat puzzling in a situation in which New Labour planned to spend at least £600 million on inspectorial activity in 2001 (Winchester 2000: 11) and in the face of evidence that only 27 per cent of local authorities in England and Wales thought that inspections led to innovation (Improvement and Development Agency 2001). Given the amount of regulatory activity, there is surprisingly little interest within the quasi-business discourse's own terms in the marginal utility of successive waves of regulation. How much improvement results from how much regulation? Could more have been achieved by spending the money tied up in regulation on more services? What is the most efficient ratio between the effort and time spent accounting for tasks as compared to actually doing them? In other words, there is a surprisingly low degree of attention to 'Best Value' by its proponents in relation to their own regulatory activities. There is, however, evidence that regulatory activity (and quasi-markets) have added to the labour costs of Social Services Departments. The number of social services staff in England fell by 7 per cent between 1995 (233,900) and 2000 (217,200). However, central and strategic staff increased by 4,100 in the same period, with the biggest percentage increase taking place in senior directing staff (50 per cent), from 400 to 600, and senior professional support staff rising from 3,000 to 4,300 (Department of Health 2001a). Two of the three reasons given by the Association of Directors of Social Services to account for this rise related to the quasi-market and regulation, namely 'increasing externalisation of services' and 'performance management work'. The spokesperson said: 'There continues to be an increase in the number of services we purchase from external organisations. We have to ensure we have senior staff to commission and manage those external services' (McKitterick, quoted in *Community Care* 2001c).

Notwithstanding the lack of scrutiny of the impact of regulation itself, expectations of what it can achieve are constantly talked up (Power 1997: 144). Power argues that the 'expectations gap' is audit's constitutive principle. Further, it is impossible to know when an audit is justified or effective, because it puts 'itself beyond empirical knowledge about its own effects in favour of a constant programmatic affirmation of its potential' (Power 1997: 142). For example, the *Joint Reviews* (2000b) concludes that the prospects for improvement are increasingly promising but there is still much to do. Presumably, this is the best type of conclusion a regulatory body can hope to produce: 'We're having an impact but you need more of what we do.' Given the notion of continuous improvement in the quasi-business discourse, the job can, in any case, never be completed, particularly as the solution to failed managerialism is 'more of the same'. In this scenario, there is a kind of cognitive dissonance involved. The more the quasi-business discourse fails, the stronger the belief generated in regulation, because it is required to be omniscient and omnipresent. In circumstances when belief might be in danger of wavering, there is always an escape clause to divert attention elsewhere. For example, Joint Reviews gave Haringey Social Services Department a glowing review three months before Anna Climbié's death. It described child protection as a highly targeted service in which 'the practice appears safe, the systems appear sound'. Four months after Anna Climbié died, a Social Services Inspectorate report on children's services found that in three out of ten of the cases inspected standards of practice were unsatisfactory to the extent that children's safety was not assured. John Bolton (head of Joint Reviews) commented: 'Our role is not to inspect services as such and local authorities should not depend on any inspection regime to assure the quality of their service. Our role is to help them put in place their own systems to check that their services are safe' (quoted in *Community Care* 2001a: 3).

In contrast to this very limited view of the role of the regulator, because of factors seen as outside the regulators' control, services are never seen as performing differently from each other because of factors outside professionals' and managers' control. The regulators' mantra is that there is never any excuse for poor services; services can never be considered poor for good reasons. Managers are expected to perform well regardless of the degree of influence they have over the variables impacting on the services for which they are held responsible (Flynn

1993: 124). The regulatory framework has thus emphasised a decon-textualised approach to quality and business excellence. We can iden-tify two consequences of this approach.

First, the framing of quality in terms of business excellence shifts it onto the ground of corporate organisational concerns, with a pressure for managers to be less interested in the quality of social workers' prac-tice than in achieving corporate objectives (Hunt and Campbell 1998). Second, even if an emphasis on standards and regulation were pro-ducing high quality services, that would help only those receiving a service. All the attention is focused on current service users, not on those refused a service (Tanner 2001), because regulation zooms in on efficiency in delivering 'core business' (Newman 2000: 54). Not only does this mean an exclusive concentration on existing customers, it also means not questioning the sources of the customers' problems, as the social work business is reduced to a series of service transactions, translated into categories for judgement, for the purposes of regulation and audit. This is one aspect of the way in which the social work busi-ness is depoliticised and represented as a neutral machine for the pro-duction of services, divorced from wider questions about equity and social justice. Questions in relation to the latter are compartmentalised in the 'value base' of the people providing the service (see Ch. 6) or in New Labour's presentation of an ideal of total inclusion in a perfect consensus (O'Sullivan 2000: 8), rather than the ineliminable place of conflict (Mouffe 2000) in the constitution of anything so politically charged as social work. Regulation insulates itself from the potentially conflictual politics of organisational complexity in order to make things auditable and produce 'certificates of comfort' (Power 1997: 140. This results in settling for a superficial appearance of what is going on:

> The panoply of performance monitoring and management sys-tems . . . has provided a means of separating workers from the lived experience of users. The detailed documentation of virtually everything that is done for clients . . . which is now embodied in care . . . planning documents, assessments and reviews . . . monitor-ing reports etc. is fast becoming a vast simulacrum, a deceptive substitute, for real contact. The point is that such documen-tation is not designed to promote emotional contact, dialogue and learning but to enable the organisation to look *as if* it is doing these things. Appearance has become inextricably confused with reality or, semiotically speaking, the system of signification

(the documentation) has become a thing in itself, masking rather than revealing actual social relations of welfare.

(Hoggett 2000: 151–2; emphasis original)

Conclusion

Government guidance and professional journals reiterate constantly the importance of the social work business being committed to individual holistic assessment of service users and the provision of individually tailored high-quality 'packages of care'. This implies the need for a degree of professional discretion, if such goals are to be achieved. At the same time, we have seen that there is a high degree of centralisation and regulation in New Labour's conduct of the social work business. Modernising the business is a strategy for contesting power that subsumes social work within a new framework of production – reconstructing its practice, regulating and controlling professional discretion, setting standards, publicising local (authority) franchisees' performance against them, promoting 'beacon' franchisees as heroic, castigating 'failing' ones as villainous (Newman 2000: 51) and threatening the latter with takeovers of their operations. All of this pushes towards the standardisation of production processes in the social work business, rather than encouraging the creativity, flexibility, innovation and engaged commitment with service users demanded by the rhetoric of the quasi-business discourse. The 'successful' social work business franchise is responsive to requirements and specified targets from New Labour's corporate headquarters and searches for key tactical improvements that will result in moving up the quasi-business performance indicators. Best practice in social work now involves the ability to know 'what works' and to follow rules and procedures competently. In New Labour's modernised social work business, the overarching goal could easily be mistaken as being the search for the regulatory processes which will finally, and to great fanfare from corporate headquarters, produce from its franchisees the social work practice equivalent of the (mass-produced, predictable and cheap) fast-food hamburger, topped with a dash of social inclusion relish.

6   Learning the business

In Chapter 2 the pre-business era was explored as a precursor to considering the establishing of the social work business under Conservative governments in the 1980s and 1990s (see Chs 3 and 4), before moving on to the modernisation of the business under New Labour (see Ch. 5). In the pre-business era, the emergence of the bureau-professional regime, following the implementation of the Seebohm Report (Cmnd. 3703 1968), was accompanied by the placement of social work education within a validation framework. A quango, the Central Council for the Education and Training of Social Workers (CCETSW), developed this framework following its founding in 1971. For much of the 1970s and 1980s, the framework that was in place was by today's standards permissive, with social work education enjoying an academic variant of 'professional self-regulation' (Jones 1999: 37). CCETSW accredited educational programmes, and reviewed them every five years on the basis of their academic and practice coherence, but there was wide variation in the orientations of particular courses, from the most traditional psychodynamic casework to radical social work. However, in the 1980s and 1990s, in parallel with the establishing of the social work business, CCETSW instituted a process of reform in social work education, which culminated in the restructuring of the arrangements for providing social work programmes and the reshaping of their content. As a result of the reform process, a significant measure of academic self-regulation was replaced by external regulation. This consolidation of external authority over social work education reinforced, and served as another avenue for, the establishment of the social work business. The process was extended following the election in 1997 of the New Labour government which, as part of its modernisation agenda, charged the Training Organisation for the Personal Social Services and the General Social Care Council with the responsibility for setting standards and monitoring the arrangements for providing social work education (see Ch. 5). This chapter analyses this series of changes in the context of their contribution to the consolidation of the social work business.

Dabbling in a debate

During the late 1970s, having set in place the Certificate of Qualification in Social Work (CQSW), CCETSW engaged in a wide-ranging process of consultation with educational institutions, social work agencies and professional bodies about the future direction of higher education social work programmes. Three consultative documents were published. The third, written by Reg Wright, an assistant director of CCETSW, attracted the most attention (CCETSW 1977). At the time, it was widely regarded as a controversial attempt to shape the direction and nature of social work education, and it sparked intense coverage in the social work press. As an organisation, CCETSW distanced itself from the document, neither formally endorsing it nor even putting it to CCETSW's Council for discussion. CCETSW's Council did, however, agree to its circulation (CCETSW 1977: 1). In today's terms, *Consultative Document 3*'s central proposals, which sparked such controversy at the time, were modest in scope: namely, the suggestion that senior staff at CCETSW should seek to arrive at a statement about the aims of CQSW programmes and the types of social worker that the programmes were aiming to produce. The statement was envisaged as continuing to allow considerable variation in the orientations of social work programmes, and this was seen as positive. In a Foreword to *Consultative Document 3*, Priscilla Young, director of CCETSW, stated: 'Although diversity is desirable in the style and detail of qualifying courses, a more clearly defined and explicit identity of purpose is needed' (CCETSW 1977: 2).

From the range of issues raised in *Consultative Document 3*, one of the most significant was the proposal that social work programmes should instil in student social workers a 'system of shared professional values, to enable them to begin to practise competently' (CCETSW 1977: 10). This appears to be one of the earliest references to 'competence' in the social work context, a concept that was, as will be seen, to become a guiding principle in years to come in terms of bringing social work education into line with the social work business. Together with the emphasis on 'shared professional values', the proposal was widely interpreted as an attack on 'radical' approaches to social work, especially as *Consultative Document 3* went on to suggest that students should eschew action to 'change the system' and should limit themselves to actions which involved functioning as 'agents of controlled social change' (CCETSW 1977: 11). However, despite such (for their time) forcefully worded statements about CQSW programmes, CCETSW's official position was that 'it is not consistent with the Council's general approach to education and training for social work to establish national requirements for a uniform curriculum' (CCETSW 1977: 6). In other words, CCETSW depicted *Consultative Document 3* as a contribution to a professional debate among peers about where social work education should be heading.

Social work programmes were highly critical in their response to *Consultative Document 3*, which was seen as possessing 'a certain anti-intellectual attitude towards the contribution of the social sciences to social work education . . . and a failure to appreciate the use of research findings' (Timms 1991: 207). One group of social work academics issued a publication in response to the *Consultative Document* in which they agreed with such criticisms, but also saw in the document – notwithstanding protestations to the contrary – evidence of CCETSW's ambition 'to impose centralist control, not only on social work education, but thereby, on thinking about social work itself' (University of Warwick 1978: 2). However, at the conclusion of the consultation period, CCETSW stated: 'on the basis of the comments received, we do not believe that the Council has evidence that it should institute immediate and radical changes in any particular direction' (CCETSW 1983: 29).

Consultation and change

Despite the cautious and inconclusive statement with which the 1970s consultation was terminated, the 1980s witnessed CCETSW moving on to propose major changes in social work education through a further period of review and consultation, beginning in 1982. Central to its case for reforming social work education, and significant later on in developments related to the interests of the social work business, was CCETSW's view that the existing Certificate of Social Service (CSS) and Certificate of Qualification in Social Work programmes were inadequate in respect of preparing social workers to undertake competently their statutory duties:

> Neither programme (CSS and CQSW) provides adequate education and training in length and depth for the increasingly complex

demands imposed on social workers. Indeed, some of those hold-ing existing qualifications who are given professional and statutory responsibility to protect the vulnerable have demonstrably lacked the knowledge and skills to do so.

(CCETSW 1987: 10)

Although CCETSW had levelled criticism at both the CSS and CQSW programmes, once the Council had announced its intention to review social work education the Association of Directors of Social Services, while supporting CCETSW's wish to abolish the distinction between the two programmes, insisted that 'the best of CSS' should be adopted and adapted to the rules and requirements of the new social work qualification (ADSS 1985). Jones suggested (1989: 18) that 'the best of CSS' was seen as 'the joint management of courses and the centrality accorded to practice competence in course design and student experi-ence' (see also Sibeon 1990: 102). This prepared the ground for the joint management of programmes, which was to become a central plank of subsequent reforms in the 1990s.

At the end of a protracted consultation, *Care for Tomorrow* (CCETSW 1987) was published. This report constituted CCETSW's submission to government for an extra £40 million per annum in order to reform social work education. The report proposed that, by the 1990s, a new three-year Qualifying Diploma in Social Work would be launched to replace the existing CSS and CQSW pro-grammes. In 1988 the government responded by rejecting CCETSW's *Care for Tomorrow* and withholding finance for the proposed three-year social work qualification. Instead, the government committed finance for the development of National Vocational Qualifications and Scottish Vocational Qualifications in Social Care, a two-year Diploma in Social Work and a post-qualifying framework.

As far as the Diploma in Social Work was concerned, the govern-ment's decision resulted in the publication of *Paper 30: Rules and Requirements for the Diploma in Social Work* (CCETSW 1989), setting out the details for the replacement for the CQSW and CSS Programmes. *Paper 30* marked a substantial shift from CCETSW's concerns in the 1970s and early 1980s in terms of opening up consideration of the impact of discrimination and oppression in relation to official debates about the future of social work education. A previous CCETSW publication, *Paper 20.6 Three Years and Different Routes. Expectations and Intentions for Social Work Training* (CCETSW 1986), had already proposed that the distinctive characteristics of social work resided in a social worker's commitment to 'challenging within his/her professional/employee role, racism, sexism, ageism and other institutional and oppressive attitudes which affect the delivery of services to the clients of his/her employing agency' (CCETSW 1986: 5). This theme was developed further in *Paper 30* (1989) in which CCETSW expressed its commitment to furthering anti-racist and anti-discriminatory practice, requiring qualifying social workers to combat discrimination based on age, gender, sexual orientation, class, disability, culture and religion (CCETSW 1989: 16).[1] In an introductory statement, CCETSW gave a definition of social work:

> Social work promotes social welfare and responds to wider social needs, promoting equal opportunities for every age, gender, sexual preference, class, disability, race, culture and creed. Social work has the responsibility to protect the vulnerable and exercise authority under statute.
>
> (CCETSW 1989: 8)

CCETSW's new requirements for social work programmes, contained in *Paper 30*, did not introduce a mandatory uniform curriculum. Instead, each programme's curriculum had to be adjudged by CCETSW as satisfying the national criteria of 'competence',[2] which CCETSW laid down. These competences were seen as the summative product of knowledge, values and skills, which were in turn set out in detail (CCETSW 1989: 14–17) as a preamble to the elaboration of the competences (CCETSW 1989: 17–20). The headings under which qualifying social workers had to demonstrate competence in practice were as follows:

- Assess needs, strengths, situations and risks
- Plan appropriate action
- Intervene to provide an initial response
- Implement action in an area of particular practice within the relevant legal and organisational structures
- Evaluate their work
- Transfer their knowledge and skills to new situations
- Take responsibility for their professional practice

(CCETSW 1989: 17–18)

1 The *Revised Paper 30* (CCETSW 1991b) added language, sign language and nationality.
2 'Competence' is discussed further on pp. 111–12.

In parallel, the organisational structures for delivering social work programmes were standardised through partnership arrangements,[3] in a way which gave Social Services Departments the potential to secure a dominant voice in shaping and developing the curricula of the programmes and in the procedures for selecting and assessing students.

Tightening the vocational mandate

In *Paper 30*, people were seen as firmly located within sets of oppressive experiences. Although some general references were made to interconnections between these experiences, the overall emphasis implied fairly rigid membership of particular social divisions (CCETSW 1989, 1991b). As a consequence, in seeking to fulfil CCETSW's requirements there was a tendency for social work education to search for forms of practice that relied on categories and procedures. As many Diploma in Social Work (DipSW) programmes encouraged category construction, students found it hard to 'break out of the language of monoliths' and to engage with more fluid understandings of oppression and discrimination (Featherstone and Fawcett 1995: 14) than those implied by CCETSW's rhetoric of opposition and oppression. Students were required, for example, to 'challenge and confront institutional and other forms of racism . . . and combat other forms of discrimination' (CCETSW 1989: 10).

CCETSW's rhetorical stance perhaps explains why, despite only minor revisions having been made to *Paper 30* in its second edition (CCETSW 1991b), it nevertheless received extensive media coverage following its publication. The coverage focused on implementation of the sections that dealt with discrimination and oppression. Claims were made in national newspapers and journals that social work and social work education had fallen prey to 'political correctness' (see, for example, Appleyard 1993; Phillips 1993; Pinker 1993) and more sustained critiques of this phenomenon emerged (Dunant 1994). In the aftermath of this public campaign against political correctness, substantial revisions were made to *Paper 30*, which re-emerged with a new title, reflecting a more business-like approach: *Assuring Quality in the Diploma in Social Work 1: Rules and Requirements for the DipSW* (CCETSW 1995a). In this version, CCETSW removed anti-discriminatory practice as a central element of the qualification, under the influence of central government concerns 'that social work education was far too preoccupied with "ologies and isms"' (Preston-Shoot

3 'Partnership' is discussed further on pp. 113–15.

1996: 13). In the run-up to the appearance of the revised rules and requirements, Virginia Bottomley, then the secretary of state for health and previously a social worker, announced in a speech to the Conservative Local Government Conference that 'a National Core Curriculum for Social Work Training . . . will be no place for trendy theories or the theory that isms or ologies come before common sense and practical skills' (quoted in Preston-Shoot 1996: 13). Clearly the *Assuring Quality* agenda was intended to lead in the direction of a no-nonsense vocational training which prepared people for employment in the social work business, with anti-discriminatory practice reduced in scope and seen as an individualised and personalised guiding ethic for individual social workers' practice. This new agenda was pursued through a partnership between CCETSW and the Care Sector Consortium, in the Care Sector Consortium's role as the NVQ Occupational Standards Council for Health and Social Care. The relationship forged between the two organisations presumably was central to the amplification of the importance of competence in social work by CCETSW, given that the Care Sector Consortium was charged with pursuing the competence agenda and was a potential threat to CCETSW's continued existence.

The review that led to the publication of the revised rules and requirements, in the *Assuring Quality* format, had five stated aims:

- to achieve contemporary relevance for the qualification in the context of changing needs, legislation and service delivery
- to establish more consistent standards of outcome from DipSW Programmes
- to provide a sound professional base for a career in social work, firmly located in higher education
- to secure the place of the DipSW in the continuum of qualifications
- to promote flexible opportunities for access to education, training and qualification

(CCETSW 1995a: 4)

CCETSW and the Care Sector Consortium employed consultants – the National Institute for Social Work and Mainframe – to develop 'national occupational standards' for social workers. In order to develop the standards, Mainframe used occupational mapping techniques derived from functional analysis. These techniques were consistent with the government's general concern to place competence at the centre of training, learning and assessment for employment across a wide range of occupations, validated by nationally agreed occupational standards (CCETSW 1994b). Mainframe's methodology appears to have drawn heavily on that set out earlier by the National Council for Vocational Qualifications (NCVQ 1988) and involved a descending level of detail about the social work job. There were overarching 'units of competence' ('core competencies').[4] Each 'unit of competence' was sub-divided into 'elements of competence' ('practice requirements'). 'Performance indicators' ('evidence indicators') were then identified in the form of behaviours which suggested that each 'element of competence' ('practice requirement') was being met. The core competencies were:

- Communicate and Engage
- Promote and Enable
- Assess and Plan
- Intervene and Provide Services
- Work in Organisations
- Develop Professional Competence

(CCETSW 1995a: 16)

The descending level of detail approach to the job is illustrated in Table 1 by taking the shortest of the competences, 'Communicate and Engage'.

CCETSW maintained that in undertaking this process, there was 'extensive consultation, within the tight timetable requested by government' (CCETSW 1995a: 4), but the exercise was very different from previous consultations on the future of social work education. It was swift and prescriptive, with consultation on the detail of the proposals rather than debate about their general direction. Following the consultation period, substantial revisions to the requirements for the DipSW were approved by CCETSW's Council in February 1995. The *Assuring Quality* revisions were heralded as a great success in securing the vocational emphasis required by the social work business. Tony Hall (then director of CCETSW) stated that 'no other profession defines so precisely and comprehensively the competencies required for its newly qualified practitioners' (CCETSW 1995b). One of the major changes in adjusting social work education to the social work business context, contained in *Assuring Quality in the Diploma in Social Work 1* (CCETSW 1995a), was the move away from what was then depicted as the previous combative emphasis on anti-discriminatory and anti-

---

4　The NCVQ terms are given first (followed by the DipSW terms in brackets).

Table 1 Practice requirements and evidence indicators for the core competence 'Communicate and Engage'

Practice requirement	Evidence indicators
Form and develop working relationships with children, adults, families, carers and groups	Establish initial contact and the reason for contact with children, adults, families, carers and groups
	Communicate effectively with children, adults, families, carers and groups
	Identify shared and differing perspectives, values and aims
	Develop working relationships with children, adults, families, carers and groups
Communicate and engage with people in communities and seek to minimise factors which cause risk and need	Identify and evaluate the key economic, social, cultural, educational, environmental and political factors which impact on the service and its users
	Identify and evaluate the roles, responsibilities, polices and potential contributions of agencies, community resources, volunteers and other professionals
	Contribute to preventative work which minimises risk and need in the community
Network and form effective working relationships with and between individuals, agencies, community resources, volunteers and other professionals	Establish contact with individuals, agencies, community resources, volunteers and other professionals
	Communicate effectively with and between individuals, agencies, community resources, volunteers and other professionals
	Develop and sustain networking relationships with individuals, agencies, volunteers, community resources and other professionals, acknowledging and working with differing perspectives

oppressive practices and towards a more modest mandate for social work. This required students to develop knowledge and understanding of 'diversity and difference' (CCETSW 1995a: 9) and the assessment of students' competence was to be in terms of how each of them managed diversity, using an individualistic approach of the kind described by Williams (1992: 226):

> This approach proclaims difference as essential in distinguishing need and prescribes responses to that need as a technical activity stripped of critical or radical ambition for change. It is essentially individualist, populist and pragmatic, and effectively operates to dissipate the politicisation of need by holding that everyone's needs are unique and special. The model holds no hope of inter-sectionality between groups as it serves essentially to fragment them, but it can accommodate notions of multi-oppression in that everyone is unique.

CCETSW's individualistic emphasis on diversity[5] in *Assuring Quality* can be substantiated by the shift away from the previous focus on social divisions and the experience of oppression to a view of diversity as the reflection of a range of differences which social work students would encounter: 'Diversity is reflected through religion, ethnicity, culture, language, social status, family structures and lifestyle' (CCETSW 1995a: 28). When such differences are encountered, students are enjoined to respect them and not to make things any worse than they already are, as they gain

> practice experience in delivering social work services to children, families and communities in ways which are responsive to and respectful of different faiths and cultural traditions, neither compounding disadvantage arising from race and social class, nor stigmatising people by reason of age, disability, illness, poverty or other difference.
>
> (CCETSW 1995a: 9)

Anti-discriminatory and anti-oppressive practice no longer appeared as requirements in relation to any of the core competences. The only point at which sources and forms of oppression emerged as part of the

5 Again, this perhaps illustrates the influence of the NCVQ framework, which treated anti-discriminatory practice in an individualised and personalised way.

requirements for the qualification was under the heading 'Ethics and values in social work'. Here, it was stated that students should be aware of 'sources and forms of oppression, disadvantage and discrimination based on race, gender, religion, language, age, class, disability and being gay and lesbian, their impact at a structural and individual level, and strategies and actions to deal with them' (CCETSW 1995a: 23). Any action on the part of students to 'counter discrimination, racism, disadvantage, inequality and injustice' had to take account of 'strategies appropriate to role and context' (CCETSW 1995a: 18). The failure to self-censor strategies appropriately in relation to 'role and context' presumably would serve to indicate a student who was not competent.

Competence and partnership have been mentioned thus far in passing as components in a reformed social work education that is more attuned to the social work business. These components are now considered further.

Competence

The term 'competence' was not adequately defined[6] in any of the three main publications about the Diploma in Social Work (CCETSW 1990, 1991b, 1995a). Nevertheless, competences were seen as the key to establishing national criteria for standardising social work education and training in ways that brought preparation for social work closer to the quasi-business discourse in which practice was embedded. (It has been argued that higher education policy more generally has been directed increasingly towards constructing future workforce members whose sense of identity and understanding of the world correspond with the demands of business culture [Dudley 1999]). This emphasis on competence led to allegations that the managerialism associated with the social work business had driven social work education to the point where it had 'reached the end of the road: stuck in a cul-de-sac of regulation and conformity that stifles innovation and change' (Committee for Social Work Education and Policy, quoted in O'Hagan 1996: 3). Particular criticism was directed at the emphasis on making competences – 'increasingly defined by legal statute and underpinned by bureaucratic procedure' (Jones 1993: 15) – relevant to the needs of

6 Given the influence of the NCVQ framework on CCETSW's proposals, perhaps a definition from the National Council for Vocational Qualifications could be substituted as a working definition: 'The ability to perform work activities to the standards required in employment' (NCVQ 1988: 2).

social workers' employers. The competence-based approach to social work was seen as: preparing practitioners for a market-driven environment (Dominelli 1997: 171); subordinating social work education to the concerns of management (Langan 1998: 216); and 'reinforcing managerial practices' (Adams 1998: 257). It was argued that students would be made ready for practice by regulating the way in which they worked (Jones 1993: 15; Humphries 1997: 656), through the reduction of social work to its technical components: 'Service delivery has become fragmented and reduced to discretely identified parts or empirically stated technical competencies and quantifiable indicators' (Dominelli and Hoogvelt 1996: 52). Adams's pessimistic conclusion was that social workers were transformed from professionals into technicians as a result of the narrowing of ideas that were consistent with outcome-based activity, the focus on easily measurable aspects of people's performance and the concentration on techniques rather than critically reflective practice (Adams 1998). This focus on competence as individual performance, determined by functional analysis, reflects the broader emphasis on performance in the social work business (see Chs 3–5). It is also consistent with that emphasis in that competence-based practice is employer-led and involves implementing what management requires for the measurable performance of the business: 'The system must be planned and led by employers as it is they who are best placed to judge skill needs' (Department of Employment 1992).

By such means, competence was first articulated and then consolidated as the overarching dimension of the quasi-business discourse within which discussion of social work education was henceforth to take place, in accordance with governmental regulation and surveillance (Jones 1995: 7; Dominelli 1996: 165). The subordination of social work education to the concerns of management, the marginalisation of academic social science and the elevation of vocational training (Langan 1998: 216) were consistent with the concerns and priorities of the social work business. Jones (1993: 15), for example, condemned CCETSW for yielding to 'employer pressure for a social work qualification which has been intellectually gutted to conform to their demands for a bureaucratically compliant workforce' represented in a 'shift towards an instrumental vocational assessment'. Brewster (1992: 88–9) pointed to the minimal representation from social work educators on the reconstituted CCETSW Council, which was responsible for making the shift to competence-based education and the overwhelming representation of the interests of the new managers of social work. The presence of these managers was indicative of the shift towards a partnership model for social work education.

Partnership

As we saw earlier in this chapter, ideas about partnership between social work agencies and educational institutions were in circulation from the late 1970s onwards and guided the gradual development of CCETSW policy (Payne 1994: 59). For example, in its report on the 1970s' consultations, referred to earlier, CCETSW began to recognise the tensions that existed between higher education institutions and social work agencies, centred mainly around the planning and monitoring of placements and the disparity in views about social work skills and objectives (CCETSW 1983). At that time, in parallel with its review of CQSW programmes, CCETSW was engaged in setting up the Certificate of Social Service (CSS). The CSS was seen as embodying a feature that employers wanted: social work training that was tailored to meet the needs of the particular social work agency (CCETSW 1983). During the 1970s, employers had expressed their discontent with CQSW programmes, which they perceived as populated by academics who were failing to inculcate in students a familiarity with the law and a due respect for agency procedure, rendering them unable to do the job employers required of them (Dominelli 1997: 159–62; Jones 1999: 45). Or, as Webb succinctly put it, there was considered to be a 'failure to deliver reliability of product' (Webb 1996: 177; see also Marsh and Triseliotis 1996). Nowhere was this more apt than in the field of child protection. Negative media coverage of child abuse investigations resulted in the Association of Directors of Social Services complaining that social workers were no longer being equipped during their training to deal with childcare issues (Cannan 1994 95: 12). The CSS had offered a different, partnership-based, approach that began to address some of the shortcomings about which employing agencies had complained.

The next stage in CCETSW's development of partnership came in the 1980s, when CCETSW asked for comments from agencies on CQSW programmes. Although the response was mixed, CCETSW observed that several agencies had emphasised

> the importance of harnessing together educational and agency resources, citing the value of their experience in planning CSS training through joint management committees, and contrasting this with their view that there was little opportunity for employers to exert influence on CQSW courses.
>
> (CCETSW 1983: 17)

These pressures from employers led CCETSW to emphasise collaboration between agencies and educational institutions in deciding to set up a new form of social work education, embracing both the CSS and the CQSW (Payne 1994: 61). In *Care for Tomorrow* CCETSW (1987: 21), argued that the primary aim of social work education and training was to produce a 'competent and accountable professional', and if that were to be achieved educational institutions and agencies would be required to collaborate in the development and provision of the new programmes. Accordingly, the introduction of the Diploma in Social Work brought with it compulsory partnerships between educational institutions and social work agencies, partnership with at least one Social Services Department being required for a programme to be considered for validation. CCETSW stated in *Paper 30* (CCETSW 1989) that the success of the Diploma was dependent on universities, polytechnics and colleges working collaboratively with social work agencies and that such collaboration was to be 'a central feature' (CCETSW 1990: 1). In order to support these collaborative partnerships, development money was made available by central government, although it was hoped that savings would be made through effective partnership arrangements.

CCETSW's arguments in support of partnership-based social work education were:

- Both field and academic learning are equally important and need to be closely integrated (CCETSW 1991a: 43).
- By having agency input, programmes could make the curriculum more relevant in preparing students for work in the personal social services (CCETSW 1987: 9).
- Partnerships are essential to achieving a high quality of education and training and in order to increase the quantity of DipSW holders as the personal social services require. More output would be achieved if resources were pooled (CCETSW 1991a: 43).
- Programmes would be more relevant. This required 'programmes to be more responsive and permeable to contemporary social work practice' (CCETSW 1991a: 43).

Brewster argued that the emphasis on partnership, geared to employment-led training, was a smoke-screen: 'When CCETSW talks about employment-led training it should really be saying managerial-led training' (1992: 88). Further, Brewster stated that new appointments to the advisory staff of CCETSW were drawn almost exclusively from the lower managerial positions in social work agencies. Managers also dominated representation on DipSW Programmes' partnership bodies, leading to allegations that a direct and subordinate relationship was established for academic staff with social services managers (Webb 1996: 186).

New Labour lends a hand

Decisive shifts were made in the nature and content of social work education during the time of the Thatcher and Major Conservative governments. These shifts were consonant with changes taking place in the social work business and with the perceived need for future social workers to learn how to function in that business. From 1997 onwards, social work education was swept up in New Labour's modernisation agenda, discussed in Chapter 5. As we saw in that chapter, the Labour government established four institutions to reform social work:

- The General Social Care Council – regulating the workforce through a statutory code of conduct for staff and a code of practice for employers.
- The Commission for Care Standards – regulating service quality.
- The Training Organisation for the Personal Social Services – an employer-led body producing occupational standards.
- The Social Care Institute for Excellence – identifying and promoting best practice with regard to 'what works'.

(Department of Health 1998b)

These proposals followed a review of CCETSW, which announced changes in the regulation of education and training in social work and in its organisational arrangements (Department of Health 1997). This proposed the possibility of CCETSW's development, regulation and awarding functions being transferred to a General Social Care Council,[7] with its other functions being taken over by the 'industry-led' Training Organisation for the Personal Social Services,[8] licensed by the Department for Education and Employment, which became responsible for workforce planning and occupational standards

7 And, later on, its counterparts – the Scottish Social Services Council (SSSC), the Cygnor Gofal Cymru/Care Council for Wales (CGC/CCW) and the Northern Ireland Social Care Council (NISCC).
8 A UK-wide body which operates through four national committees, with only England having a separate organisational structure for TOPSS. In the other three countries, the work of TOPSS has been transferred to the councils referred to in 7.

(TOPSS 1998, 1999a). The elaboration of occupational standards required that TOPSS should decide the tasks which needed to be done at different levels of the workforce and then should identify the knowledge and skills needed by those employed to undertake those tasks (TOPSS 1998). The anticipated scenario seemed to be that TOPSS would define the occupational standards, the GSCC would designate the training required to deliver them, and higher education institutions would provide the training (Orme 2001: 617), using the knowledge base developed by the Social Care Institute of Excellence:

> New knowledge must inform training, so that changes in service and practice are sustained. SCIE will have a strong role in working with the national organisations for training (GSCC, TOPSS) and the providers of social care training to communicate its findings and guidelines.
>
> (J M Consulting Ltd 1999: para. 51)

In March 2001, the Department of Health announced that a three-year course of undergraduate training for social work would be put in place from 2003, following consultation on *A Quality Strategy for Social Care* (Department of Health 2000a), and that this three-year programme would have a greater emphasis on practice learning and would be based on a national curriculum (Department of Health 2000a: para. 106). The government envisaged that this would produce social workers more acceptable to the social work business: 'The new courses will strengthen the practice learning undertaken by students and ensure that they are able to do the job required by employers at the end of their training' (Department of Health 2001b: 2). TOPSS similarly stressed the needs of the social work business: 'Social care needs to have a framework of qualifications to provide a basis for registration and to show whether work is meeting the requirements of the performance culture in our sector' (TOPSS 1999b: 1). This was reinforced by the announcement by the chair of TOPSS (England) of the setting up of regional training forums. Included in their remit was the benchmarking of training and workforce development between employers and training providers (Keefe 2000).

In total, what do these developments represent? Social work is to move from

> being a (quasi-) profession with central governance and a fairly cohesive, if not coherent, infrastructure for education and training, to a regulated and accredited profession, but accountable to, if not

directly governed by, many different bodies . . . the regulatory systems as currently envisaged represent a fragmentation of responsibilities and a proliferation of lines of accountability . . . while the structures may appear to be fragmented the desired outcomes are centrally driven.

(Orme 2001: 612–3)

The last point is significant. We saw in Chapter 5 that New Labour has a highly centralised top–down approach to the management of performance and outcomes in the social work business. Within the framework of a competence-based approach to education and training and a centralised managerialist approach to business performance, it might be anticipated that the modernising institutions will be firmly committed to carrying out central government's policies, with a built-in bias towards delivering outcomes in line with the interests of the employers in the social work business: 'New Labour is an interventionist, regulatory government, which is optimistic and ambitious about the possibilities of changing individuals and cultures, but relies on crude notions of reward and punishment to implement its plans' (Jordan and Jordan 2000: 80).

Conclusion

The original agenda of *Paper 30* (CCETSW 1989) can be regarded, in part, as having been influenced by a range of interests in placing emphasis on the need for social work to address discrimination and oppression. Hugman (1996: 142–3) argued that the dominant view pressed upon CCETSW, from various perspectives but nevertheless across this range of interests, was that social work would become increasingly incompetent and irrelevant unless it transformed its mandate in accordance with societal developments. However, the anti-discriminatory and anti-oppressive content of *Paper 30* was attacked by, among others, the Conservative government, which, as we have seen, ordered a review. The review adopted a much narrower and functional analysis of the sort of social work needed to deliver objectives that the government considered to be acceptable for the social work business. The end result was a technical, formulaic and prescriptive approach to students' behavioural performance in assessed practice placements, geared to on-the-job competences. Accountability to employers for educational provision, against the backcloth of the social work business, framed the social work tasks to be undertaken. The end result allowed Jones to claim that 'there is no comparable system of social work education in the world, which is so nationally uniform, uninspired and tailored so closely to the requirements of major state employers' (Jones 1996: 191; and see Lymberry *et al.* 2000).

As a result, alternative definitions of, and perspectives on, social work were downgraded and the interests of the social work business prevailed. This was achieved in part because there always existed within CCETSW's framework for the Diploma in Social Work a tension between on the one hand a traditional liberal social work agenda, framed within the statutory context, and on the other hand an agenda of promoting anti-discriminatory practice and confronting structural oppression. Traditionally, the values of social work have been seen as 'clients' rights to dignity, privacy, confidentiality and choice and protection against abuse and violence' (CCETSW 1989: para 2.2.2). Jordan suggests that this traditional list of values has its roots in liberal ethics, market-minded politics, casework and law. These values fit with the 'overall tone of the [*Paper 30*] requirements, with their priority on legal and procedural knowledge, and the application of technical skills' (Jordan 1991: 5). The radical agenda, on the other hand, has been satirised as CCETSW's prescription concerning 'which values social workers should hold, thereby determining the moral ground which practitioners should occupy. Possessed of the moral truth, CCETSW's high priests have sent out the word which all must follow and by which all will be judged, censured and watched' (Webb 1991: 151).

These 'surface' exhortations from CCETSW for social work to repudiate discrimination sat alongside what was in effect an endorsement of neo-liberalism (Webb 1996: 186). The net effect of the reforms was that power, privilege and prejudice were to be taken into account at the individual's level, but without upsetting the legal and moral foundation (economic and political individualism) on which they were built (Jordan 1991: 5). The strengthening in the revised rules and requirements (CCETSW 1995a) of the emphasis on traditional social work values reinforced a move towards a more individualised way of working, with an emphasis on 'appropriate client–worker relationships' and 'contractual arrangements' (Dominelli 1996: 171). Dominelli (*ibid.*) suggested that in such a context it is difficult for social workers to consider organisational and structural oppression, and that they are just 'tinkering at the edges'. This argument is reinforced by Jones (1995: 6), who maintained that

> CCETSW has successfully managed a transformation of social work education where the concerns of the disadvantaged and

marginalised, which should figure at the centre of social work education, have been swallowed up and have disappeared into the needs of the state agencies.

Thus the establishment and modernisation of the social work business (see Chs 3–5) can be seen as reflected in the parallel reforms to social work education and the arrangements they instituted for students to learn the business. For some, the Conservative reforms of social work education were seen as simply increased employer interference over what was being taught on the Diploma in Social Work, with the involvement by agencies representing an increased level of surveillance and supervision which tied social work programmes up in time-consuming partnerships and bureaucratic procedures that were often of little benefit (Novak 1995: 5). New Labour has been able to build its regulatory mechanisms for learning the social work business on the foundation of the Conservatives' reforms of social work education, with an assumption that the best ways of doing social work can be uncovered and codified, allowing Jones (1999: 47) to depict the current state of affairs, in pessimistic terms:

> In the contemporary welfare system, state social work agencies do not require highly informed or educated, research-aware social workers. These are now regarded as positively unhelpful qualities that make for questioning and criticism. Rather what is now demanded is agency loyalty, an ability to follow instructions, to complete procedures and assessments on time, to modify and placate client demand, to manage inadequate budgets and to work in such ways that will not expose the agency to public ridicule or exposure. . . . Simply, the tasks expected of state social workers in the contemporary welfare system are such that professional self-regulation is hopelessly inadequate; what is required is a managed workforce with no illusions about professional autonomy or ideals that service to the clients is paramount. . . . Professional social work education – for so long held to be the key to the regulation and reproduction of the occupation – is consequently becoming increasingly marginalised. . . . As state social work has become more concerned with rationing and gatekeeping scarce resources and the surveillance of clients . . . so the need for professional education will increasingly diminish.

7   Creating the customer base

This chapter provides an account of the attempts made to create customers for the social work business, by re-imaging, or perhaps more accurately re-imagining, the people on the receiving end of social work. After considering the significance attached to the customer identity, both in general and in the specific customer focus espoused in the social work business, the background to how the latter position was reached is explored. The shift to a customer focus in the social work business is located in the Conservative governments' reforms of the late 1980s and early 1990s, and in the consolidation of those reforms by New Labour. The customer base of the social work business is then scrutinised in order to discuss whether the creation of customers is a feasible or desirable goal.

Consuming the customer identity

Bauman argues that once the market has made people dependent upon itself, people's identities relate first and foremost to their role as customers and that, as a consequence, consumerism spills over into all other aspects of contemporary life:

> Consumer conduct (consumer freedom geared to the consumer market) moves steadily into the position of, simultaneously, the cognitive and moral focus of life, the integrative bond of society and the focus of systematic management. In other words, it moves into the selfsame position which in the past – during the 'modern' phase of capitalist society – was occupied by work in the form of wage-labour. This means that in our time individuals are engaged (morally by society, functionally by the social system) first and foremost as consumers rather than as producers.
>
> (Bauman 1992: 49)

In this context, the exercise of choice by a consumer is represented as an expression of identity, rooted in the celebration of free choice, so that freedom is now depicted as consumer freedom (Bauman 1988: 88). That viewpoint was given a major boost by Thatcherism, which cast

> the shadow of a rampant and theoretically naive notion of consumer choice, part of a discourse deriving from the abstract model of consumer economics, adapted and popularised as political principle by the New Right, which insinuates that the maximum level of personal freedom is found in the market place.
>
> (Warde 1996: 304)

The alleged power of the consumer identity is seen as an overwhelmingly 'good thing', as part of the more widespread rhetoric in capitalist economies of seeing customers as co-producers of services and as a key component in the business discourse. The exercise of choice as a customer is thus presented as not only the key to identity and freedom but also as a deeply democratising feature of what capitalism has to offer. According to some commentators, the trend towards pluralisation, made possible by markets, expanded the 'potentialities and identities' available to ordinary people in their everyday lives (Hall 1989: 129). Without the hallowed status and alleged power and potential accorded to the customer, the business discourse would fall apart. The status of 'customer' is revered, even when it is unattainable, as will be seen later, indicating the economic, political and social significance now attaching to consumerism (Lyotard 1984) and to its expression through differentiated and segmented patterns of consumption (Loader and Burrows 1994: 1). In short, the customer is often depicted as a modern-day heroine/hero (Warde 1994: 228–9).

In this customised context, Bauman (1988: 88) predicts the continued decline of state-provided welfare because of the changing role of consumption and the refined orientations of individual consumers as they use the purchase of commodities to establish their self-identities. Notwithstanding Bauman's pessimism about the future of state welfare, if his analysis of the experience, status and significance of consumption is correct we might expect that there would be attempts to shape the status and experience of social work's 'customers' in ways that are consistent with the broad societal trends he identifies. In other words, we might expect social work to be presented as operating 'in the way things normally work' in the rest of society.

The general trends in consumerism within capitalist societies, identified by Bauman and others, were given a fillip by saturated market conditions and intensified competition for market share (Parton 1996a), which prompted a tendency towards stressing customer sovereignty (Abercrombie 1991). A central tenet of the business discourse, developed in response to these trends and conditions, was the commercial value of the customer base and the generation and maintenance of customer loyalty. This type of thinking spread to public services operating under very different conditions, through the transplantation of the work of management gurus (see, for example, Peters and Waterman 1984) who stressed the desirability of enterprises being 'close to the customer'. In these management discourses, customers were presented as in the driving seat of private sector enterprises. They said what they required, and businesses provided it. In contrast, public services were seen to lack such customer sovereignty, and so were able to shelter from business pressures and to serve their own interests in large inefficient empires. These empires were considered to be providing basic services that were unacceptable to their contemporary, more discriminating, customers: 'The legitimate demand for a more differentiated state product . . . comes directly from a new actor whose appearance over the last decade corresponds to another important change in the environment of most welfare state organisations – the "differentiated consumer"' (Hoggett quoted in Williams 1994: 65). In similar vein, Warde identifies 'a type of consumer who cannot possibly derive satisfaction from universally provided, collectively financed and state-allocated services' (1994: 223). This type of customer has entered everyday political discourse: 'If government is going to be effective at delivering services in the way people want them for today, it has to be modernised, it has to be updated' (Blair quoted in Newman 2000: 46). Williams (1994: 49) traces a direct link between the trends in the wider economy and aspirations for developments in welfare services:

> Changes in the organisation of both production and consumption in the wider economy have influenced and even been reproduced within the provision of welfare: mass production to flexible production; mass consumption to diverse patterns of consumption; production-led to consumer-led; from mass, universal needs met by monolithic, bureaucratic/professional-led provision to the diversity of individual needs met by welfare pluralism, quasi-markets, reorganised welfare work and consumer sovereignty.

The impact of the changes referred to by Williams underscores the erosion of the distinctiveness of public sector services and the installation of quasi-capitalist rationality within them, as part of a quasi-business discourse (see Chs 3–5). Within this wider trend, how did the representation of citizens as customers of the social work business come about?

From citizens to customers

Chapter 2 showed how, in the pre-business era of the social democratic welfare state, social problems were seen as the outcome of unregulated market forces. The state was seen as acting to protect citizens against the ravages of the market, with faith being placed in public services – and in the professionals within those services – as providing an in-built form of 'consumer protection' (May 2001). In that model of consumer protection, the general appeal of bureaucracies, such as Social Services Departments, can be readily understood in terms of their being seen as an advance on earlier organisational regimes, as structures based upon equality before the law and upon notions of order, reason and justice (Leonard 1997: 89). Thus, welfare bureaucracies were presented as providing a uniform standard of service, with impartial decision making by professionals subject to hierarchical accountability. However, those welfare bureaucracies came to smack of paternalism, intrusion, authoritarianism and insensitivity, and professionals were regarded as being over-confident about their knowledge of what service users required. This was the seedbed in which the Conservatives' emphasis on customer choice was planted.

Customer choice

One of the widely acknowledged sources of the Conservative governments' success in pursuing their programme of reform of the public sector generally – and specifically in relation to the establishment of the social work business – was their claim that only the Conservatives embodied a central concern with 'freedom' and 'choice'. They contrasted their safeguarding of this concern with citizens' everyday experience of being clients of the social democratic welfare state (see Ch. 2), portraying citizens as being subjected to heavy-handed bureaucratic services insensitive to their individual needs (Wilding 1992). The Conservatives argued that this was illustrative of a conflict of principle between egalitarianism and freedom, as competing political aims and ideals (Roche 1987: 370) in the public sector. This critique of the tarnished egalitarianism of the welfare state included a sceptical view of social workers and their main employers, Social Services Departments (Loney 1986: 142; Jones and Novak 1993; Midgley and Jones

1994). Social work was attacked (see, for example, Brewer and Lait 1980) as a state power bloc ranged oppressively against the people's interests. The Conservatives proclaimed that they were committed to dismantling this power bloc through a transformation of the culture and style of welfare services, with the adoption of customer choice as the guiding principle (Ranson and Stewart 1994).

Customer choice undermined the authority of the professions, which had traditionally relied on the creation of boundaries between themselves and their clients, based on the possession of mysterious knowledge beyond the scrutiny of the uninitiated (Fournier 2000: 74–5). With the Conservatives regarding the professions as a major stumbling block lying in the path of the reconstruction of the welfare state (see Ch. 3), symbolically boosting the status of the customer must have been an attractive prospect. The more the service user could be elevated as a customer, the more the notion of social workers having any particular knowledge and expertise could be repudiated (Howe 1994, 1996; Aldridge 1996). Thus in attacking social work, the Conservatives took up challenges to state welfare provision and siphoned them into the rhetoric of overcoming the professional power bloc of social work by instituting customer choice. Barnes and Prior (2000: 14ff.) set out the main characteristics of the Conservatives' position as follows:

- The universalist approach to welfare was capable of delivering only inflexible and unresponsive services that were mass-produced for a mass market rather than designed around individual needs and aspirations.
- The state should make it possible for people to make their own decisions rather than taking responsibility for their welfare.
- Installing quasi-markets would enable the exercise of rational choice – rooted in active self-interest instead of passive citizenship – by individual customers and would encourage greater flexibility and responsiveness to those individual choices between service providers.
- Social services departments would facilitate the operation of quasi-markets, expanding the service suppliers in the voluntary and private sectors. Quasi-markets would produce economy (lower costs), efficiency (through competition between providers) and effectiveness.
- More assertive customers would be created, by providing better information about the services. Such customers would be enabled to make better choices and would be able to exit from services.

- Giving customers the right to make complaints would empower the customer against recalcitrant professionals.

That was the vision conveyed by the Conservatives of allowing the customers of social work to live their own lives as they wanted, assisted by rapid and flexible responses to customer preferences in post-bureaucratic services (Hoggett 1991: 247). Thus, the White Paper *Caring for People* (Cm. 849 1989: para 3.4.3.) identified anticipated benefits in terms of a wider range of flexible social services from which customers would be able to choose and subsequently claims were made that the separation of the purchase and provision of services would result both in greater cost-effectiveness and in heightened levels of choice, flexibility, responsiveness and quality (Audit Commission 1992). In this vision, the exercise of choice by customers was seen as the key to securing responsive and accountable services that followed their demands and preferences and took precedence over the judgement of professionals. Redefining service users as 'customers' was premissed on promises to enhance their status, offer them greater choice and ensure responsiveness to their individual needs (Exworthy and Halford 1999: 5).

Managerialism speaking for the customer

The imagery, or imagining, of the customer empowered managers to purport to speak for service users as a core component in advancing managerialist agendas (see Ch. 3). Given that social workers were accused of professional self-interest that was hostile to customers' interests, managers could represent themselves as on the side of customers against professionals (Barnes 1997: 32). This managerial alignment could be used to justify subjecting social workers to the disciplines of the market and the managerial constraints of the quasi-business discourse in the interest of services becoming 'customer-focused' and concerned with the 'empowerment' of service users. Managerialism was presented as being concerned about making services appeal to their customers and improving relationships with them (Stewart and Stoker 1994), as well as emancipating them by reproducing market-type conditions and by introducing quasi-capitalist rationality. Thus, limiting the powers of local government and curtailing the discretion of professionals (see Ch. 3) were carried through under the banner of introducing customer responsiveness.

With promises of widening the choice of services and recasting provision on more competitive and more business-like lines, the

Conservatives were well placed to go on the offensive against the established pattern of social work services, ironically through their inheritance of central government powers and mechanisms associated with the social democratic welfare state (Taylor-Gooby 1993: 466). In mounting their offensive, customers' jeopardy in the hands of social workers was depicted as remediable through the forces exerted by marketisation and managerialisation (see Chs 3 and 4), as the twin routes to the freedom and choice promised by the Conservatives through state-sponsored consumerism. The aim of the Conservatives was 'to discredit the social democratic concept of universal citizenship rights, guaranteed and enforced through public agencies, and to replace it with a concept of citizenship rights achieved through property ownership and participation in markets' (Gamble 1988: 16). By breaking the monopoly of public services, the Conservatives argued, service users would have not only a greater degree of choice in the services on offer but control over the services they received. Thus the marketisation and managerialisation of social work were seen as compatible with notions of empowerment for individual citizens because legal and political rights were presented as the defining aspects of the citizen-as-customer, while the validity of social rights was denied (Glennerster and Midgley 1991: 173). The implication of this set of arguments was a double-shift, away from the universalism to which the Seebohm Report aspired (see Ch. 2) and towards greater targeting of social work at those unable to provide for themselves (Alcock 1989; Baldock 1994). Dependence on social workers was to be avoided and self-help and support by informal carers were much prized (Phillipson 1994). (The implications for the latter are considered further in Chapter 8.) The resultant changes in the practical mechanics of service funding and delivery involved in establishing the social work business (see Ch. 3) were seen by many commentators as inseparable from the rejection of social democratic citizenship values and the embrace of consumerism (see, for example, Baldock and Ungerson 1994).

Active citizenship

The reappraisal of citizenship with regard to social services, represented by an appeal to customer identity, was complemented and reinforced by the promotion of 'active citizenship', from 1988 to 1990, during the last stages of Thatcherism. Active citizenship was launched by Douglas Hurd, then Home Secretary (Hurd 1988). At the 1988 Conservative Party Conference it was endorsed as the key theme for Conservative politics in the 1990s (Gyford 1991: 170) and was taken up by Margaret Thatcher in an attempt to present a more compassionate variant of Thatcherism (Oliver and Heater 1994: 123–6). This concerned and actively involved citizenship was constructed on assumptions of privilege:

> In speeches by the Prime Minister and the Home Secretary, the active citizen is frequently evoked: the good-hearted, property-owning patriot, who serves as an unpaid JP if asked, does jury service, gives a day a week to meals-on-wheels, checks that the old age pensioner next door is tucked in on cold days and so on. The accent is on good neighbourliness, public spiritedness and, above all, on property. For it is property that makes the active citizen active. Without property, a citizen cannot be independent; without the income of property an individual will not have the leisure necessary to be a good citizen. Without property the citizen is passive, a ward of the state, a dependent on the benefit cheque, the social services and the council housing department.
>
> (Ignatieff 1991: 26)

Lister (1990), in similar vein, argued that citizens were depicted as successful, self-reliant, enterprising, consuming and property owning. Despite the rhetoric of 'community' found in 'active citizenship', active citizens were seen as those able to stand alone, independent in the market; their freedom guaranteed (by economic rather than social rights) from the culture of dependence and the welfare state, the Conservatives' symbol of subjecthood. Subjects were those in poverty, prevented from belonging to the enterprise culture, the new symbol of full citizenship.

Two kinds of citizens' rights now came into collision and both had implications for social work: 'The right of the wealthy citizen to maintain his or her property relatively inviolate is incompatible with the social right of the less advantaged citizen to welfare state benefits' (Oliver and Heater 1994: 37). In this context, the concept of the worthy active citizen emphasised personal rather than public responsibilities, depoliticising the provision of social services: 'The impression is given that in order to become a *good* citizen, the individual must surrender positive, critical, political interests. The active citizen is a depoliticised voluntary worker in his or her local community' (Oliver and Heater 1994: 130; emphasis original). Such a person was portrayed as magnanimously contributing to social services from the position of having been justly rewarded for her or his enterprise in the market. When not actively engaged in civic duties, the active citizen was represented as a compulsory shareholder in local government services, anxious to see investment used prudently and sparingly and countering any excessive calls on her or his purse (Gyford 1991: 160–1). But what of those citizens in receipt of social work services? The Conservatives' response was the creation of the 'customer–citizen', seen as capable of entering into responsible relations with the restructured social services through the quasi-markets of the mixed economy of welfare (Le Grand 1993).

Customer citizenship

From 1991 onwards, a key initiative for the promotion of the customer– citizen was Prime Minister Major's *Citizen's Charter*, ostensibly concerned with the transplanting of best private sector customer-centred practice into the public sector (Deakin 1994). The *Charter* set out the means by which services were to be made more responsive to their users (Prime Minister 1991: 2), particularly through the specific charters that were developed. By 1996 there were forty-two charters for public services, accompanied by over 100,000 local charters (May 2001: 288). Amongst this welter of charters, the *Framework for Local Community Care Charters* (Department of Health 1994) fleshed out the original *Citizen's Charter* themes in relation to social work. The emphasis in this more specific charter was on the extension of quasi-capitalist rationality to the relationship between the service user and social services, through the introduction of practices associated with the private sector. For example, getting what was promised by the *Framework* depended on customer vigilance, operating from the basis of rational self-interested calculation, as it was seen as desirable for the service–customer relationship to be treated as if it were taking place on a commercial basis in the private sector: 'Through these Charters the citizen can increasingly put pressure upon those responsible for providing services to deliver them to a high standard rather as commercial competition puts consumer pressure on the performance of private sector organisations' (Prime Minister 1991: 1). The *Citizen's Charter* (Prime Minister 1991: 4) had four main themes that were seen as contributing to this customer pressure on services:

- *quality* – a sustained programme for improving the quality of public services;

- *choice* – choice, whenever possible between competing providers, is the best spur to quality improvement;
- *standards* – the customer must be told what service standards are and be able to act when services are unacceptable;
- *value* – the customer is also a tax-payer; public services must give value for money within a tax bill the nation can afford.

This emphasis on situating the individual citizen's interests in accordance with the principles of capitalist economics and business practices drew the language of the *Citizen's Charter* inexorably towards that of consumerism. (In the text, 'customer' is used interchangeably with 'citizen'.) The means set out (ibid. 1991: 5) to advance the customer's interests covered a range of initiatives including:

- privatisation of services;
- increased competition;
- the publication of national and local performance standards;
- publication of information on the standards achieved;
- more effective complaints procedures;
- tougher and more independent inspectorates.

These measures by implication undermined some aspects of citizenship. Service users were to be encouraged to act as individual customers and to complain rather than take collective political action, which is what citizens might do if they were dissatisfied with public services (Oliver and Heater 1994: 109 10). This reflected a wider implication of the creation of customers through marketisation and managerialisation, namely that the objectives of providing social services were changed fundamentally. In the social democratic welfare state of the pre-business era, two objectives existed: efficiency and equity. Judgements about efficiency were frequently linked to questions of equity. For example, *efficiency* in the pre-business era welfare state required the pursuit of the goal of providing services that would give the greatest level of overall benefit to citizens; and *equity* required the pursuit of fairness in the distribution of services between different citizens. In the case of social work, these twin objectives of efficiency and equity were pursued through Social Services Departments as public sector financers and providers of services. In the establishment of the social work business, the concern with the equity of the distribution of services between citizens was swept away. For example, the shift to a quasi-market system had a primary focus on efficiency, narrowly defined in terms of value for money (see Chs 3 and 8). For the Conservative governments, questions of equity were seen to fall within the political domain, as they require value judgements about the distribution of services between citizens. It was precisely those value judgements that the Conservatives were at pains to obscure through the drive for economic efficiency. Such efficiency could be portrayed as belonging on the ground of supposedly value-free economics. By collapsing the twin objectives of social work into the single objective of efficiency – expressed as value for money – the Conservative governments attempted to side-step and depoliticise questions of equity as it set about establishing the social work business.

In the pre-business era welfare state, equity carried with it, at the least, some notions of justice and equality. Where equity appeared at all in the social work business, it was tightly prescribed in a very different notion of fairness to social work's customers, for example requiring local government Social Services Departments to set down minimum standards for service provision, having complaints procedures for dissatisfied customers and inspecting services to check on standards. Social services departments were required to conduct market research to find out what their local population needed in the way of services and to ensure that this was made available through service contracts and purchasing. They were required to publish (business) plans for public inspection (local Community Care Plans) and to make information available about what services were on offer and which people were eligible for them. In the *Framework for Local Community Care Charters* (Department of Health 1994), the emphasis was on simple output measures through which the performance of individual services could be monitored against indicators drawn up by the Audit Commission, with the results published locally. All of these measures were consistent with a view of equity as making services more accountable to individual customers. The users of social services were thus re-imagined as customers choosing between a range of options on offer from public, private and voluntary agencies; options which were envisaged as henceforth giving precise and identifiable outputs to the individual (Department of Health 1994). Achieving this emphasis on the customer was seen as requiring a 'cultural revolution' in the personal social services (Audit Commission 1992: 19). As we have seen, the spirit of this cultural revolution had been established at the outset as explicitly consumerist.

As was mentioned briefly earlier, the other thread that ran through the *Citizen's Charter* initiative, alongside that of the service user as customer, was the bulk of the citizenry casting in the role of local shareholders. The implication was clear: the social work business should be operating along quasi-commercial rather than political lines, with citizens seen as compulsory local shareholders in local government, anxious to see their investment used prudently and sparingly, and keen to protect themselves against any excessive calls upon their funds. The shareholder model of local government was represented as envisaging a more active role on the part of those who were the funders of local government in place of the rather more passive role of tax-payer (Gyford 1991: 160–1). The *Citizen's Charter* initiative thus aimed at co-opting the public on to the side of central government in the surveillance of performance at the local level (Taylor-Gooby and Lawson 1993b: 135).

The consensus built around the customer

Although much derided at the time as Major's desperate attempt to come up with a 'big idea' which would allow his premiership to move out from the long shadow cast by Thatcherism, the *Citizen's Charter* (Prime Minister 1991) initiative was a turning point in terms of embedding emergent official recognition of the importance of consumerism in the public services. It was to become a core component in the culture of the social work business, introducing the notion of the responsiveness of services to 'customers' and 'shareholders'. It was a quasi-capitalist approach that was essentially managerialist. Its impact was such that, from the early 1990s onwards, the range of language used in debates about the future of social work narrowed across the political spectrum. The Conservatives, as we have seen, presented a strategic vision of empowering the individual citizen as a customer, a vision which they claimed would be realised by transferring services and resources outside of the public sector and setting in place quasi-market arrangements. In parallel, the Labour Party sought to distance citizens' social entitlements from what it perceived as outdated and unpopular notions of state clienthood (see Chs 2 and 5). It articulated a new concern with the individual citizen, as a reaction to the perceived shortcomings of the authoritarian power inherent in the social democratic welfare state's previous service arrangements in the pre-business era. In this context, state-sponsored consumerism was embraced by the Labour Party as a mechanism for empowering individuals against the dominance of the state. In Labour's *Citizen's Charter* (Labour Party 1991) although individuals were identified as both 'customers' and 'citizens', no clear distinction was made and the emphasis was much more on the individual as a customer than as a citizen. The hope was that the hostility of a disenchanted public to the imagery of a bureaucratic and domineering welfare state (Taylor-Gooby 1987: 199–201) would be overcome through advocating the re-allocation of power from the state to the individual (Pierson 1991: 196–7). This represented a departure from the way in which the issue of professional power in the public sector had often been represented by the Labour Party: namely, that the way to limit professional power was to make it more accountable to democratic bodies (Plant 1992: 27).

The emergent political consensus converged in the allegation that state provision tended to be unresponsive, unaccountable and alienating. This tapped into a disquiet that the welfare state provided an unsatisfactory level of service which produced uncertain results and unsympathetic treatment by service providers over whom the service user had little control (Taylor-Gooby 1987: 199–201). In the statements on citizenship produced by the Conservative government and the Labour Party the establishing of a consensus was evident on a number of key points:

- Services should be flexible in meeting individual needs.
- Individuals should have more say in how their needs were met.
- Services should be specified and standards set for them.
- Service users should have access to complaints procedures.

(Prime Minister 1991; Labour Party 1991)

In summary, by the early 1990s a new and enduring consensus was established that saw the citizen as a customer in a mixed economy of social services. For example, the Labour Party's manifesto that was issued in 1992 included the proposal that local authorities should carry out yearly surveys of consumer satisfaction (Labour Party 1992: 20). This emphasis on the citizen-as-customer was evident in the bi-partisan support for the Conservative government's reforms of the early 1990s, which provided the vehicle for introducing the language of consumerism into social work.

The Griffiths Report (1988: 5), which ushered in the reforms (see Ch. 3), anticipated that there would be 'value in a multiplicity of providers, not least from the consumer's point of view, because of the widening choice, flexibility, innovation and competition it should stimulate'. The White Paper, *Caring for People*, which followed the Griffiths Report, stressed that the reforms were focused on 'enhancing choice and independence' (Cm. 849 1989: para. 1.8). The first two of the key components of community care listed in *Caring for People* referred to services that respond flexibly and sensitively to needs and to the provision of a range of services from which to choose (Cm. 849: para. 1.10).

Competition, it was argued, would increase choice and responsiveness, and customer choices would determine the nature and range of provision in a quasi-market system. Such claims were reinforced in the run-up to the implementation of the NHS and Community Care Act (1990):

> The rationale for this reorganisation is the empowerment of users and carers. Instead of users and carers being subordinate to the wishes of service providers, the roles will be progressively adjusted. In this way, users and carers will be enabled to exercise the same power as consumers of other services.
>
> (Social Services Inspectorate 1991a: 9)

Later in the chapter, some of the limitations of the citizen-as-customer are explored in more detail (p. 139ff.), but suffice it to say at this point that behind such consumerist rhetoric glimpses of the reality of practice could be obtained, particularly in the advice given to social services departments about how to set up the new system. For example, assessment was seen as 'the process of objectively defining needs and determining eligibility for assistance against stated policy criteria' (Department of Health 1990: Appendix B). In this example, 'customers' have their needs 'objectively defined' and they have their 'eligibility for assistance determined'. In other words, it was envisaged that judgements about the customers' needs would be made by social workers, who would decide whether customers would receive any assistance to meet those needs. It would have been more accurate in these circumstances to refer to increased customer choice through the empowerment of care managers, acting on the customers' behalf. Social workers, the 'anti-user villains of state welfare', were thus transformed into the 'user-champions of the market place' (Drakeford 2000: 109; and see Lewis *et al.* 1996: 3). The care manager was charged with ensuring that the rhetoric of individual customer choice was realised by providing an individualised service to meet the needs of a particular person, rather than requiring the person to fit whatever was already available. Smale *et al.* (1993: 4) capture the essence of what was involved for the customer in entering this 'social services supermarket' and being greeted by the care manager:

> On entering the shop . . . the person explains that their job is to work with you to identify your needs and form an opinion as to what kind of package of goods you need and what resources can be called upon to obtain them. The shopping manager also explains that this supermarket no longer provides many goods

themselves, but the manager will contract with a supplier who does.

This is very different from Griffiths's view of the 'social services supermarket', in *Community Care: An Agenda for Action*:

> There is no reason why, on a controlled basis, social services authorities should not experiment with vouchers or credits for particular levels of community care, allowing individuals to spend them on particular forms of domiciliary care and to choose between particular suppliers as they wish.
>
> (Griffiths 1988: para. 40)

While Griffiths's version envisaged a form of quasi-market as close to market conditions as possible, the depiction by Smale *et al.* recognised that the aim of setting up the system was ostensibly to make social workers think like surrogate customers, by making them purchasers on the customers' behalf. However, setting up the social services supermarket with the care manager as purchaser also undermined consumer sovereignty. It meant that 'empowerment of care managers on behalf of clients does not mean absolute choice. Professional views, departmental policy, budgetary constraints and availability will all have a major impact on the package of care provided' (Department of Health–Price Waterhouse 1991). This was acknowledged in the guidance issued for social workers about what 'need' was: 'Need is a dynamic concept, the definition of which will vary over time in accordance with: changes in national legislation, changes in local policy, the availability of resources, the patterns of local demand (Social Services Inspectorate 1991a: para. 12.) Or, to put it simply, as far as care managers were concerned, '[t]he aim of assessment should be to arrive at a decision on whether services should be provided and in what form' (Cm. 849 1989: 3.2.12). Despite these glimpses of the reality behind the rhetoric of the social work business, the consumerism that permeated government reports was underpinned by the bi-partisan political consensus that regarded managers and users as having shared interests in more customer-focused services.

New Labour

After coming to power in 1997, New Labour maintained its support for the bi-partisan consensus on state-sponsored consumerism that had developed in the early 1990s (Johnson 1999). 'Third way' thinking had already embraced markets, the diversity of providers and customer choice (Giddens 1991), and the focus on the customer was maintained when New Labour took office, as the *Citizen's Charter* programme was replaced by *Service First* (Cabinet Office 1998). The government's modernisation agenda for social work began by declaring that 'social services are for all of us' (Department of Health 1998b). Setting to one side the falsity of this claim – social services are clearly nowhere near being a universal service – it nevertheless set the tone for an agenda which was concerned with customer choice. The *Quality Strategy for Social Care* that followed embraced a 'new vision and culture', which would be concerned with 'extending choice, control and flexibility' and emphasised that 'second best will never be good enough. We want everyone who uses . . . social services to expect only the best' (Department of Health 2000a: Foreword). 'That best' was defined as 'flexible, user-centred services tailored to individual needs' (Department of Health 2000a: para. 19). The relationship between services and customers would be changed: 'Staff will be working with people who are informed and know what they can expect. Users' expertise will be respected. Such empowerment can only lead to better outcomes' (Department of Health 2000a: para. 13). Despite this commitment to consumerism, the Labour government faced difficulty over safeguards for customers, not least under pressure from Audit Commission and Social Services Inspectorate reports, and instituted a more rigorous system of quality assurance and control (May 2001: 290), with greater surveillance of providers, national performance frameworks, league tables and sanctions for poor performers (see Ch. 5). As with the Conservatives' reforms, the gap between rhetoric and reality has been visible at times. For example, the 'best value plan' of one Social Services Department states that 'best values' will be promoted 'for example by ensuring that any training . . . will reinforce the need to focus on the customer's priorities'. In the same department's 'commissioning document', the customer's priorities recede: 'we will be looking at our services to ensure that they are provided equitably in relation to need', and by the time potential customers are addressed directly – in a leaflet on community care, produced for widespread distribution to the public – they are told:

> Your assessor will take responsibility for arranging the assessment. . . .Your assessor's job is to find out the best way of helping you within the available resources. . . . Your assessor will discuss

with you the outcome of the assessment and try to agree with you exactly what needs you have. He or she will explain the eligibility criteria for particular services and advise you of the sort of help for which you qualify.

Similarly, in another Social Services Department, a document called 'Responding to your needs' runs in turn through the services available, setting out their aims and what they offer, and dealing with the issue of 'How do we decide if you qualify for this service?' Conflicts between the customer rhetoric and the glimpses of the reality of accessing services, such as those provided, stem from the use of consumerist language to obscure the gatekeeping role played by social workers (see pp. 148–51 for a more detailed discussion).

   The bi-partisan consensus supporting the shift from citizens to customers has regarded commercial private sector businesses as having much to teach social work about focusing on the customer.

Customer focus

In the early days of the newly established social work business, a much discussed inspiration for 'customer focus' was Peters and Waterman's *In Search of Excellence* (1984), referred to earlier, which claimed to distil what made the USA's top-performing companies successful. Being 'close to the customer' was seen as a key ingredient in their success and proximity to customers was embraced evangelically by many Social Services Departments. One social services director was so taken with *In Search of Excellence* that every social worker and manager in the department was required to attend a screening of the spin-off *In Search of Excellence* video. 'Close to the customer' was adopted as the motto and rallying cry in the department's new business-style culture. (The life of the motto was short, however, as or the posters in social services locations across the local authority, customers added a 'd' and produced the motto 'Closed to the customer'.)

   Such initiatives represented the most extreme examples of attempts to make rapid changes in the culture of social work and have been largely abandoned, in part because they have been rendered unnecessary by the quiet consolidation, at least in terms of its rhetoric, of the customer focus as a dimension of social work's quasi-business discourse. As part of this discourse, customer focus has become a central element in addressing some of the difficulties faced by managers in controlling social workers' performance and represents a further twist to the controls instituted as a result of managerialisation. As was seen in Chapter 4, the managerialisation of the social work business tilted the balance of control over day-to-day work more towards managers, who required social workers to behave in ways consistent with the imperatives of quasi-capitalist rationality. Inculcation of 'customer focus' meshes with that managerialism. It serves, first, to let social workers know that the environment in which they work has changed and that changes are required of them by the quasi-business culture. Second, customer focus provides a means of bolstering the compliance of social workers with the quasi-business culture in ways that draw on their sentiments towards, and commitments to, service users. It can be used by management to encourage social workers to undertake their work in particular ways on the basis of self-control, as is the case in other occupations (Knights and Sturdy 1990), rather than by enforcing compliance through management control. In addition, social workers may, wittingly or unwittingly, draw on their wider experiences of consumerism in adapting themselves to working within the quasi-capitalist rationality of the social work business. Whether or not they do so, customer focus is encouraged through training courses, mission statements, the development of core values, and so on. By such means, customer focus is embedded in the social work business's organisational structure and culture as an aspect of management control.

The well-established practice of supervision can be used to illustrate this. Although supervision sessions can now be rooted in the 'hard data' provided by information technology, and thus have the potential for greater management control of social workers' performance (see Ch. 4), they can be conducted in ways which seek to foster social workers' commitment and involvement through qualitative dialogue about the circumstances of individual customers. A straightforwardly hierarchical accountability relationship, concerned solely with monitoring quantitative performance against management standards, is still unusual. However, the basis of the dialogue is not customer sovereignty. There is no sense in social work, other than in the most abstracted and remote managerial business rhetoric, that the customer is always right. Instead, the social work business has appropriated what were previously professional notions of empathy and has re-worked them into the need for social workers to empathise with the service user as a customer, on a similar plain to that of social workers themselves. They are enjoined to involve customers in terms of negotiation and the creation of shared meanings, rather than in terms of the customer issuing them with instructions. This dominant customer focus guides social workers to respond to the varying situations of customers in ways that the social work business requires, but which cannot always be pre-designed. Further, the customer focus induces acceptance by social workers of the pervasive systems of information technology observation and data collection. This is achieved by arguing that the technology has been established in order to sharpen the customer focus. Social workers should therefore embrace managerial monitoring as it supports the achievement of the aim, to which social workers are committed, of putting the customer at the centre of services; management and social workers share that aim, and control of what social workers do is merely a method to achieve that common goal. In these ways, focusing on the customer builds on and transforms the tradition of professional empathy towards service users dating back to the bureau-professional regimes of the social democratic welfare state (see Ch. 2).

Although customer focus can be incorporated into managerial control strategies, it is not a straightforward means of extending control over social workers. For example, while there may be a shared aim of increasing the attention paid to the customer, the matter of who constitutes the customer is open to debate. Managers' definition of 'the customer' is more likely than that of social workers to be preoccupied with those people waiting for a service (see Ch. 4 for a discussion of management concern to maintain throughput) and cutting the time that those customers spend waiting, particularly given the standards set by regulatory regimes (see Ch. 5). In contrast, social workers are more likely to be preoccupied with providing assistance to their current caseload of customers. The longer the periods of time spent by social workers in completing work with existing customers, the less time is available to reduce the waiting list of potential customers. Thus, addressing a customer's difficulties may possess intrinsic satisfaction for the social worker and may promote customer satisfaction with the outcome, while damaging customer service as defined by management in terms of time spent by potential customers waiting for a service. Much of the material covered in Chapter 4 can be interpreted as management's attempts at addressing this conflict and as part of a wider struggle in which management seeks to impose its definitions of the 'customer' and 'good service' over those of social workers. The more managers attempt to impose their definition by intervening in social workers' practice, the more negative social workers' reactions are likely to be. For example, if supervisors in their meetings with social workers only focused mechanically on task-lists generated by the computer software for each of their cases, as a way of trying to free up social workers' time to deal with customers waiting for a service, they might undermine any job satisfaction social workers gain from engaging with the problems of their current customers.

While customer focus is a key aspect of management control, the role of information gained directly from customers has not been well developed thus far. Nevertheless, the introduction of complaints procedures, as part of establishing the social work business, led to a more broadly based facility in many Social Services Departments for customers to lodge their comments and compliments, as well as their complaints. In most Social Services Departments, social workers are required to give customers a copy of the complaints procedure on first meeting and, in many departments, compliance with this requirement is one of the 'core standards'. The other side of the coin of customer feedback is the use of information from customers in the form of 'Thank you' cards and letters of praise to promote commitment to the customer focus. Some managers display these in social services settings or read them out at team meetings, sometimes even accompanied by applause in recognition of the work of a colleague. However, at present, the role of customers as direct providers of information is relatively undeveloped and is largely confined to such *ad hoc* complaints and expressions of thanks. If management seeks in future to combine the customer focus with a more systematic collection of information from the customer, further conflicts might ensue. The role of the customer as provider of information to management might undermine the generation of customer focus among social workers, if social workers identify customers with management's interests because of their information-providing role.

Having seen that much has been made of the need to create customers for the social work business, the remainder of the chapter is concerned with whether such customer creation is a feasible or desirable goal.

Scrutinising the customer base

Rational self-interested customers

The way in which customers are conceived of, and are meant to conceive of themselves, has important implications for the social work business and its customers. As we have seen, the nature and effectiveness of services are discussed rhetorically, in ideal–typical terms of the way things are supposed to be (Warde 1994: 238). There is less concern with whether citizens want to be customers than with how they should function in relation to the quasi-market and a social work business operating on the basis of quasi-capitalist rationality, because that is what is considered to be best for them. As a result, the customer focus embodies a view of people as competent economic and social actors, capable of pursuing their best interests in the marketplace (Drakeford 2000: 24). Muetzelfeldt identifies the origins of such assumptions about customers in neo-liberal theory

> that both describes and prescribes society as made up of atomised individuals with their own distinct interests, capacities and resources. It involves a rejection of any social theory that acknowledges that people are more than atomised individuals, that they have shared identities through which they and their interests are formed, and that society is constituted by bonds of mutuality that go well beyond the instrumental transactions between atomised individuals.
>
> (1994: 139–40)

This neo-liberal discourse promoted entrepreneurial selves: individualistic, autonomous, competitive, self-interested, rational and informed (Froggett 2000: 7); selves who used 'choice to maximise their individual utility based on their self-interest' (Muetzelfeldt 1994: 148). In that discourse, customers have only their individual interest in getting the best deal they can, determined by the power and personal resources they bring to the market. Thus, customers with resources, high expectations and information will be best placed to enter the quasi-market of social work (Stanley 1999). The lack of resources available to many of social work's customers to purchase from the market (Parker 2000) does not diminish the extolling of choice and competition (Baldock 1998).

The influential (Conservative and Labour) *Citizen's Charters* reflected exactly this image of individual customers consuming specific services. This customer orientation resulted in a view of citizenship in the *Charters* that consisted of aggregating the outcomes of the exercise of rational, self-interested, individual choice at the point of service use and ignored the public and collective nature of services. The logical flaw is immediately apparent. Existing individual customer choices cannot determine the overall pattern of services for citizens who are potential customers, otherwise meeting existing customers' demands equitably would mean meeting overall need inequitably. There are questions about what should be provided for whom; those questions are inherently political and are obscured by an exclusive emphasis on rational self-interested customers making choices.

Making choices from the available options

In any market, active choice from available options is the key to the authority of the customer (Keat *et al.* 1994). Rational, self-interested and utility-maximising customers can function only 'when there are a variety of options of quality from which choices can be made' (Rustin 1994: 199) and when they enter the marketplace equipped to choose from the options available. Both of these requirements for functioning as a customer are explored in relation to the social work business.

First, what is the evidence that the reforms of the early 1990s, under-pinned ostensibly by a commitment to state-sponsored consumerism, produced a variety of options from which customers can choose?

Henwood *et al.* (1996) noted that the approach based on assessment and care management processes and supported by devolved budgets was intended to enable packages of care to be assembled in line with individual needs and preferences. However, on the basis of their monitoring of the impact of the approach, they questioned the extent to which the objective of promoting choice was achieved. They had no difficulty unearthing new systems and processes, but questioned whether they produced the proclaimed user outcomes. Further, they suggested that the emphasis on user outcomes receded, as implementa-tion progressed, with the desired outputs and outcomes deflected from ends to means. The criteria against which the managers assessed the success of the implementation were essentially those relating to admin-istrative systems and processes. They concluded that using such criteria to suggest that the new arrangements for funding, assessing and pur-chasing services had been introduced without significant disruption was an essentially neutral finding and that the more appropriate ques-tion was whether the changes had made a positive difference in terms of improved opportunities for service users to exercise choice and live independently. While management interest focused on tangible evi-dence that new administrative structures and processes were in place, service users and carers pointed to the absence of hard evidence to contradict their personal experiences of there being little change in the extent and availability of services in the community:

> With the exception of a few individual examples, hard evidence of service improvement was thin and the [*management*] belief in improvement was often not grounded in firm data. Indeed, in some instances, the belief that services were becoming more flexible and better suited to individuals' needs was contradicted by objec-tive evidence that the range of options remained restricted.
>
> (Henwood *et al.* 1996: 5)

Similarly, in their implementation study, Lewis and Glennerster (1996) found that an enormous investment had been made in terms of the development of structures and procedures, producing a considerable increase in bureaucracy for social workers, in order to produce changes in the pattern of services, which they anticipated would benefit relatively few service users (1996: 203). They pointed out that providing customer choice through genuinely individualised needs-led care packaging that does not use off-the-shelf services is expensive, probably more expensive than the cost of residential provision (Lewis and Glennerster 1996: 164): 'The main aim of introducing market principles into community care was to increase choice for users and to ensure the provision of more flexible, appropriate care. Authorities are a long way from delivering tailor-made packages to meet assessed need' (1996: 116).

In part, the failure to deliver choice from a range of options was a result of the '85 per cent rule', requiring Social Services Departments to spend 85 per cent of the funding on services provided by the independent sector (see Ch. 3). The bulk of independent provision was in residential care, so that was where resources continued to be channelled (Lewis and Glennerster 1996: 200). In other words, the existing market, rather than customers' preferences, shaped supply. When efforts were made to diversify the options available, the main concern was with providing plurality of supply to social workers, not choices for service users (Schorr 1992). This was because commissioners negotiated block-contracts for groups of service users, rather than individual social workers purchasing services for individual users, as in the Kent community care scheme (Challis and Davies 1980), which had impressed Griffiths in reaching his recommendations for reform. Block-contracts, and set-list services drawn from them, placed social workers in a position akin to that of the travel agent who produces a package holiday brochure and tells the customer what is available. The attractions of block-contracts, as compared to a succession of spot-contracts, are clear – lower unit costs, reduced transaction costs and ease of monitoring quality. In any case, providers were resistant to providing the small units of service required by spot-contracts and preferred the guaranteed level of funding available to them under block-contracts (Lewis *et al.* 1996: 15). Spot-contracts were not recommended on a large scale in the Department of Health's guidance on purchasing services (Department of Health 1991: para. 4.61), despite the fact that the use of block-contracts minimises customer choice. The priority was achieving economy and efficiency in contracting by seeking high volume from a limited range of standardised services.

As a result, assessment was shaped by social workers' awareness of the services that were available, rather than the customer choosing from a range of options (Davis *et al.* 1997; Baldwin 2000). In addition, given constrained resources, the initial stress on 'needs' has increasingly been replaced in practice by the detailed assessment of dependence and/or risk in relation to the social work business's eligibility criteria.

There are questions, then, about the extent to which options are available from which customers can choose. Putting those questions to one side for the moment, what about the second issue: do customers enter the marketplace equipped to make choices, assuming for the time being that those choices are available?

Service users have been shown to have difficulty in making demands as customers because they have little conception of what type of help to expect from both statutory and independent sector services (Ellis 1993; Davis *et al.* 1997; Clark *et al.* 1998; Richards 2000). The words that appear in the information provided by Social Services Departments can themselves be a barrier. For example, a survey of service users found that 'none understood "network" and few understood "gender", "criteria" and "equitable manner". Some thought that "voluntary agency" meant "people with no experience", "sensitive" meant "tender and sore" and "agencies" meant "second-hand clothes shops"' (Payne 1995: 186). However, lack of information about services may not always be the issue. Baldock and Ungerson's 1994 research highlights that obstacles to market use may be a matter of users' values and culture, rather than lack of facts and information. They term these 'habits of the heart', which act as barriers to purchasing help on the part of those who have a history of low participation in the market.

It is not just lack of knowledge and value clashes that mitigate against the entrance of confident customers into the market place. Contact with the social work business might be unwelcome; it might have been initiated by someone else and it might be misunderstood. The emphasis on customer choice, and the acceptance at face value of a shared focus between the customer and the social worker, disguises the reality of how many people come into contact with the social work business. The majority of the social work business's customers are not choosing to use its services. They are involved with the business as a result of their life experiences or through aspects of their social context that have a coercive element (Flynn 1993: 162; Forbes and Sashidharan 1997). Yet service users are presented as enterprising and active choice makers in a way that isolates their experiences from problematic and stressful conditions which may have brought them into contact with the social work business (Barnes and Prior 1995). This isolation of service users from their material and emotional circumstances is compounded by the word 'customer' itself, which is suggestive of impersonal, largely one-off, transactions in temporary trading relationships. While this might be consistent with the message that citizens should avoid dependence on the state, it is out of kilter with the often complex interpersonal relationships between service user and social worker (Hadley and Clough 1996: 196; Hoggett 2000: 147), which are quite unlike the customer–salesperson relationships of the market:

> There is a fundamental conflict between the impersonal and formal relations of contract which prevail in the market and the relationships which prevail in social services and which place a high premium on personal and informal contacts. Factors which play a very limited role in commerce – the helping and caring roles of individuals, family members and local networks – are the essence of the work of social services. The statutory responsibilities of official agencies are also a crucial part of the social services framework in a way they are not for a normal commercial enterprise. Another key distinction arises form the fact that SSDs [Social Services Departments] provide public rather than consumer goods. Whereas the ordinary entrepreneur needs to satisfy only the customer, workers in social services have a 'multi-dimensional agenda': they have to satisfy service users (who may have carers or families with conflicting interests and needs), but also have important responsibilities to the common, public, interest.
>
> (Langan 2000: 163–4)

All of this complexity is set to one side in the notion of rational self-interested customers making choices. It is as though being a competent customer will just happen or can be effected easily. However, people who have been disadvantaged may need massive amounts of support to acquire the assertiveness this implies, as the experience of user self-advocacy demonstrates (McNally 2000). Being in need and functioning as a customer may be a contradiction (Biggs 2000), and in reality customers may be preoccupied with finding *any* service (Barnes 1997: 34), rather than in judiciously deciding whether alternative services would meet their needs more effectively:

> The notion of users of social care services exercising rational choice in a way which is consistent with the notion of economic agents maximising personal benefits ignores the reality of the way in which people come to be in the position of 'needing' such services

and the way in which such services are used. . . . Entry to the social care system is often an indication of lack of choice rather than the positive exercise of choice . . . (or it) has the characteristics of the 'least worst' option rather than a positive choice.

(Barnes and Prior 2000: 85)

Some service users, however, do enter the assessment process 'decided'. Such service users seem to have a clear idea of their difficulties and what help they would like, and look to social services to provide this specific help (Richards 2000; Tanner 2001). These service users would appear to be more equipped to enter the marketplace and to exercise customer choice. However, there is a 'Catch 22'. Assessment and care management begin from the assumption that social workers will assist them in identifying their needs and will then involve them in deciding on the most appropriate services to meet those needs (Social Services Inspectorate 1991a, 1991b). As this process unfolds, these previously 'decided' customers may have little say about which needs are met or which services are considered to best meet them (Myers and MacDonald 1996). An example of a 'decided' group of customers whose choices are not respected is provided by residents of local authority residential establishments. There have been protests by older people and attempts to use the Human Rights Act (1998) to ensure that local authorities continue to provide and run homes for older people. The Residents Action Group for the Elderly issued a writ for an injunction against Birmingham Council under the Human Rights Act (1998) to try to prevent thirty homes being transferred on the basis that this was a violation of residents' human rights. Their clear choice as customers was frustrated by the local authority being unable to afford to bring the homes up to the standard required by regulation. (The capital budget for Birmingham Social Services was £7 million, and £35 million was needed to bring the homes up to registration standards [Winchester 2001: 11].)

Barnes and Prior (1995) question whether it is customer choice or confidence in services meeting their needs that people most want, but suggest that whether or not customer choice leads to a sense of empowerment depends on five dimensions:

- The degree of coercion associated with using the service.
- Predictability – can the user determine the likely effects of services in advance of their use?
- Frequency – does the user develop expertise in determining the likely outcomes of service use?

- The significance of the services in relation to different types of need.
- Participation – the extent to which outcomes depend on the involvement of the user as a co-producer of services.

These are tough requirements to satisfy, and they suggest that the 'proxy customer' of social work is situated at some distance from the self-interested, active, rational, utility-maximising customer of consumerist rhetoric. Perhaps, it might be objected, the latter might be created through the use of direct payments? However welcome direct payments might be as an option for service users, the conclusion that only cash transactions will enable them to exercise control over services implies a faith in market forces which is not well founded, judging by the earlier discussion, and may not work for people with complex emotional and interpersonal needs (Barnes 1997: 142).

The myth of 'the customer experience'

The discussion has raised questions about whether 'the customer experience' functions in the way suggested by the consumerist rhetoric. That rhetoric is fed by a myth, generated by comparing images of 'best experience' in the private sector with a depiction of what is worst in the public sector. The image of 'the customer' that is conveyed by the rhetoric is, either explicitly or implicitly, drawn from the commercial sector at the level of a range of companies like Marks & Spencer, Next or Benetton. It is an image that involves a choice from quality options and an ability on the part of the customer to change her mind, if she decides she does not like her purchase. In other words, the consumerist rhetoric sounds suspiciously middle class (Pollitt 1994: 11). What seems to be forgotten in this portrayal of the customer experience is that the market also produces everything-for-a-pound shops, dodgy back-street second-hand car dealers and cafés and restaurants with indifferent food. Interestingly, in relation to the latter, the imagery of customer choice in consumerist rhetoric implies the choice of an *à la carte* menu in an upmarket restaurant, rather than the limitations and predictability of McDonalds. Care management is not able to conjure up a sense of high-end customer luxury derived from this rhetoric, but nevertheless purports to make a customer's experience memorable, just as fast-food restaurants and supermarkets do.

In other words, the imagery of the customer that is derived from the market is highly selective. In any case, many of social work's customers know the 'lower end' of the market all too well, in the daily struggle to get by. There is little recognition in the consumerist rhetoric of the limitations in the range of goods available and affordable from which many people have to choose, or that the ability to consume at a basic level is precarious for growing numbers of people (Hills 1997, 1998). This is the customer status and experience which many people carry into their interaction with social work. They do not have high expectations of what being a customer involves. Consumerism does not, therefore, have the effect of necessarily heightening their expectations, and some of the trappings of consumerism are unfamiliar to social work's customers. For example, in one Social Services Department, the introduction of 'smart cards' in connection with home care services caused widespread confusion, which turned to consternation when customers received their first statements through the post. As the vast majority of them had never had a credit card, they panicked at the sight of minus symbols, not realising that these represented payments they had made to their account rather than sums that were outstanding. Notwithstanding such difficulties in maintaining the myth of the customer status and experience, presentation rather than the intrinsic worth of what is on offer counts for a great deal in consumerist rhetoric, and so the 'customer' is still present in many mission statements and business plans. The reality may be very different:

> A pressurized [*sic*] public authority comes to rely on pre-selected 'packages of care', which are not really tailored to individual needs, so the experience becomes more like that of a 'consumer' under a communist regime – queuing up for commodities which are strictly rationed by the authorities according to their own criteria of risk and need, and then being given something which does not fit or suit and certainly is not chosen.
>
> (Jordan and Jordan 2000: 23)

In contrast, the myth of the customer experience obscures what is required in order to be a competent customer and how far away those requirements are from the status and experience of being a customer of social work. Being a competent customer of anything requires:

- resources to purchase (access);
- knowledge and ability to choose between options (information and choice);
- knowledge and ability to evaluate the purchase (evaluation);
- knowledge and the ability to seek redress for unsatisfactory goods and services (redress);

- ability to substitute a more satisfactory product for a less satisfactory one (substitution).

(Adapted from Potter 1994 and Warde 1994)

The distance from these requirements experienced by customers of the social work business is in part due to the gatekeeping role played by social workers.

Gatekeeping

Earlier in the chapter, examples were given of the way in which the consumerist rhetoric is harder to discern the closer one gets to detailed practice guidance in the social work business. This is because as the rhetoric encounters actual practice it is confronted by the gatekeeping role played by social work, and that role exposes the shortcomings of the customer status and experience still further.

Flynn (1993: xiii) points out that in private sector commercial transactions the sale connects customers with the organisation. Sales make profits, and so customers are persuaded to purchase. Success is measured by the achievement of sales targets and profit levels. However in social services, customers who cannot pay are entitled to services on the basis of their citizenship. The customer orientation encourages buying, whereas social services are concerned with ensuring that only people whose needs are defined as satisfying certain policy criteria receive a service (Flynn 1993: 145). As the gatekeepers of resources in these circumstances, social workers regulate the distribution of rights and obligations on behalf of the state. As we saw in the discussion of policy developments earlier in the chapter, needs are essentially what the state decides to recognise and provides the resources to meet (Blackman and Atkinson 1997). As a consequence, social workers' accountability is to managers charged with implementing and monitoring the criteria for receiving a service. As one social worker, reflecting on twenty-five years' experience, put it: 'Although there was always an element of rationing resources, today, under the guise of managerialism, with its focus on routines and procedures, one is largely engaged in explaining why needs cannot be met' (Rogowski 2001: 15). In the consumerist rhetoric, this is obscured and accountability to users is presented as though it is predominant. The contradictions between customer choice and the constraints and responsibilities of gatekeeping can be summarised as follows:

Table 2 Customer choice versus gatekeeping

Customer choice	Gatekeeping
Needs-led	Budget-led
Budget flexibility	Budget inflexibility/strict control of costs
Tailor-made services	Maximising the amount of service provision available as economically and efficiently as possible
Freedom to purchase services from wherever on the basis of individual choice	Constraints on purchase of service and choice in order to ensure value for money for taxpayers
Individual influence on the style and content of the service	Standardised services

Any social worker who took the consumerist rhetoric at face value and operated on the basis of the features presented in the left-hand column would be rapidly disabused concerning the reality of customer choice, when faced with rationing and channelling constrained resources, through a relationship that has dimensions of power and authority. Regardless of their intentions, stances, motivations or orientations, social workers are involved in determining eligibility for services through rules, regulations and procedures.

> Many SSD workers were enthusiastic about the possibility of user empowerment, but have found it difficult to separate needs-based assessment from the ever-present issue of resources and what services are actually available, and have been subject to a vast increase in bureaucracy. Thus, from a bottom-up perspective, it is less clear that such a managerial and organisational approach to change has been successful.
>
> (Lewis and Glennerster 1996: 206)

Two examples illustrate this: the use of eligibility criteria; and the establishment of resource allocation panels. The intention behind eligibility criteria is to prioritise the allocation of resources to people considered to be at high risk and to ration resources according to pre-defined criteria (Ellis 1993; Barnes 1997: 40; Stanley 1999). (Or, as one senior manager put it to me: 'They convey the message "come back when you're worse".') The infamous Laming circular warned social services departments not to make explicit statements of need against such criteria unless they were confident that they could supply a service (Social Services Inspectorate 1992). This sounded surprisingly 'service-led' for a set of reforms that were alleged to be concerned with 'needs-led' assessment that would enable services to be tailored to customers' individual requirements (Social Services Inspectorate 1991a, 1991b). In reality, the use of eligibility criteria allows Social Services Depart-ments to ration services in line with the resources they have available. They are able to adjust their eligibility criteria, if faced with resourcing difficulties, so that fewer people qualify for a service, thus making transparent that need is defined in the context of what a Social Services Department can provide (Tanner 1998). In this context, social workers have been increasingly providing 'a service of last resort' (Langan 1993: 163; and see Ellis 1993; Richardson and Pearson 1995; Stanley 1999), rather than the comprehensive and preventive services envisaged at the time of the Seebohm Report (Harris 1999; White and Harris 1999). The home care service, for example, is being provided in greater volume to a smaller number of households (Department of Health 2000b). This is a tangible example of eligibility criteria being used to channel resources to people in greatest need. The advantage of eligibil-ity criteria for the social work business is that they assume a technical–managerial guise, rather than being seen as political decisions. In that guise, they are far more likely to produce passive service users than active customers:

> [Rationing is] very powerful precisely because it gradually redraws the parameters of available social services and entitlements. . . . The incremental and relatively invisible nature of these cost-containment practices makes it very difficult to identify a policy that is hurting a class of people, and thus to mobilise resistance.
> (Fabricant and Burghardt 1992: 76)

The second example of determining the eligibility for services as part of the gatekeeping role is the operation of resource allocation panels. Their operation can be illustrated by their functioning in a particular Social Services Department. In the guidance about the panels given to social workers, they are described as

> identifying, comparing and keeping a watching brief on individuals with similar needs for resources, who are a high priority. . . . Their purpose is to ensure that the most appropriate options to meet

these needs are explored and the best use is made of the total resources available to meet these needs.

A script is provided for social workers to use if they need to explain the existence and role of the panel to the customers. They are told to say:

> The panel is a group of senior managers from the social services department and the health service whose job is to consider all individuals who appear to have similar needs, to make sure that all the options for meeting those needs are explored, and that priority for the use of the money available is given to those most in need.

Social workers are told that the use of such a script 'will ensure that their expectations are not raised beyond what the department is likely to be able to deliver' and that they should 'identify all the options for meeting the individual's needs, including information about the relative cost/benefits in any written assessment, whatever the initial request for a service'. They are asked to remember that they are 'undertaking the assessment on behalf of the department and that the assessment process is not finally completed until a decision has been made by the panel which matches the individual's potential needs to the resources available'. Referring to service users as 'customers' takes us no further forward in resolving such conflicts for resources or in setting priorities. In fact, it obscures those conflicts, in contrast to the advice to social workers above, which makes the conflicts admirably clear. The consumer rhetoric mystifies social workers' involvement in deciding on customers' needs and whether they will be met, or referring them to resource allocation panels for decisions on whether they will be met. In reality, social workers' and managers' judgements still have a central role (MacDonald 1995: 134–5) in what the customers get.

Conclusion

The creation of customers was instigated by Conservative governments, as a facet of establishing the social work business, particularly through the development of the *Citizen's Charter* (Prime Minister 1991) in the context of a bi-partisan political consensus around a focus on the customer. Of course, there are elements within the shift from citizen to customer that can be used to promote the interests of service users (Harris 1999; White and Harris 2001):

[I]t would be wrong to dismiss out of hand the idea that people want more than to 'take what is given'. . . . Indeed for those whose lives are likely to be lived in contact with social care agencies for lengthy periods and in circumstances in which such services enter into the intimate sphere and fundamentally affect day-to-day opportunities for any type of social interaction, then a degree of choice over how, where and by whom services are to be provided has considerable significance.

(Barnes and Prior 2000: 85)

The question is whether we need to transform people into customers in order to address issues that have emerged from the consumerist critique of social work. As we have seen, that critique emerges from a wider analysis of changes in society that positions individuals as constructing their identities through the choices they make as customers. This analysis has been applied to social work's 'customers', most of whom are detached from the material and emotional circumstances out of which the consumerist rhetoric sprang. Social work's service users are not the affluent, identity-enhancing customers of the consumerist rhetoric. They are what Bauman (1988) refers to as 'flawed consumers', unable to make meaningful personal decisions in the market because of their lack of material resources. They are turning to the state because they are unable to turn to the market as individual customers in their own right. The way the consumer is conceived in the wider society colours evaluation of the effectiveness and desirability of public sector provision and of the people who use it (Warde 1994: 225–6). Some of them might even be looking for an escape from atomised individualism, rather than seeking ways of being thrust further into it through consumerism. In addition, although consumerism is presented as extending users' involvement in the social work business, it is concerned with modes of service delivery in ways which curtail that involvement to a universalised managerial set of expectations about what being treated well as a customer means (Clarke and Newman 1997: 121–2), effectively leaving overall control with the business and side-stepping questions of rights and justice. Thus, reliance on customer satisfaction legitimises the power of management by giving a mandate for what is being done, without changing the power relations: managers consult customers, managers act.

This is one example of the way in which consumerist rhetoric functions to obscure the systems of production that lead to the services that are provided. A further example is provided by the floating off of local authority services to independent operators. That option is presented as offering more choice to customers through diversifying provision in the quasi-market, conveniently omitting that, in the process, pay for the workers concerned can be driven down to the minimum wage. If we are to advance our understanding of the social work business, we need an analysis of the whole process. Different systems of provision are the consequence of distinct relationships between various material and cultural practices comprising the production, distribution, circulation and consumption of the goods or services concerned (Fine and Leopold 1993). It is salutary to remind ourselves that the business world, whose discourse social work has adopted and adapted, is not concerned ultimately with meeting human needs through sovereign customer choice. Portraying the system of production 'as a servant to the needs and wishes of consumers' (Fine and Leopold 1993: 20) is a comparatively recent ideological gloss (see pp. 121–22). Profit is the end towards which business is directed, and it is profit that drives the production, distribution and consumption of goods and services: 'Consumption can also be viewed as a passive response to the goods that manufacturers offer, with tastes manipulated to guarantee sales and profitability' (Fine and Leopold 1993: 5). Adopting a quasi-business discourse in social work means adapting social work to quasi-capitalist rationality: seeing it as though it were a business concerned with making profit. Trying to present an altruistic customer focus as the defining characteristic of the social work business is as much of an illusion as seeking to do so for a capitalist firm. Yet, in the quasi-business discourse of social work, the message comes across that if only social workers would somehow sort themselves out and really concentrate on refining the customer focus, all would be well. On the contrary, even if key elements in the dream offered by the consumerist rhetoric could be realised, the material conditions of a *state*-managed *quasi*-market would rapidly shatter the dream. The public sector has different purposes from those of businesses and different relationships with service users (Flynn 1993: 76). If we inject that reality into following through the rhetoric of the consumerist dream, the dream's inherent contradiction becomes clear: the more customer-oriented the social work business became, the more choice of services it offered, the more customers' and potential customers' expectations were raised, the more demand that was generated, the more rationing would be needed and the less responsive it would be forced to become.

8   Sorting out the supply chain

The sweeping changes that have taken place following the establishment and modernisation of the social work business have been examined in terms of the influence exerted by the quasi-business discourse on social work generally (see Chs 3–5) and, more specifically, in relation to its customer base (see Ch. 7). This chapter moves consideration of the impact of the quasi-business discourse onto another aspect of the social work business's operation: its supply chain. More specifically, the chapter considers the changes which have taken place with regard to two of the business's core suppliers: the voluntary sector and informal carers. As far as the voluntary sector is concerned, the key changes are seen to consist in the implications for that sector of the shift to quasi-markets, managed by the social work business, and especially the repercussions of the introduction of contractual trading relationships. In the case of informal care, stress is laid on the way in which caring has been repositioned politically as an aspect of citizenship obligation, reconceptualised as an overt resource and incorporated as the main source of supply in packages of care assembled by the social work business.

The voluntary sector

It is perhaps unsurprising that in establishing the social work business Conservative governments brought the private sector into a position of prominence in the supply chain (see Ch. 3). If there was to be a social work business, operating in a quasi-market place, reducing the amount of public service provision and lauding the contribution of the private sector were obvious strategies for a Conservative government wishing to take its political agenda forward (Johnson 1995; Bartlett *et al.* 1998). The implications for the supply chain of the shift to quasi-capitalist rationality did not end with the private sector, however.

Setting up the social work business involved extending a quasi-business discourse to the voluntary sector. The use of competition and contracting was signalled when the Conservative government placed a requirement on Social Services Departments to promote the development of a 'flourishing independent sector' (Cm. 849 1989: para. 1.11) and, where independent (for-profit and voluntary) providers were unavailable, for Social Services Departments to identify to central government how they proposed to stimulate them into activity (Cm. 849 1989: paras 3.4.5 and 3.4.6). The overriding message concerning the independent sector was that local authorities should make maximal use of it (Henwood *et al.* 1996: 42). As we saw in Chapter 3, in order to ensure greater employment of independent sector services, when central government funds were transferred to Social Services Departments for the implementation of the Conservative reforms, the stipulation placed on their use was that 85 per cent of the funding had to be expended on that sector (Department of Health 1992: Annex C, para. 3). Promoting this independent 'market' was seen by the Conservatives as essential to the development of competitive cost-effective services (Social Services Inspectorate 1991a: para. 1; 1991b: para. 1).

The introduction of the term 'independent sector' is significant in this context. It was a new term that embraced both commercial organisations and voluntary organisations, collapsing some of the previous distinctions between them and cloaking the embrace of the profit motive through use of private sector social services provision. As a result, the composition, management style and ethos of voluntary organisations were constrained to change (Leat 1995: 171). In classic business-like fashion, the term 'independent sector' was meant to enhance the perception of the quality of the products being supplied under this 're-branding', by virtue of a change in their collective name (Fine and Leopold 1993: 30). The name change was deceptive in relation to the voluntary sector. Whereas previously state expenditure on the voluntary sector had been used to finance provision of services subject to the sector's independently applied terms of reference, paradoxically, the introduction of the term 'independent sector' signified the managerial sweeping aside of the independent social objectives that distinguished the voluntary sector from commercial care businesses and the public sector, as a result of situating the voluntary sector in competition with the private sector in a market managed by the social work business. The voluntary sector was thus entering a more dependent relationship with the state at precisely that moment when the state was designating the sector as 'independent'. The choice between the voluntary sector and the commercial sector was no longer seen as a choice between different ideologies of social services. Rather, the choice became subject to cost–benefit calculations, developed by the social work business to manage the quasi-market as part of the 'competition state' (see Cerny 1990: 204–32). Thus, as the availability of funding through the quasi-market determined the services provided by voluntary organisations, those organisations shifted to being *alternative* (rather than supplementary or complementary) providers of welfare, competing for their customer base with commercial service providers (Lewis 1995: 20).

When these developments were instituted by the Conservative government, the National Council for Voluntary Organisations (NCVO) unsurprisingly opposed contracting on the basis of price-based competition (NCVO 1989). Its response typified a widely held view at a time when there were difficulties in introducing into voluntary organisations contractual relations which were intended to mimic those operating in private sector businesses. There was, therefore, resentment over the imposition of commercial business values and practices (Walsh *et al.* 1997). One of the points at issue in this resentment was that the way in which a market is framed and organised through the public sphere advantages some participants and disadvantages others:

> [A]ll markets are made possible by, and are framed and organised through, the public sphere. The particulars of how this is done advantage some actual or potential market participants and disadvantage others, a point that tends to slip from sight because of the assertions of the naturalness of the market by those who have been advantaged through it.
>
> (Muetzelfeldt 1994: 150)

Not only were voluntary organisations potentially disadvantaged by having to compete against the commercial sector: there was differential advantage within the voluntary sector itself. Strong national organisations with a history of service provision were better placed than smaller organisations engaged in advocacy or self-help activities, such as much of the voluntary effort in minority ethnic communities (Johnson 1991). In addition, those voluntary organisations which, in the pre-business era, might have been pressuring the public sector to provide services by pointing to shortfalls in provision were now themselves constrained to bid for contracts to supply those services.

Bidding for contracts was envisaged as the means of producing more cost-effective services from voluntary organisations (Cm. 849 1989: para. 3.4.12) and was to result in their managerialisation through their incorporation into the quasi-business discourse: 'Local authority Social Services Departments will develop an increasingly contractual relationship with providers. Contracts will require clear specifications, be enforceable in law, by or against the parties concerned' (Department of Health 1990: para. 4.23). This statement typifies the notions that underpin the operation of the 'contract state'. For example:

- Social and political life can be understood as a series of contracts in which the agent agrees to perform tasks on behalf of the principal and in return the principal agrees to reward the agent.
- The parties to an exchange are made distinct from each other, as are their interests. The interdependence of participating parties is reduced and they are increasingly expected to see themselves as independent of each other. Any shared values and interests are replaced by sanctions and incentives.
- Exchanges become more specific and concrete. There is a shift from a focus on inputs, outcomes and public goods to a concern with outputs and private goods.
- Evaluation criteria become more specific and measurable, with evaluation on the basis of being a party to a contract.

(adapted from Muetzelfeldt 1994: 136–9)

As a consequence of the application of these notions, and contrary to the arguments of the proponents of quasi-capitalist rationality concerning service diversification and choice, the introduction of the quasi-market constrained the range of voluntary sector provision (Cutler and Waine 1994: 141), as the sector's services become more formalised and standardised. In summary, in the Conservatives' reforms there were implications for the future shape of voluntary organisations in terms of their management, the balance of their activities and their distinctive identity, as they were re-branded as contracted suppliers to the social work business.

As has been implied, much of the changed shape of voluntary organisations was achieved through the introduction of contracts, which were the most significant aspect of the reforms as far as the introduction of business trading processes was concerned. The use of contracts had far-reaching implications. The findings of one research project suggested that no sector had a majority which thought that contracts improved service quality, but there was a lack of uniformity in response within this overall pattern across the two actions of the now amalgamated independent sector:

Broadly, both sets of providers from outside the statutory sector were more sceptical than others about the level of bureaucracy involved in contracting, the complexity of the additional administrative tasks involved and the emphasis in contracts on controls and sanctions. Respondents from the voluntary sector and those from for-profit organisations differed sharply, however, on the overall objectives of contracting and the likely beneficiaries from the process. Private sector providers were more optimistic about likely improvements in the quality of services, enhanced efficiency as a result of the introduction of contracts and the adoption of a more 'businesslike' approach. Voluntary sector providers were more sceptical about the potential benefits to users, the change of values implied in joining a contract culture and the impact on organisations involved in the contracting process.

(Deakin 1996: 31)

The nub of voluntary sector scepticism was that what were previously understood primarily as relationships of reciprocity, between local government Social Services Departments and the voluntary sector, were converted into exchange relationships – the voluntary sector was to engage henceforth in direct exchange, for cash, of specified activities or outputs with the social work business. The contract was not simply a practical tool but a social construction. It was the foundation for exchange relationships internal to Social Services Departments (between purchasers and providers) and for contracting out services to commercial and voluntary organisations through competitive tendering and repeat contracting from approved lists of external suppliers (Mackintosh 2000: 291). However imperfect such business practices were in establishing markets – indeed such imperfection is signalled by referring to *quasi*-markets (Le Grand 1993) – that imperfection was no barrier to the importation of the quasi-business discourse through the introduction of contracts. The contract held a vital symbolic position as

a device transplanted from the market world which represents the crucial virtues of the market as presented by its advocates: clarity of purpose and allocation of responsibilities, simplicity in operation, and working with the grain of motivation in tapping entrepreneurial and competitive instincts and harnessing them to quality in service delivery. . . . Approached in this light, contracts can be seen . . . as a metaphor for the change process as a whole.

(Deakin 1996: 20)

Thus, whether or not quasi-markets would offer more choice to service users was, in reality, a side issue in the reforms (see Ch. 7). The central issue was establishing managerialised business trading relationships, with competition between voluntary and commercial organisations on price and with little regard to the strong potential for downward pressure on quality (Mackintosh 2000: 298) as a result of the tendency towards formalisation and standardisation of modes of operation (Lewis 1993; Taylor *et al.* 1995). This pressure on quality was frequently compounded by social workers stretching their budgets (Mackintosh 2000: 299) by the only means they had available – using the cheapest services they could find. What is apparent, despite all the rhetoric of customer responsiveness which accompanied the introduction of contracts, is the exclusion of the service user from the economic culture in which the business trading relationships, surrounding the purchase of services between organisations, were embedded (Mackintosh 2000: 298, 302). There is no obvious reason why the use of contracts should empower the service user. The key movement was to a set of contractual arrangements in a managed system that would increase efficiency and lower costs, rather than towards enhancing customer choice (see Ch. 7). In addition, contracts are usually defined exclusively or primarily in terms of inputs rather than outcomes. Day-to-day power lies with the providers of services rather than the purchasers or users, and it is more difficult for the social work business to monitor the quality of outcomes at arm's-length than it would be if the services were provided from within the business (Barnes and Prior 2000: 32).

Having marginalised service users, and contrary to the idea of partnership between the voluntary sector and the social work business, these contractual trading relationships assumed that their participants had distinct interests and would act on the basis of them. The introduction of contracts reinforced, indeed often created, these different interests. Voluntary organisations with general interests and functions were restructured to make those interests and functions as specific as possible, in order to make them contractable. The social work business, as the purchaser, then controlled the allocation of contracts for services with tightly specified activities or outputs. Any shared values and interests were replaced by sanctions and incentives to act in accordance with self-interest, as money began to be directly exchanged for the delivery of services. The impact of contracts on the voluntary sector can be summed up as follows:

> The introduction of contracts has been presented at its starkest as whipping away the comfort blanket of the familiar grants regime

and allowing the chill winds of competition to blow unchecked on the most vulnerable. Voluntary agencies are portrayed as unwilling parties to that process, their independence compromised, their competence frequently in doubt and their flexibility and capacity to innovate put at risk.

[. . .]

The gradual evolution of the process of market-making in care which is placing new responsibilities on some voluntary agencies has forced many of them to change their operational style and objectives [and], as a result, they are abandoning the role of complementing local authority service provision and becoming not just alternative providers but often the dominant source of services. For many organisations . . . this is a different script which prescribes different lines for the key actors – not just voluntary sector managers but also their management committees. . . . These are parts that have to be performed convincingly if voluntary organisations are to be transformed into effective providers operating in a competitive market.

(Deakin 1996: 22, 25)

If we turn to the contribution of New Labour, we see that it accepted the supply chain inheritance from the Conservative governments that preceded it and then took that inheritance a step further. In 1998, eighteen months after New Labour came to power, the Home Office promulgated a compact on relations between government and the voluntary sector, which sought to introduce a framework for relations at every level and proceeded to link funding to objectives, performance indicators and their associated targets (Home Office 1998). An inspection of working relationships by the Social Services Inspectorate advocated that local authorities and voluntary organisations make 'common cause', with the diversity of the sector seen as a barrier to the realisation of this cause (Barwood 2000). The voluntary sector's concerns about the contract culture were acknowledged – loss of independence, being required to do more for less money and the increase in costs associated with greater accountability – but were seen as surmountable barriers rather than issues for legitimate debate.

New Labour's emphasis that the state has a 'common cause' with the voluntary sector is an apposite summary of the position to which developments to date have led. The voluntary sector's sense of distinctiveness – in terms of its nature, purpose and autonomy (as compared to the public and commercial sectors) – has been eroded as voluntary organisations have sought to accommodate to a reconstructed relationship with the state, premissed on the business disciplines of the market and managed by the social work business. We should not under-estimate the advantages to the state of transferring a series of poten-tially damaging risks in the name of partnership: 'Governments cannot afford to respond whole-heartedly to problems themselves. . . . Instead, a shunting yard is required, where problems can be shelved or transferred, while giving the appearance of state responsiveness' (McDonald 2000: 88). In the USA, where these trends are significantly further advanced, the emphasis has been increasingly on the advan-tages derived from cost-containment through productive and efficient budgeting, with a consequent 'narrowing of the service encounter' as not-for-profit organisations have been constrained to become leaner and meaner (Fabricant and Burghardt 1992: Ch. 4). However, there can be disadvantages to the use of contracts, even when viewed narrowly from within a quasi-capitalist frame of reference. If contracts are complex to write and monitor and/or if there are few suppliers there are increases in the transaction costs of contracting, and in such circumstances there may be an advantage in internalising the trans-actions. Whether markets and contracts have the potential to be efficient depends on the number of suppliers and the complexity of the contracts (Flynn 1993: 140).

Carers

The establishment and modernisation of the social work business has not been simply a matter of sorting out policies and reshaping organi-sational structures and processes. It has also been about changing what social work is meant to represent as an aspect of the state's intervention in people's lives. Specifically, an aspect of the quasi-business discourse is the shift in expectations of what social work is and what it will pro-vide. In relation to informal carers, that shift in expectations centres around the role of the social work business in strengthening self-reliance.

Caring in the pre-business era

As was seen in Chapter 2, social work was incorporated into the pre-business era's social democratic vision of the state's responsibility for its citizens with the publication of the Seebohm Report (Cmnd. 3703 1968). The Report contained a commitment to the promotion of social citizenship rights, enshrined in a vision of universal social services, through the agency of social work. Such social democratic representations of the pre-business era have been questioned by feminists. They have cast doubt on the portrayal of the welfare state as progressing towards an inclusive concept of citizenship, through aspirations for comprehensive and universal services. Their exposure of the welfare state's patriarchal underpinnings opened up new understandings of social citizenship, in particular revealing it to be a gendered concept, premissed upon specific assumptions about the roles of women and men. The core of these assumptions rsted on men being engaged in full-time employment, while women were to concentrate their energies on homemaking and care-giving, from their location in stable heterosexual marriages (Wilson 1977; Williams 1989; Lister 1990, 1997, 1998; Lewis 1997). The assumptions were present from the outset, with Beveridge, as the architect of the post-war welfare state, arguing that insuring women via their husbands, rather than in their own right, recognised their valuable contribution to caring (Lewis 1997: 170). At the heart of the welfare state, then, was an established boundary between men's paid work in the public domain and women's unpaid work (including caring) in the private sphere (Stacey 1981; Lister 1990, 1997, 1998; Lewis 1997). This dominant social democratic understanding of citizenship in the pre-business era accorded a privileged position to publicly visible paid work (Stacey 1981; Finch 1989; Kingdom 1996; Lister 1998), with caring as a taken-for-granted resource in the invisible arena of households:

> The informal sector provides the objective background to provision. It represents the given against which agencies act, and against which they structure their services. It is a frame of reference which has a neutral quality to it. Agencies relate to the informal sector as an object-like reality. They read the situation and act in its context.
>
> (Twigg 1989: 61)

Consistent with the general acceptance of caring as a taken-for-granted resource, the Seebohm Report emphasised that as far as social work was concerned:

> The care which a family gives to its older members is of prime importance and nothing is quite an adequate substitute. Therefore the social services and the social service departments in particular, should make every effort to support and assist the family which is caring for an older member.
>
> (Cmnd. 3703 1968: para. 294)

However, we have seen that, in the era of the social democratic welfare state, this emphasis on informal care was accompanied by a stress on the state's parallel obligations to provide services, as an aspect of social citizenship, through the agency of social work: 'We believe that the social service department should undertake the co-ordination of various services which the old person may require . . . as well as advice and support to any relatives or friends who may be able to help look after him [*sic*]' (Cmnd. 3703 1968: para. 308). With the establishing of the social work business, this stress on the state's parallel obligations began to be undermined.

Caring and the social work business

It might be considered unremarkable that, once the social work business got into full swing, the voluntary sector was re-jigged as part of the business supply chain. Attempting a similar consolidation of the position of informal care in the supply chain might be regarded as more remarkable. However, given that the difficulty in meshing informal care and public sector care was attributed by the Conservatives to the previous rigidity of local authority services, it was envisaged that this would change if flexible packages of care were assembled from commercial and voluntary providers, allowing the contribution of informal care to be slotted into the packages. In addition, the existence of 5.7 million carers, estimated to be saving the taxpayer £34 billion a year (HM Government 1999: 17), has attracted increasing government attention in terms of their existing and potential contribution to the social work business supply chain. This is part of more deep-seated changes:

> Today, as the world of consumption is conceptually broadened, it is increasingly being understood without a sharp division being drawn between its incidence and origins in the commercial world and its roots elsewhere, whether through state or household provision. Our lives are being interpreted in terms of the broad categories of services and users, as producers and consumers. Whilst the language employed exhibits a degree of neutrality, the underlying model and logic is to emulate, if not to replicate, the corporate world. It is a process that treats the social and the commercial as commensurate, if not identical, the better to subject the former to the more exacting and targeted economic calculation associated with the latter. The notion of 'value for money' extracts the essence of the supposed condensing of social relations into the world of

consumption, making explicit its association with the purchase of commodities, irrespective of what explicit values are used to assess 'value' for money.

(Fine and Leopold 1993: 16–17)

Consistent with these deep-seated changes, the re-positioning of caring began as a result of the Conservative governments' reforms in the early 1990s (see Ch. 3). Changes in the practical mechanics of service funding and delivery were seen by many commentators as inseparable from the rejection of social democratic citizenship values (see, for example, Baldock and Ungerson 1994). Notions of community and collectivism were replaced by an emphasis on enterprise and individualism (Marquand 1996), which served to reduce expectations of what the state should provide and to construct a vision of the 'good society' based on individual self-interest and individual moral responsibility (Jordan 1989). A new concept of citizenship was promoted in which dependence was to be avoided and self-help and support by informal carers came to the fore (see Ch. 7). By the late 1980s, this new orthodoxy had run into difficulty. The primacy accorded to the market and the extra-state social solidarity within households were proving to be two distinct threads which were difficult to interweave in the New Right's, by then, established political agenda (Jordan 1994). The privileging of atomistic individualism within New Right discourse, rendered personal relationships provisional and revocable (Gray 1999: 37). The New Right needed 'new modes of social integration, solidarity and citizenship. The market may indeed be an efficient mechanism of allocation, but not of building solidarities' (Esping-Andersen 1998: 27).

As we saw in Chapter 7, the new mode of integration, solidarity and citizenship employed by the Conservatives was 'active citizenship', emphasising the need for social bonds of obligation. The overall impact of the notion of the 'active citizen' was to emphasise still further personal and private, rather than the state's, responsibilities to provide care. Aimed at shedding the individualistic self-interested image of Thatcherism, this political re-positioning of caring was recovering a tradition of Conservative communitarianism which had lain dormant in conceptions of one-nation Toryism, hitherto marginalised and discredited (Gray 1999: 35). This tradition emphasised a sense of common purpose consonant with individualism (Cowen 1999: 199). Neighbourliness, kindness and voluntary action were rediscovered as crucial functions, and caring for kin was ripe for incorporation into this moral conception of citizenship, with active citizens taking more responsibility for others as well as of themselves (Johnson 1993). One arena in which this citizenship reclamation project took place was in the establishment of the social work business and, in particular, the reform of community care policy and practice:

> [A] number of government-sponsored social policies have brought the term 'community' to new prominence in political and social discourses – policies such as community care. . . . In a number of industrial societies they were introduced by right-wing governments who attempted to yoke them together with the freest possible markets.
>
> (Frazer 2000: 179)

The Conservative governments not only heralded the benefits to be gained from quasi-capitalist rationality in market arrangements (see Ch. 3), but trumpeted the importance of a willingness to care within households and the imperative to make maximal use of this 'resource':

> [A]ssessment/case management in its most comprehensive form covers . . . taking account of what can be done to meet the identified needs *first through informal support* and then through available resources. . . . Once a user's individual needs for care have been identified the next step will be to decide what services can be provided at the public expense, in the light of the resources available. . . . Most support for vulnerable people is provided through care by family, friends and neighbours. The assessment will need to take account of the support from carers that is available or can be arranged, and *social services support will often be a matter of supplementing the carer's likely future ability to care* . . .
>
> (Department of Health undated: 5–8; my emphasis)

Such references to 'the public expense' hint that although the managerial reforms of the early 1990s onwards were cast rhetorically in terms of citizens' rights (White and Harris 1999), their introduction was inextricably interlinked with constraints on public expenditure and the move to a quasi-market (Harris 1999), prompting some commentators to conclude that the community care reforms were driven by financial priorities (Mooney 1997; Dominelli 1998; Twigg 1998):

> [The reforms] were not primarily driven by a desire to improve the relations between the various statutory authorities, or to improve services for elderly people, or to help those emerging from mental hospital. They were driven by the need to stop the haemorrhage

in the social security budget and to do so in a way that would mini-
mise political outcry and not give additional resources to the local
authorities themselves. Most of the rest of the policy was, as the
Americans would say, for the birds.

(Lewis and Glennerster 1996: 8)

These financial considerations had their origins in concerns about the
costs of welfare provision that had turned the spotlight on an ageing
population. Something approaching a 'moral panic' had been engen-
dered by a discourse that represented older people as a drain on the
public purse, with phrases like 'pension time-bomb', 'rising tide' and
'demographic burden' commonly being used to describe the demographic trends: 'A whole research industry has been generating panic
reports on how much it is going to cost the young to support the old'
(Thompson 1993: 94). Running parallel with this concern about the
costs of population ageing, Conservative governments, as we have
seen, had promoted the virtues of self-responsibility and self-reliance,
virtues which implied that only people who could take care of themselves could be proud of themselves. The preoccupation with dependence in the community care reforms was positioned in a discourse in
which being dependent on others was seen as having very negative cultural connotations. Dependent people were seen as not self-supporting
and as a burden on the state or on other individuals. The high value
placed on independence was graphically expounded in the Conservative government's White Paper on social services (published shortly
before the 1997 General Election) which said that 'responsible people
should meet their own care needs' (quoted in *Professional Social
Work*, July 1997: 5), with the implication that people who needed
social services were likely to have been irresponsible or to have had
irresponsible kin.

Against that backdrop, reinforcing the informal caring role was
financially more attractive in the government's plans for the social
work business than was care based on state-provided domiciliary
services. The centrality of 'the family' as the primary unit of care for
older people was reinforced, though, as feminist commentators have
pointed out, 'family care' is frequently used as a euphemism for 'care
by women' (see, for example, Graham 1983; Dalley 1988; Williams
1989). At the time of the establishing of the social work business,
care provided by women from within households already constituted
the largest proportion of the welfare mix (Graham 1991; Lewis 1997),
not surprisingly given the assumption that women would be available

to provide care, implicit from the outset in the male bread-winner model of the pre-business era welfare state. In such a constrained context, the significance of the Conservatives' reforms for informal caring was that its positioning shifted from being an assumed to an overt resource (Graham 1991; Lewis 1997): 'The contribution of carers *should be formally recognised* in new procedures for care management and assessment' (Social Services Inspectorate 1991a: 14; 1991b: 16; emphasis added). The shift was signalled clearly from the beginning of the Conservatives' reform process in the Griffiths Report (1988: para. 3.2):

> Publicly provided services constitute only a small part of the total care provided to people in need. Families, friends, neighbours and other local people provide the majority of care in response to needs which they are uniquely well placed to identify and respond to. This will continue to be the primary means by which people are enabled to live normal lives in community settings. The proposals take as their starting point that this is as it should be and that the first task of publicly provided services is to support and where possible strengthen these networks of carers.

The assumptions that informal caring – as an expected standard of behaviour predicated on individual willingness and a sense of responsibility – would be the first port of call, and that it required active management by social workers, became axiomatic from that point onwards. The potential success of the community care reforms rested on the preparedness of informal carers to continue to undertake primary caring responsibility (Barnes 1997: 105). The White Paper *Caring for People* (Cm. 849 1989) which followed the Griffiths Report (1988) reinforced the message. It was centred around the themes of 'home', 'choice' and 'independence', with the worthy nature of the 'choice' to care being emphasised (Bauld *et al.* 2000: 12):

> The government acknowledges that the great bulk of community care is provided by friends, family and neighbours. The majority of carers take on these responsibilities willingly. The decision to take on a caring role is never an easy one. However, many people make that choice and it is right that they should be able to play their part in looking after those close to them.
>
> (Cm. 849 1989: para. 1.9)

Closely following the worthiness of the choice to care was the economic expediency associated with quasi-capitalist business rationality: 'Helping carers to maintain their valuable contribution to the spectrum of care is both right and a sound investment' (Cm. 849 1989: para. 2.3). This is one of the few references to the economic benefits of placing even greater reliance on informal care, benefits which some commentators see as situated at the heart of the changes which have taken place:

> For all the rhetoric of choice, flexibility and enhanced efficiency, the single most important political consideration surrounding the welfare state over the last twenty years has been its cost. The major reforms of the late 1980s sought efficiency gains, so as to extract a greater welfare *output* from a welfare *input* which could not rise in line with either social expectations or demographically driven need. It is a process in which women, with their greater reliance on public services and their much greater role in delivering unpaid welfare services within the family, have been disproportionately disadvantaged.
>
> (Pierson 1994: 112; emphasis original)

The Conservatives' assumptions about informal caring were at odds with research findings that were contemporaneous with their reforms. Finch, who undertook a review of research on kinship caring obligations during this period, found that willingness to care did not follow a straightforward trajectory. She found that kinship was highly variable and located in specific social and biographical contexts, rather than being derived from a set of abstract moral values (Finch 1989). Informal carers were negotiated into the caring role through family processes arising from these contexts (Finch and Mason 1993). These findings have been confirmed in more recent work (Clark, Dyer and Horwood 1998; Tulle-Winton 1999). Other studies have found that public services are often seen as preferable to informal care (Wilson 1993; Minichiello *et al*. 2000). Requiring a family member to provide intimate care can undermine the relationship that already exists (Barnes and Prior 2000: 90–1). Nevertheless, carers were cemented into the social work business supply chain through Social Services Departments' public statements on eligibility criteria for the provision of services, with service allocation based on the inability of carers to cope (Brown and Smith 1993: 186). What were previously intimately negotiated[1] voluntaristic[2] caring arrangements were transformed into actively identified, carefully managed and negotiated, formal agreements about the scope and nature of the care which was to be traded in return for social services assistance. In the process, normative assumptions about the role of families were explicitly exposed and linked to formalising the care they provided (Barnes and Prior 2000: 91). In this context, the community care practice curriculum for social work education, produced by the Central Council for Education and Training in Social Work, included assessment of carers' 'willingness to contribute to care packages' as an element of competence required by social work students (CCETSW 1991b: 17). This concern with formalising the contribution of carers to the supply chain has not always been received with enthusiasm by those on the Right:

> Neglect of family responsibilities should be stigmatised and heroic service should be honoured; but self-care by families should be regarded as normal. . . . If community care is to comprise an alternative, its voluntary nature must be left uncorrupted by ideological and financial incorporation into state machinery.
>
> (Marsland 1996: 187)

Nevertheless, as the Conservatives' reforms bedded down, incorporation into the state machinery was in evidence. As carers were rapidly established as part of the social work business supply chain, their services were quantified in assessments and care plans, and commodified as supplier components in packages of care. Exploiting hostility towards bureaucratised professional-dominated care and drawing on dissatisfaction with state-provided services, the new arrangements emphasised the message that people were to be made more responsible for their own care arrangements and thus were to be reconstituted as 'empowered' participants in caring (Leonard 1997: 58–9). While this rhetoric stressed independence from the state's power to control people's lives through Social Services Departments, in reality the arrangements represented an extension and dispersal of state managerial power through the social work business into detailed and intimate

---

1 In the pre-business era, a carer's contribution might have been taken into account as it became more public through contact with a social services department, but the extent to which this happened was determined by the values and vagaries of individual social workers. Although this had its own problems of inconsistency, the point being made here is that the existence of this inconsistency indicates that quantifying carers' contributions as an overt resource was not something with which the state was centrally concerned at that time.
2 Voluntaristic to varying degrees and with the assumption that women would be the main 'volunteers'.

aspects of daily life within households. The drive to end the 'culture of dependence' was essentially an attempt to manage the displacement of dependence on state services with state-monitored dependence on the supply of informal care: 'For the great majority of carers the community care changes so far seem to have meant "business as usual" with carers trying to cope with little help from the public agencies apart from some promises of a better tomorrow' (Warner 1994: 38). This comment about 'business as usual' reminds us again that informal carers have always been the most significant resource in the provision of care, primarily through the contributions of women in their homes, on which the state has relied heavily:

> Feminist analysis has helped to puncture the myth that in the modern welfare state, the state has taken over the welfare functions of the family. It reveals the myriad ways in which the family continues to operate as a site not just of welfare consumption but also of production. Families still represent the main source of care of children and of older people. Much of this care is provided by women.
>
> (Lister 2000: 24)

The formalisation of the state's use of informal care had knock-on consequences in introducing the notion that if informal carers were to be maintained as suppliers to the social work business they needed the business's support. The White Paper *Caring for People*, provided the first official intimation that local authorities should make 'practical support for carers' a high priority (Cm. 849 1989: para. 1.11). As the community care system rendered explicit the demands made on carers by the social work business, and increased those demands, carers came to realise how crucial they were to its success. Support groups and pressure groups lobbied for recognition of their role (Twigg and Atkin 1994; Nocon and Qureshi 1996). The evidence to support this attempt to increase public recognition and change the perceived status of carers was found in a vast amount of detailed information on the numbers of people involved in caring, in what kinds of tasks, for how many hours each week, how much money this saved the state, and so on. According to a survey by Age Concern, one woman in five was caring for her children and her parents (reported in *Community Care*, 15–21 October 1998: 3). One in four women aged between 45 and 64 and one in six men were providing care,[3] although women still spent more time in caring and continued to provide the more intensive forms of care (Lewis 1997: 172). Carers' groups invested considerable energy and resources in analysing this kind of information about the services provided by carers, without which carers would have been unlikely to have secured increased recognition (Parker 1999).

The tangible expression of that recognition came in the Carers (Recognition and Services) Act (1995), implemented in July 1996, not long before the Conservative government left power, which enables carers to request that local authorities make a separate assessment of their 'ability to provide and continue to provide care' (Carers [Recognition and Services] Act [1995]: Section 1).[4] In other words, official recognition for carers emerged in the form of a right to request an assessment of their continuing capacity to function as part of the supply chain. Ten months after the implementation of the Act, New Labour came to power.

Caring and New Labour

The Conservative governments' project to formalise the contribution of care provided by kin, as a component in 'packages' of supply chain services managed by the social work business, was inherited

3 The increasing influence of the carers' lobby raises a question about whether the increasing numbers of men as carers might account, at least in part, for carers' voices being heard more readily. The downturn in male employment and the upturn in the numbers of male carers (especially in the area of spousal care) have coincided with the new thinking about caring as an expression of citizenship obligation. Such thinking has begun to reflect the concerns that feminists have been raising for decades – that unpaid care work in the household is, in the context of citizenship, as important as labour market participation.

4 This Act to date may be more significant as a symbolic valuing of carers. It is the responsibility of carers to request an assessment (Clements and Ruan 1997) and Social Services Departments have been criticised for not informing carers of their right to do so (Heron 1998). In a telephone survey of 80 carers in one local authority, 69 carers said they had not been offered a separate assessment, 8 said they had and 3 remembered talking to a social worker but were not sure whether this counted as an assessment (Collins 1999). Assumptions about the availability of carers and inadequate services for them have continued (Twigg 1998; Parker 1999), with the implication that the sole purpose of services is to maintain carers in their role (Nolan and Caldock 1996), leading the Royal Commission on Long Term Care (1999: para. 8.24) to suggest that services should be provided on the basis of the needs of the service user, rather than assumptions about what carers are providing or could provide. This was seen as a means of ensuring that the presence of carers does not lead to the provision of inadequate services. This suggestion strikes at the heart of the current political positioning of caring.

approvingly by New Labour, consolidated as an expression of citizenship obligation and accorded a more specific status. It resonated with the general New Labour sentiment that: 'For too long, the demand for rights from the state was separated from the duties of citizenship and the imperative for mutual responsibility on the part of individual' (Blair 1998: 3–4). This accorded with Etzioni's approach to communitarianism, which identifies the line of responsibility for welfare as running from the individual to the family to the local community. Etzioni (1994) argued that only when that line of responsibility has been exhausted should 'society at large' take responsibility, targeting public welfare on the minority who cannot help themselves and engaging them in responsible involvement in seeking solutions to their difficulties. With the advent of New Labour, this communitarian approach is increasingly evident in the expectation that ordinary citizens, through the choices and actions which make up their everyday private lives, will themselves increasingly be the primary resources for delivering the government's objectives (Barnes and Prior 2000: 6).

For New Labour, then, as much as it had been for the Conservatives, it remained economically expedient and politically imperative to depict informal carers as 'active citizens' who make a vital and valued contribution to the economic and moral good of the country. Frank Field identified the control of welfare expenditure as a central aspect of New Labour's plans for reform (cited in Mooney 1997).[5] He made clear that this goal could be achieved only if 'the family' plugged the gaps created by constrained public spending. Following Field's announcement, the moral responsibility of families to care for dependent relatives was stressed by the New Labour government in much the same way as it had been by the Conservatives: 'What carers do should be properly recognised. Carers should be able to take pride in what they do. And in turn, we should take pride in carers. I am determined to see that they do – and that we all do' (Prime Minister, in HM Government 1999: 4).

Some commentators saw the Conservatives' approach as part of a re-moralising project aimed at reinforcing the hegemony of the heterosexual nuclear family (see, for example, Carabine 1996; Pascall, 1997). In Labour's manifesto, in the lead-up to the party's 1997 victory, this emphasis continued; a pledge to strengthen family life was illustrated with a photograph of a bride in a traditional white wedding dress

5 With which Field was later initially entrusted, in a New Labour government that had committed itself to not exceeding the previous Conservative government's expenditure plans.

which signalled the kind of household that was seen as 'the cornerstone of a decent society' (Labour Party 1997: 27). Once in office, it became clear that the New Labour government intended to deliver on its manifesto's vision of the family which, the Prime Minister reiterated, was the 'foundation of society' (address to 1997 Labour Party Conference, quoted in Lloyd 1997: 12). An Inter-Ministerial Committee on the Family was set up, chaired by the then Home Secretary Jack Straw, and the rhetoric extolling the family and re-privileging marriage was stepped up (Lloyd 1997). In New Labour's portrayal of the family, a weak liberal equal opportunities agenda was eclipsed by a moralising Christian-Socialist communitarianism, in which 'marriage and the traditional family are a panacea for the virus of dependency' and 'families [are seen] as islands of altruism within a sea of competitive individualism' (Bruegel 1998: 11). While much of the rhetoric was concerned with addressing the perceived failures and the need for the re-moralisation of heterosexual families with children,

> [a]nother argument for marriage is becoming increasingly impor-
> tant . . . continued cohabitation provides both partners with care
> in old age. As people live longer, so the state costs of care rise;
> these are reduced when the family continues to function. The
> state's economic interest in marriage is thus not just with depen-
> dent children; it is also with dependent adults.
>
> (Lloyd 1997: 12–13)

In addition to this general concern to bolster family sources of care, New Labour's introduction of 'Best Value'[6] has provided an ethos in which carers are seen – even more readily than previously – as the 'stakeholders' providing the greatest value for money. 'Stakeholding' is one element in New Labour's discourse. Another, and key, element for carers is 'social exclusion', given tangible expression in the establishing of the Social Exclusion Unit. As the focus of the Labour Party shifted from structural inequality to a preoccupation with individual character as shaped by personal circumstance, New Labour's mission became reduction in individuals' social exclusion (Lund 1999: 454). The main strategy adopted in pursuit of that mission was

---

6 'Best Value' (Department of the Environment Transport and the Regions 1998) imposes a duty on social services departments (and other areas) to deliver services to clear standards of quality and cost, efficiently, economically and effectively (Department of Health 1999: para. 7.14). See pp. 80–83, this volume.

inclusion through integration into the labour market (Levitas 1996; Driver and Martell 1997). The strategy of devaluing unpaid work (Levitas 1996: 5) allowed an exception for only one group – carers for adult kin. Their social inclusion was to be achieved by the enhanced recognition and representation of caring as a valued activity, an expression of citizenship obligation, which accords carers honourable status. The state-as-community, identified as coterminous with the public interest, is presented as responding to carers as a community-in-adversity. How has New Labour's strategy of social inclusion for carers found political expression?

The main emphasis from New Labour has been on the strengthening of carers' rights and status, cognisant of the economic advantages to be gained from doing so. The White Paper *Modernising Social Services* promised carers enhanced status in the planning and delivery of services (Department of Health 1998b: para. 7.6). In a speech given at a carers' conference, the then Junior Health Minister Paul Boateng linked this enhanced status to financial considerations: 'Carers could save the government even more money if they were properly listened to. . . . We have to find a way of giving carers status. Just as someone is registered disabled, should not a carer have something that says "I'm a carer"?' (reported in *Community Care*, 15–21 October 1998). These concerns culminated in the production of the National Carers' Strategy *Caring About Carers* (HM Government 1999), to which the Prime Minister attached his personal support. Its development was announced during the Carers' National Association's 'National Carers' Week' in June 1998. When it was published, on 8 February 1999, the main evening news on BBC television highlighted government proposals for 'carers to have breaks from their *duties*', a statement which emphasises the distance travelled in formalising carers' contributions to the business supply chain on behalf of the state. This emphasis on performance of duties is at odds with research evidence on informal care relationships which suggests that if such relationships are based on equality and mutual support, what would normally be seen as 'cared-for' people are more independent and more positive about themselves (Wenger 1984; Langan *et al.* 1996). Nevertheless, the carers' strategy suggested measures which promoted further formalisation of the duties associated with carers' supplier status:

- The NHS must help carers to learn skills which will prevent injuries.
- Filling gaps in carers' support groups must be given priority in joint investment plans.

- Health and local authorities acting jointly will bring together carers' organisations in order to assess the needs of carers and to consider how local support services should be provided, for example, through making application for National Lottery funding.
- The Carers' National Association, the Princess Royal Trust for Carers and Crossroads will develop a quality assurance scheme for local carers' support services (HM Government 1999).

The promotion of the national carers' strategy was followed by the Carers and Disabled Children Act (2000, most provisions implemented from April 2001) – the culmination to date of carers' struggles for recognition as suppliers to the social work business and government responses to them. The Act allows both for the possibility of an assessment and for the provision of services, including services to the cared-for person, in order to support carers, if they are providing a substantial amount of care on a regular basis to a person (over 18) for whom the local authority would have the power to provide services.

The Act builds on the carers' strategy, confirming that caring has been officially articulated as a service of choice for the user and as a relationship of choice for the carer:

- Caring may affect *every one* of us
- We may all *need care*, or need to provide care
- Caring forms a vital part of the *fabric and character* of Britain
                          (HM Government 1999: 5; emphasis original)

The government's strategy – 'Carers should not be pitied, but respected and admired' (HM Government 1999: 81) – may be attractive to a group of people who, as we have seen, have been marginalised historically from citizenship. Simultaneously, however, carers may feel even more obliged to supply caring to the social work business. The other side of the recognition coin is that coercing carers into 'compulsory altruism' (Jordan 1989) has potential dangers and disadvantages for both carer and cared-for.

At a time when caring poses acute social policy challenges for the future (Lewis 1997: 171) a concept of citizenship which confers rights on resources has become increasingly eroded by Conservative and New Labour governments. Worthy citizens are those who look to their own resources and slot into their position in the supply chain. In the case of carers, the reward for unpaid caring is a higher public profile, acknowledging the expression of citizenship obligation in which carers are seen to be engaged. An overriding emphasis on the value of caring-as-citizenship-obligation has led to a situation in which carers' voices are privileged over the voices of cared-for people (in relation to assessments, for example; see Rummery *et al.* 1999), with the former portrayed as virtuous suppliers and the latter seen as customers who drain off resources:

> As state responsibility is reconstituted as enabling family, friends and neighbours to take liabilities on, so a new morality is arguably emerging within community care. Positioned as the 'deserving' is an active citizenry of carers who must be supported in discharging their duties towards a 'second class' citizenry of older, sick and disabled people.
>
> (Ellis 1995: 2)

As a consequence of social work business costs being displaced on to households, people's private lives have become sites for the delivery of public policy (Barnes and Prior 2000: 9 and 31), with 'caring' now encompassing an active and formalised relationship with the state, managed by the social work business. Not only does this emphasise a 'burden' model of old age: it underscores a model of citizenship based solely on active participation, 'usefulness' and self-reliance, from which many recipients of social services will feel excluded. This is not an argument against recognition and support for carers by the social work business. Rather it is to suggest that the strengthening of carers' rights, in an approach to caring which enhances the citizenship status of those providing it, should not neglect the citizenship of those receiving care. Citizenship discourses need to take into account the interdependence of both the giver and the receiver of care (Twigg 1992) as 'active human subjects' (Leonard 1997: 59). For example, the allegation has been made that care *giving* has become a central feminist issue but care *receiving* has not (Begum 1992). While some feminist writers (for example, Finch and Dalley 1984; Dalley 1988) have asserted that 'collective' (i.e. institutional) forms of care for older and disabled people are the only way to prevent the exploitation of women as carers, the disability movement has challenged this construction of disabled people as passive victims and demanded that the principle 'the personal is political' is applied equally to both carer and cared-for (Morris 1993). An example of this lacuna is provided by the debate leading up to the introduction of the Carers (Recognition and Assessment) Act (1995). The views of recipients of care were not sought, whilst the views of carers were canvassed, perhaps suggesting that carers are perceived as a resource and an asset in the supply chain, while those who need care are not valued as customers (see Ch. 7). In addition, the introduction of policies for carers has not seen an equivalent surge of measures aimed at empowering the cared-for, providing an indication of the relative power of the carers' lobby.

It might be argued that New Labour initiatives were put in place to correct this imbalance. The 'Better Government for Older People' programme and the Inter-Ministerial Group on Older People might be seen as examples of such initiatives. However, their predominant emphasis was on 'active ageing' and on the right of older people to lead 'active, independent lives' (*Community Care*, 19 November 1998b: 2). Age Concern (England), for example, was involved in a campaign against ageism in the workplace, with government guidance being issued; but, again, the emphasis is on older people's ability to produce and perform. While these strategies are important as a way of countering a view of older people as a passive burden, they inadvertently reinforce a concept of citizenship that defines people's status according to their contribution to the economy, as well as reinforcing sharp distinctions between the young–old and the old–old and between the grey pound and the grey drain.

Finally, there are dangers for both carer and cared-for in the idealisation of the family as the most appropriate locus of care. Concerns about the breakdown of the supply chain in the form of family violence, potential or actual, have been compartmentalised in 'vulnerable adults' policies by governments determined to contain the growth of state welfare and to ensure that caring for others should be seen as a function of the family and an expression of citizenship obligation. For example, the right of families to privacy was a central plank in the Conservative government's 1997 election manifesto. It promised 'anti-political correctness' guidance to ensure that social workers did not 'unnecessarily interfere' in the lives of families (*Community Care*, 13–20 March 1997: 3). Protecting carers from 'interference' by social workers continues to be a financially attractive option, particularly in a situation where carers are expensive to replace. There are dangers for carers, too: attempts to boost the notion of 'family care' may create difficulties for carers in just the same way that the concept of 'wonderful children' (Ong 1985) places immense pressure on women to conform to the idealised norm of a happy, contented mother. Valorising carers and caring may make some carers reluctant to ask for help, for fear of seeming a failure, and may squeeze the last remnants of the right not to care (Land and Rose 1985) out of existence.

New Labour's approach to informal carers is consistent with the broad sweep of its policy in which people's private lives have become sites for the delivery of public policy. Barnes and Prior suggest that the general policy emphasis is on reinforcing agency by enjoining people to take action to improve their lives, in what may be highly disadvantageous circumstances, and by connecting public services more closely to the relationships and networks of support that people already have. In other words, services are seen as supporting, strengthening and facilitating existing strategies to deal with problems, which have been developed between individuals and those who care for them. The role of New Labour's policy is to provide guidance and to shape intentions. Policy objectives are delivered and demand is managed by exhorting people to become their own welfare providers, acting in accordance with the responsibilities the state says that they bear and which are worked out through engagement with professionals, who mediate active and formalised relationships between citizens and the state (Barnes and Prior 2000: 25–31).

Conclusion

This chapter has reviewed developments in the social work business's supply chain in so far as the voluntary sector and informal carers are concerned. Voluntary organisations have been enveloped in a new term, the 'independent sector', and have had to compete for funding against other voluntary organisations and against the commercial sector. Contractual trading relationships have subjected the sector to a quasi-capitalist rationality and have eroded aspects of its distinctiveness from the commercial sector. The introduction of contracts and trading relationships placed pressure on the quality and variety of services supplied by the voluntary sector. As the tendency towards formalisation and standardisation took hold, a risk-averse and price-focused economic culture became institutionalised (Mackintosh 2000: 302–4).

Following the Conservative governments' reforms, caring was positioned overtly as the core resource in packages of care. It was seen as requiring quantification and management by social workers. Caring arrangements in households became actively identified, publicly negotiated, carefully organised and subject to formal agreements about the scope and nature of the care provided, often with the goal of averting service provision. New Labour articulated and consolidated this shift to caring as an expression of citizenship obligation, refining its ideological basis and securing its position in the social work business supply chain. The promotion of a National Carers' Strategy represents the culmination to date of carers' incorporation into the social work business, with caring officially articulated as the service of choice for the user and as the relationship of choice for the carer.

9 Seeing through the social work business

Looking back

Consideration of the development of the social work business began with the pre-business era (Ch. 2), the era of the social democratic welfare state. In that era, public sector services like social work were regarded as driven by a dynamic different from that of the private sector. The distinctiveness involved in organising services such as social work was considered to derive from their connection with citizenship: 'Values of equity and justice have to play a part in management in a way which would be irrelevant to most businesses' (Flynn 1993: xiii).

The establishment of the social work business by Conservative governments (Chs 3 and 4) and its modernisation by New Labour (Ch. 5) was an aspect of the undermining of much of the distinctive dynamic underpinning public services, as their former distinctiveness was collapsed into a quasi-business discourse, with an economic culture institutionalised in increasingly taken-for-granted meanings and behaviour (Du Gay 2000; Mackintosh 2000). This economic culture has been built around a quasi-capitalist rationality, the embrace of the methods and culture of the capitalist sector, founded on the principles of efficiency, calculability, predictability and control by non-human technology (Ritzer 2000: 9–11). The nature of the large-scale shift that has taken place is captured by Fine and Leopold (1993: 300–1):

> Services made available through public sector systems of provision . . . signalled a commitment to collective rather than individual interests; social and political objectives took precedence over narrowly economic concerns. . . . State expenditure used to finance public systems of provision was subject to its own terms of reference and its own performance criteria, independently

applied and evaluated. . . . Free market economics . . . seeks to sweep aside all the political and social objectives that distinguish public from private provision in order to subject all economic activity across the board to the iron-clad rules of the market. Stripped of it special features, public provision is treated simply as an alternative to private sector provision . . . the degradation of public services has been achieved as much by the privatisation of language as by the actual privatisation of goods and services. Atomised individuals are now cast as 'consumers'. . . . Public services are reduced to commodities like beer and soap. . . . In other words, the concept of consumption has been crudely expanded to accommodate the expansion in commitment to market economics. . . . This distorts the nature of the relationship between individuals and a variety of social services and activities they are now thought to 'consume'. Moreover, at the macroeconomic level, if considerations of consumption and investment alone govern decision-making across the economy as a whole, then the choice between one sector and another is no longer a choice between ideologies but simply one based on cost–benefit calculations prescribed by market economics.

The term 'the social work business' has been used throughout the book to suggest a specific coherent trend, of the kind described by Fine and Leopold (1993), a trend underpinning a wide-ranging set of developments in social work. Those developments resulted in major changes to social work's boundaries, working methods and relationships, operating procedures, accountability and culture; changes driven by the central dynamic of the quasi-business discourse. The quasi-business discourse provides a hegemonic 'common-sense' view of the world. It lets social work have access to knowledge and expertise about how the social and economic world works and how best to do things. Social work has been aligned with this discourse through managerialism (Chs 4 and 5), 'made up of a blend of notions that inform, and values that legitimate its practical prescriptions' (Muetzelfeldt 1994: 139). Parallel developments occurred in social work education (Ch. 6), as its concerns were reformulated by the Conservatives and New Labour to reflect the need to prepare students for working in the social work business: making them ready for involvement in quasi-markets as distributional mechanisms and for their role in the classification of individuals into packages of care.

Businesses have customers; the social work business re-imagined users of its services as its customer base, with a narrow focus on a series of individual service transactions (Ch. 7). The social work business also sorted out its supply chain, through greater use of the private sector, reshaping the contribution of the voluntary sector and formalising the contribution of informal carers (Ch. 8). Lewis summarises the impact of developments on customers and carers:

> The late nineteenth century British government aimed to set up a framework of rules within which society would more or less run itself. In some ways the late twentieth century state looks somewhat similar, as governments attempt to retreat from taking the responsibility for social provision. There are continuities especially in the concern to get the family to provide welfare in the form of both money/maintenance and care. But the conditions under which the contribution is being elicited are quite different. Governments in the 1990s were exerting a far more centralised control than their late nineteenth century counterparts, while at the same time, denying responsibility for provision. The introduction of quasi-markets in health, community care services, education and housing was intended to make services more responsive to the needs of 'consumers' rather than 'citizens'. But market mechanisms, while holding out the promise of a better deal for people as consumers, offer nothing by way of participation to the citizen.
>
> (Lewis, J. 2000: 48)

Looking beneath the surface

Lewis's gloomy prognosis chimes in with the small selection of reminiscences about the social work business that I included in Chapter 1. They serve as a reminder that the trends and developments impacting upon and through the social work business have a personal dimension. The changes that have taken place are not confined to 'technical' managerial changes in organisational structures and processes. They have deeply personal implications for social workers; professional practice is embodied in the person of the professional, the professional–service user relationship and the processual nature of the work (Clarke and Newman 1997: 6–7). The policies and procedures I have considered in earlier chapters re-form social workers and reformulate what it means for them to do social work. Social workers are expected to be more concerned with calculation – using 'what works' in the most efficient way. They are seen as 'human resources' to be managed in the pursuit of government's policy agendas. They are constrained to talk about themselves and think about themselves, their purposes, motivations and relationships, in new ways that reflect and testify to their affiliation to the corporate culture of the social work business. They are often uncertain about whether they are doing enough and whether they are doing the right things. The social work business has this internal emotional dimension. It is embedded in social workers' day-to-day relationships with service users, with managers and with each other. It is not that the social work business gets in the way of 'real' social work: the social work business has changed what 'social work' is and what social workers do, as the book has sought to demonstrate. As a consequence, the themes and issues raised here have implications for what social workers think, feel and are.

Increasingly, the experience of talking to social workers resonates with echoes of the semi-submerged sense of demoralisation that characterised services under state socialism in Central and Eastern Europe. Some demoralisation is almost inevitable when social workers feel they are unable to challenge the official dogma in contexts where no alternative perspective is tolerated. The typical response to the demoralisation that existed under state socialism is also evident in British social work. Overt compliance and private resistance or withdrawal (Jones 2000) appear to be rife among social workers, while many managers, like their earlier counterparts in state socialist systems, quickly adjust their vocabulary to conform to the latest shift in emphasis or tone within the quasi-business discourse. In contrast to the discourse's grey uniformity, Stewart (1992: 33) argues that debate in the public sector is by its nature unbounded. No judgement is final, nor is any performance ultimately successful – other voices can always be a source of challenge to judgements made. In relation to social work, Bauman (2000: 10) cautions:

> Clarity and unambiguity may be the ideal of the world in which 'procedural execution' is the rule. For the ethical world, however, ambivalence and uncertainty are the daily bread and cannot be stamped out without destroying the moral substance of responsibility, the foundation on which the world rests.

Looking forward

Ambivalence and uncertainty suggest the possibility of resistance. The social work business may be represented as a triumphant hegemonic discourse, but it cannot achieve complete closure on its way of seeing the world:

Because of the non-capitalist nature of some public sector organisations, capitalist solutions must always be a half measure, an
approximate fit, contested and competing with a service ideology
and wider political practices that go beyond the criteria of
profitability. . . . When examining work within the public sector
it is important to incorporate an awareness of its distinctive
characteristics.

(Smith *et al.* 1991: 3)

One of the distinctive characteristics is the search for bonds of mutu-
ality and shared identities, through which people and their interests
are formed and which go beyond instrumental transactions between
atomised individuals. This search may have been dampened, but it
has not been extinguished (Muetzelfeldt 1994: 140). There are other
discourses struggling for expression from users of social work's
services: forms of participative citizenship based on shared identities
and experiences of social divisions, grounded in concerns affecting
people's personal lives, but related to broader collective experiences
of inequality and exclusion (Prior *et al.* 1995; Harris 2001). Social
work is one of the sites where such struggles take place over the connections between the state and its citizens and the distribution of rights and
responsibilities in social welfare. It is a site on which a dynamic interplay takes place, involving: domination and resistance; establishing the
boundaries of what is 'normal' and seeking to dislodge those boundaries; applying limited criteria of access to resources and struggles to
change those criteria (Lewis, G. 2000: 12–15). In exploring any aspect
of social work practice or management, two questions can be posed:
who has the power to define the terms in which the issues or problems
are understood? Who stands to gain or lose from particular sets of
social work relations and practices? One of the arguments of the
book is that social workers have lost out as a result of the relations
and practices introduced in the social work business: social workers

have become more specialised around assessment of resources and
risks, the investigation of abuse and rule-breaking, and the setting
up and enforcement of contracts. . . . It is developing into an arm's
length, office bound, report-writing official kind of practice which
leaves face to face work to others.

(Jordan and Jordan 2000: 37)

In this context, it is easy to see why so often it feels like social work has
lost its critical edge. However, social workers show signs of not having

succumbed to complete compliance with the quasi-business discourse. As the social work business has been consolidated, it has represented a different framework for viewing the world, one that is at odds with the perspectives of many of the people working in it. This has resulted in problems with the 'fit' between the values and ideals held by many of the people who enter social work and the quasi-capitalist rationality of the organisations within which they work. Some social workers are holding on to values that are not dominated by the quasi-business discourse and creating at least small spaces in which practice can be developed (White and Harris 2001). They are learning to live creatively with, and at times move beyond the constraints of, the social work business, rather than being subordinated by it. That is possible because of the existence of tensions within the social work business which amount to

> a complex and contradictory picture of welfare whose notions of consumer-sovereignty, diversity and choice represent different and competing interests, and where notions of efficiency and equity, managerialism and professionalism, corporatism and localism, needs and budgets sit very uncomfortably with each other.
>
> (Williams 1994: 67)

Within this uncomfortable location, social work, whether wittingly or unwittingly, is bound up with conceptions of citizenship, as it engages day-to-day in mediating between the state and the service user. Seeking a politically dynamic formulation of citizenship (O'Brien and Penna 1998: 200) involves recognising that it has to be struggled for as a *practice*. It will be striven for in different services, settings and circumstances by service users and social workers trying things out, modifying, experimenting. Despite the existence of these – albeit often small – opportunities for developing tendencies contradictory to a quasi-capitalist rationality, there will surely be a continuing impetus behind the social work business's demand for contained problem categories and technical task outputs, as the political, economic and social issues raised by social work continue to be transformed into quasi-business managerial formulations. Against that demand for rendering service users manageable, social workers will no doubt seek ways of emphasising the variability and unpredictability of the social situations in which service users are located, highlighting the individual and the collective outcomes that arise from the circumstances of their lives. That, it could be argued, is social work's business.

Bibliography

Abercrombie, N. (1991) 'The privilege of the producer', in R. Keat and N. Abercrombie (eds) *Enterprise Culture*, London: Routledge.

Adams, R. (1998) 'Social work processes', in R. Adams, L. Dominelli and M. Payne (eds) *Social Work. Themes, Issues and Critical Debates*, Basingstoke: Macmillan.

Alaszewski, A. and Manthorpe, J. (1990) 'Literature review: the New Right and the professions', *British Journal of Social Work*, 20, 237–51.

Alcock, P. (1989) 'Why citizenship and welfare rights offer new hope for new welfare in Britain', *Critical Social Policy*, 9, 32–43.

Aldridge, M. (1996) 'Dragged to market: being a profession in the postmodern world', *British Journal of Social Work*, 26, 177–94.

Alexander, A. (1982) *The Politics of Local Government in the United Kingdom*, London: Longman.

Alford, J. and O'Neill, D. (eds) (1994) *The Contract State: Public Management and the Kennett Government*, Melbourne: Deakin University Press.

Anleu, S. L. (1992) 'The professionalisation of social work? A case study of three organisational settings.' *Sociology*, 26, 1, 23–43.

Appleyard, B. (1993) 'Why paint so black a picture?' *Independent*, 4 August.

Association of Directors of Social Services (1985) *Competence for Caring: The ADSS Approach*, London: ADSS.

Audit Commission (1983) *Performance Review in Local Government: A Handbook for Auditors and Local Authorities*, London: HMSO.

Audit Commission (1986) *Making a Reality of Community Care*, London: HMSO.

Audit Commission (1988) *The Competitive Council*, London: HMSO.

Audit Commission (1992) *The Community Revolution: The Personal Social Services and Community Care*, London: HMSO.

Audit Commission (1995) *Seize the Day! Guidance for Incoming Unitary Authorities*, London: HMSO.

Audit Commission (1999) *Best Value and the Audit Commission in England*, London: Audit Commission.

Bailey, R. and Brake, M. (eds) (1975) *Radical Social Work*, London: Edward Arnold.

Bains Report (1972) *The New Local Authorities. Report of the Study Group on Local Authority Management Structure*, London: HMSO.

Baldock, J. (1994) 'The personal social services: the politics of care', in V. George and S. Miller (eds) *Social Policy Towards 2000*, London: Routledge.

Baldock, J. (1998) 'Old age, consumerism and the social care market,' in E. Brunsden, H. Dean and R. Woods (eds) *Social Policy Review 10*, Canterbury: Social Policy Association.

Baldock, J. and Evers, A. (1991) 'Citizenship and frail elderly people: changing patterns of provision in Europe', in N. Manning (ed.) *Social Policy Review, 1990–91*, Harlow, Longman.

Baldock, J. and Evers, A. (1992) 'Innovations in the care of the elderly: the cutting edge of change for social welfare systems', *Ageing and Society*, 12, 3, 289–312.

Baldock, J. and Ungerson, C. (1994) *Becoming Consumers of Community Care*, York: Joseph Rowntree Foundation.

Baldwin, M. (2000) *Care Management and Community Care: Social Work Discretion and the Construction of Policy*, Aldershot: Ashgate.

Bamford, T. (1989) 'Discretion and managerialism', in S. Shardlow (ed.) *The Values of Change in Social Work*, London: Tavistock–Routledge.

Barclay Report (1982) *Social Workers: Their Roles and Tasks*, London: National Institute for Social Work–Bedford Square Press.

Barnes, M. (1997) *Care, Communities and Citizens*, Harlow, Addison Wesley Longman.

Barnes, M. and Prior, D. (1995) 'Spoilt for choice? How consumerism can disempower service users', *Public Money and Management*, July–September, 53–9.

Barnes, M. and Prior, D. (2000) *Private Lives as Public Policy*, Birmingham: Venture Press.

Barns, I., Dudley, J., Harris, P. and Petersen, A. (1999) 'Introduction: themes, context and perspectives', in A. Petersen, I. Barns, J. Dudley and P. Harris, *Poststructuralism, Citizenship and Social Policy*, London: Routledge.

Bartlett, W., Roberts, J.A. and Le Grand, J. (1998) *A Revolution in Social Policy: Quasi-Market Reforms in the 1990s*, Bristol: Policy Press.

Barwood, A. (2000) *Towards a Common Cause. A Compact for Care*, London: Social Services Inspectorate.

Bauld, L., Chesterman, J., Davies, B., Judge, K. and Mangalore, R. (2000) *Caring for Older People. An Assessment of Community Care in the 1990s*, Aldershot: Ashgate.

Bauman, Z. (1988) *Freedom*, Buckingham: Open University Press.

Bauman, Z. (1992) *Intimations of Postmodernity*, London: Routledge.

Bauman, Z. (2000) 'Am I my brother's keeper?' *European Journal of Social Work*, 3, 1, 5–11.

Beck, U. (1992) *The Risk Society*, London: Sage.

Begum, N. (1992) *Something to Be Proud Of*, London: London Borough of Waltham Forest.

Benington, J. (1976) *Local Government Becomes Big Business*, London: Home Office Community Development Project.

Benton, T. (2000) 'Reflexive modernization', in G. Browning, A. Halcli and F. Webster (eds) *Understanding Contemporary Society: Theories of the Present*, London: Sage.

Best Value Inspectorate (2001) *Another Step Forward*, London: Audit Commission.

Biggs, S. (2000) 'User voice, interprofessionalism and postmodernity', in C. Davies, L. Finlay and A. Bullman (eds) *Changing Practice in Health and Social Care*, London: Sage.

Blackman, T. and Atkinson, A. (1997) 'Needs targeting and resource allocation in community care', *Policy Studies*, 18, 2, 125–38.

Blair, T. (1998) *The Third Way: New Politics for the New Century*, London: Fabian Society.

Bolger, S., Corrigan, P., Docking, J. and Frost, N. (1981) *Towards Socialist Welfare Work. Working in the State*, London: Macmillan.

Bourdieu, P. (1991) *Language and Symbolic Power*, Cambridge: Polity.

Braverman, H. (1974) *Labor and Monopoly Capital: The Degradation of Work in the Twentieth Century*, New York: Monthly Review Press.

Brewer, C. and Lait, J. (1980) *Can Social Work Survive?* London: Temple Smith.

Brewster, R. (1992) 'The new class? Managerialism and social work education and training', *Issues in Social Work Education*, 2, 2, 81–93.

Briggs, A. (1961) 'The welfare state in historical perspective', *European Journal of Sociology*, 2, 2, 221–58.

Brown, H. and Smith, H. (1993) 'Women caring for people: the mismatch between rhetoric and women's reality', *Policy and Politics*, 21, 185–93.

Bruegel, I. (1998) 'Fighting over the family', *Red Pepper*, 11 February.

Burns, D., Hambleton, R. and Hoggett, P. (1994) *The Politics of Decentralisation*, Basingstoke: Macmillan.

Burrows, R. and Loader, B. (eds) (1994) *Towards a Post-Fordist Welfare State?*, London: Routledge.

Butcher, T. (1995) *Delivering Welfare. The Governance of the Social Services in the 1990s*, Buckingham: Open University Press.

Cabinet Office (1998) *Service First: The New Charter Programme*, London: Stationery Office.

Cabinet Office (1999) *Modernising Government*, London: Stationery Office.

Cabinet Office, Department of Environment, Transport and the Regions and Improvement and Development Agency (2000) *Guide to Quality Schemes and Best Value*, London: Cabinet Office.

Campbell, M.L. (1990) 'Information technology and the labor process. A case study in co-operation and control', *Canadian Social Work Review*, 7, 1, 84–98.

Cannan, C. (1994–95) 'Enterprise culture, professional socialisation and social work education in Britain', *Critical Social Policy*, 14, 3, 5–18.

Caporn, C. (2001) 'Need a little help?' *Community Care*, 1 February, 24–25.

Carabine, J. (1996) 'Heterosexuality and social policy', in D. Richardson (ed.) *Theorising Heterosexuality: Telling it Straight*, Buckingham: Open University.

Carchedi, G. (1977) *On the Economic Identification of Social Classes*, London: RKP.

Care and Health (2001–2) *Guide*, December–January, 4–5.

Castles, F.G. and Pierson, C. (1996) 'A new convergence? Recent policy developments in the United Kingdom, Australia and New Zealand', *Policy and Politics*, 24, 233–45.

Causer, G. and Exworthy, M. (1999) 'Professionals as managers across the public sector', in M. Exworthy and S. Halford (eds) *Professionals and the New Managerialism in the Public Sector*, Buckingham: Open University Press.

Central Council for Education and Training in Social Work (1977) *Consultative Document 3: Patterns of Education and Training Leading to the Certificate of Qualification in Social Work. Policy Issues Arising from Consultative Documents 1 and 2*, London: CCETSW.

Central Council for Education and Training in Social Work (1983) *Review of Qualifying Training Policies, Paper 20*, London: CCETSW.

Central Council for Education and Training in Social Work (1986) *Paper 20.6 Three Years and Different Routes. Council's Expectations and Intentions for Social Work Training*, London: CCETSW.

Central Council for Education and Training in Social Work (1987) *Care for Tomorrow*, London: CCETSW.

Central Council for Education and Training in Social Work (1989) *Paper 30 Rules and Requirements for the Diploma in Social Work*, London: CCETSW.

Central Council for Education and Training in Social Work (1990) *Partnerships and Collaboration in Programmes for the Diploma in Social Work. A Guidance Note on Paper 30*, London: CCETSW.

Central Council for Education and Training in Social Work (1991a) *Assessment, Care Management and Inspection in Community Care. Towards a Practice Curriculum*, London: CCETSW.

Central Council for Education and Training in Social Work (1991b) *Revised Paper 30. Rules and Requirements for the Diploma In Social Work*, London: CCETSW.

Central Council for Education and Training in Social Work (1992) *Contracting and Case Management in Community Care. The Challenges for Local Authorities*, London: CCETSW.

Central Council for Education and Training in Social Work (1994a) *Purchasing and Contracting Skills*, London: CCETSW.

Central Council for Education and Training in Social Work (1994b) *Diploma in Social Work. Update One*, London: CCETSW.

Central Council for Education and Training in Social Work (1995a) *Assuring Quality in the Diploma in Social Work 1: Rules and Requirements for the DipSW*, London: CCETSW.

Central Council for Education and Training in Social Work (1995b) *CCETSW News*, No. 2, London: CCETSW.

Cerny, P.G. (1990) *The Changing Architecture of Politics: Structure, Agency and the Future of the State*, London: Sage.

Challis, D. and Davies, B. (1980) 'A new approach to community care for the elderly', *British Journal of Social Work*, 10, 1–18.

Challis, L. (1990) *Organising Public Social Services*, Harlow: Longman.

Clark, H., Dyer, S. and Horwood, J. (1998) *That Bit of Help: The High Value of Low Level Preventative Services for Older People*, Bristol: Policy Press.

Clarke, J. (1979) 'Critical sociology and radical social work: problems of theory and practice', in N. Parry, M. Rustin and C. Satyamurti (eds) *Social Work, Welfare and the State*, London: Edward Arnold.

Clarke, J. (1998) 'Managerialisation and social welfare', in J. Carter (ed.) *Postmodernity and the Fragmentation of Welfare*, London: Routledge.

Clarke, J., Cochrane, A. and McLaughlin, E. (eds) (1994) *Managing Social Policy*, London: Sage.

Clarke, J., Gewirtz, S. and McLaughlin, E. (2000a) 'Reinventing the welfare state', in J. Clarke, S. Gewirtz and E. McLaughlin (eds) *New Managerialism, New Welfare?* London: Sage.

Clarke, J., Gewirtz, S., Highes, G. and Humphrey J. (2000b) 'Guarding the public interest? Auditing public services', in J. Clarke, S. Gewirtz and E. McLaughlin (eds) *New Managerialism, New Welfare?* London: Sage.

Clarke, J. and Langan, M. (1993a) 'Restructuring welfare: the British welfare regime in the 1980s', in A. Cochrane and J. Clarke (eds) *Comparing Welfare States. Britain in International Context*, London: Sage.

Clarke, J. and Langan, M. (1993b) 'The British welfare state: foundation and modernisation', in A. Cochrane and J. Clarke (eds) *Comparing Welfare States. Britain in International Context*, London: Sage.

Clarke, J. and Newman, J. (1993) 'Managing to survive: dilemmas of changing organisational forms in the public sector', in N. Deakin and R. Page (eds) *The Costs of Welfare*, Aldershot: Avebury.

Clarke, J. and Newman, J. (1997) *The Managerial State*, London: Sage.

Clements, L. and Ruan, G. (1997) *Signposts Through the Maze: A Guide to Carers and the Law*, London: Carers National Association.

Cm. 849 (1989) *Caring for People. Community Care in the Next Decade and Beyond*, London: HMSO.

Cmnd. 3703 (1968) *Report of the Committee on Local Authority and Allied Personal Social Services* (Seebohm Report), London: HMSO.

Cochrane, A. (1994) 'Restructuring the local welfare state', in R. Burrows and B. Loader (eds) *Towards a Post-Fordist Welfare State?* London: Routledge.

Cochrane, A. (2000) 'Local government: managerialism and modernization', in J. Clarke, S. Gerwitz and E. McLaughlin (eds) *New Managerialism, New Welfare?* London: Sage.

Cockburn, C. (1977) *The Local State. The Management of Cities and People*, London: Pluto.

Collins, A. (1999) *Survey of Carers' Experiences of Separate Assessment*, Coventry: University of Warwick, Department of Social Policy and Social Work.

Community Care (1997) News pages, 13 March, 3.

Community Care (1998a) News pages, 15–21 October, 3.

Community Care (1998b) News pages, 19 November, 2.

Community Care (2000) News pages, 7 December, 20–1.

Community Care (2001a) News pages, 18 January, 2–3.

Community Care (2001b) News pages, 1 February, 2.

Community Care (2001c) News pages, 1 March 2–3.

Community Care (2001d) Latest news, 18 June, available online: http://www.community-care.co.uk/cc_news/article.asp

Cooper, J. (1991) 'The future of social work: a pragmatic view', in M. Loney, R. Bocock, J. Clarke, A. Cochrane, P. Graham and M. Wilson (eds) *The State or the Market? Politics and Welfare in Contemporary Britain*, London: Sage.

Corrigan, P. (1999) *Shakespeare on Management*, London: Kogan Page.

Corrigan, P. and Leonard, P. (1978) *Social Work Practice Under Capitalism: A Marxist Approach*, London: Macmillan.

Cowen, H. (1999) *Community Care, Ideology and Social Policy*, Hemel Hempstead, Prentice-Hall.

Crewe, I. (1982) 'The Labour Party and the electorate', in D. Kavanagh (ed.) *The Politics of the Labour Party*, London: Allen & Unwin.

Cutler, T. and Waine, B. (1994) *Managing the Welfare State. The Politics of Public Sector Management*, Oxford: Berg.

Dalley, G. (1988) *Ideologies of Caring: Rethinking Community and Collectivism*, Basingstoke: Macmillan.

Davies, C. (2000) 'The demise of professional self-regulation: a moment to mourn?', in G. Lewis, S. Gewirtz and J. Clarke (eds) *Rethinking Social Policy*, London: Sage.

Davis, A., Ellis, K. and Rummery, K. (1997) *Access to Assessment: Perspectives of Practitioners, Disabled People and Carers*, Bristol: Policy Press.

Day, P. and Klein, N. (1990) *Inspecting the Inspectorates*, Bath: University of Bath, Centre for Analysis of Social Policy.

Deacon, B., Hulse, M. and Stubbs, P. (1997) *Global Social Policy. International Organizations and the Future of Welfare*, London: Sage.

Deakin, N. (1994) *The Politics of Welfare*, 2nd edn, Hemel Hempstead, Harvester Wheatsheaf.

Deakin, N. (1996) 'The Devil's in the detail: some reflections on contracting for social care by voluntary organizations', *Social Policy and Administration*, 30, 1, 20–38.

Department of Employment (1992) *Equal Opportunities and the Development of NVQs and SVQs*, London: DoE.

Department of the Environment, Transport and the Regions (1998) *Modern Local Government: In Touch With the People*, London: Stationery Office.

Department of the Environment, Transport and the Regions (1999) *Local Government Act 1999. Part 1: Best Value*, Circular 10/99, London: DoETR.

Department of Health (1990) *Community Care in the Next Decade and Beyond: Policy Guidance*, London: HMSO.

Department of Health (1991) *Purchase of Service: Practice Guidance*, London: HMSO.

Department of Health–Price Waterhouse (1991) *Implementing Community Care: Purchaser, Commissioner and Provider Roles*, London: HMSO.

Department of Health (1992) *Memorandum on the Financing of Community Care*, London: Department of Health.

Department of Health (1994) *A Framework for Local Community Care Charters in England*, London: HMSO.

Department of Health (1996) *Obligations of Care: A Consultation Paper on the Setting of Conduct and Practice Standards for Social Services Staff*, London: Department of Health.

Department of Health (1997) *Review of the Functions of the Central Council for Education and Training in Social Work*, London: Department of Health.

Department of Health (1998a) *Quality Protects: Framework for Action*, London: HMSO.

Department of Health (1998b) *Modernising Social Services*, London: HMSO.

Department of Health (1999) *A New Approach to Social Services Performance: Consultation Document*, London: Department of Health.

Department of Health (2000a) *A Quality Strategy for Social Care*, London: HMSO.

Department of Health (2000b) *Community Care Statistics 1999 Home Help/ Home Care Services in England*, London. Government Statistical Service.

Department of Health (2000c) *Social Services Performance in 1999–2000. The Personal Social Services Assessment Framework Indicators*, London: Government Statistical Service.

Department of Health (2001a) 'Personal Social Services Staff of Social Services Departments at 30 September 2000, England, *Bulletin 2001/16*, available online: http://www.doh.gov.uk/public/sb0116.htm

Department of Health (2001b) 'Radical Reforms to Social Work Training to Raise Social Care Standards', press release 2001/0154.

Department of Health (undated) *Caring for People. Community Care in the Next Decade and Beyond. Implementation Documents: Assessment and Case Management*, London: HMSO.

Derber, C. (1982) 'Managing professionals: ideological proletarianization and mental labor', in C. Derber (ed.) *Professionals as Workers: Mental Labor in Advanced Capitalism*, Boston, MA: G. K. Hall.

Derber, C. (1983) 'Managing professionals: ideological proletarianization and post-industrial labor', *Theory and Society*, 12, 3, 309–41.

Dominelli, L. (1996) 'Deprofessionalizing social work: anti-oppressive practice, competencies and postmodernism', *British Journal of Social Work*, 26, 153–75.

Dominelli, L. (1997) *Sociology for Social Work*, Basingstoke: Macmillan.

Dominelli, L. (1998) 'Anti-oppressive practice in context', in R. Adams, L. Dominelli and M. Payne (eds) *Social Work: Themes, Issues and Critical Debates*, Basingstoke: Macmillan.

Dominelli, L. and Hoogvelt, A. (1996) 'Globalization and the technocratization of social work', *Critical Social Policy*, 16, 2, 45–62.

Donzelot, J. (1988) 'The promotion of the social', *Economy and Society*, 17, 3, 395–427.

Drakeford, M. (2000) *Privatisation and Social Policy*, Harlow: Pearson.

Driver, S. and Martell, L. (1997) 'New Labour's communitarianisms', *Critical Social Policy*, 17, 27–46.

Dudley, J. (1999) 'Higher education policy and the learning citizen', in A. Petersen, I. Barns, J. Dudley and P. Harris (eds) *Poststructuralism, Citizenship and Social Policy*, London: Routledge.

Duff, J. and Larsen, A.-C. (2000) 'Service professions in corporate settings: the implications for autonomy and ethical practice', Paper given at the conference *Managerialism, Contractualism and Professionalism in Human Services* Melbourne: Deakin University, Centre for Citizenship and Human Rights.

Du Gay, P. (2000) 'Entrepreneurial governance and public management: the anti-bureaucrats', in J. Clarke, S. Gewirtz and E. McLaughlin (eds) *New Managerialism, New Welfare?* London: Sage.

Dunant, S. (1994) (ed.) *The War of the Words: The Political Correctness Debate*, London: Virago.

Edgell, S. and Hetherington, K. (1996) 'Introduction: consumption matters', in S. Edgell, K. Hetherington and A. Warde (eds) *Consumption Matters*, Oxford: Blackwell.

Elcock, H. (1993) 'Local Government', in D. Farnham and S. Horton (eds) *Managing the New Public Services*, Basingstoke: Macmillan.

Elcock, H., Jordan, A. G. and Midwinter, A. F. (1989) *Budgeting in Local Government: Managing the Margins*, London: Longman.

Ellis, K. (1993) *Squaring the Circle: User and Carer Participation in Needs Assessment and Community Care*, York: Joseph Rowntree Foundation.

Ellis, K. (1995) 'Are women becoming a burden? Independence, dependence and community care', *Social Services Research*, 2, 1–10.

England, H. (1986) *Social Work as Art*, London: Allen & Unwin.

Esping-Andersen, G. (1998) *Welfare States in Transition*, London: Sage.

Etzioni, A. (1994) 'Who should pay for care?' *Sunday Times*, 3–4, 9 October.

Evers, A., Haverinen, R., Leischenring, K. and Wistow, G. (eds) (1997) *Developing Quality in Personal Social Services: Concepts, Cases and Comments*, Aldershot: Ashgate.

Exworthy, M. and Halford, S. (1999) 'Professionals and managers in a changing public sector: conflict, compromise and collaboration?' in M. Exworthy and S. Halford (eds) *Professionals and the New Managerialism in the Public Sector*, Buckingham: Open University Press.

Fabricant, M. and Burghardt, S. (1992) *The Welfare State Crisis and the Transformation of Social Service Work*, New York: M.E. Sharpe.

Fairclough, N. (1992) *Discourse and Social Change*, Cambridge: Polity.

Farnham, D. and Horton, S. (1996) 'Public service managerialism: a review and evaluation', in D. Farnham and S. Horton (eds) *Managing the New Public Services*, 2nd edn, Basingstoke: Macmillan.

Featherstone, B. and Fawcett, B. (1995) 'Power, difference and social work: an exploration', *Issues in Social Work Education*, 15, 1, 3–20.

Finch, J. (1989) *Family Obligations and Social Change*, Cambridge: Polity.

Finch, J. and Dalley, G. (1984) 'Community care: developing non-sexist alternatives', *Critical Social Policy*, 9, 27–39.

Finch, J. and Mason, J. (1993) *Negotiating Family Responsibilities*, London: Routledge.

Fine, B. and Leopold, E. (1993, reprinted 2001) *The World of Consumption*, London: Routledge.

Finer Jones, C. (1997) 'The new social policy in Britain', *Social Policy and Administration*, 31, 154–70.

Fitzpatrick, T. (1998) 'The rise of market collectivism', in E. Brunsdon, H. Dean and R. Woods (eds) *Social Policy Review*, 10, 13–33.

Flösser, G. and Otto, H.-U. (eds) (1998) *Towards More Democracy in Social Services. Models and Cultures of Welfare*, Berlin: Walter de Gruyter.

Flynn, N. (1993) *Public Sector Management*, 2nd edn, Hemel Hempstead: Harvester Wheatsheaf.

Flynn, N. (2000) 'Managerialism and public services: some international trends', in J. Clarke, S. Gewirtz and E. McLaughlin (eds) *New Managerialism, New Welfare?* London: Sage.

Forbes, J. and Sashidharan, S.P. (1997) 'User involvement in services: incorporation or challenge?' *British Journal of Social Work*, 27, 481–98.

Foucault, M. (1991) 'Governmentality', in G. Burchell, C. Gordan and P. Miller (eds) *The Foucault Effect: Studies in Governmentality*, Chicago, IL: University of Chicago Press.

Fournier, V. (2000) 'Boundary work and the (un)making of the professions', in N. Malin (ed.) *Professionalism, Boundaries and the Workplace*, London: Routledge.

Frazer, E. (2000) 'Communitarianism', in G. Browning, A. Halcli and F. Webster (eds) *Understanding Contemporary Society: Theories of the Present*, London: Sage.

Freeden, M. (1999) 'The ideology of New Labour', *The Political Quarterly*, 70, 42–51.

Freidson, E. (1994) *Professionalism Reborn. Theory, Prophecy and Policy*, Cambridge: Polity Press.

Friedman, A. (1977) *Industry and Labour: Class Struggle at Work and Monopoly Capitalism*, London: Macmillan.

Friend, J. and Jessop, W. (1969) *Local Government and Strategic Choice: An Operational Research Approach to Public Planning*, London: Tavistock.

Froggett, L. (2000) 'Care and commodity aesthetics: fetishism and transformation in social welfare', in I. Paylor, L. Froggett and J. Harris (eds) *Reclaiming Social Work: The Southport Papers*, vol. 2, Birmingham: Venture Press.

Gamble, A. (1988) *The Free Economy and the Strong State*, Basingstoke: Macmillan.

George, V. (1998) 'Political ideology, globalisation and welfare futures in Europe', *Journal of Social Policy*, 27, 17–36.

George, V. and Wilding, P. (1984) *The Impact of Social Policy*, London: Routledge & Kegan Paul.

Giddens, A. (1991) *The Consequences of Modernity*, Cambridge: Polity.

Giddens, A. (1994) *Beyond Left and Right: The Future of Radical Politics*, Cambridge: Polity.

Glennerster, H. (1992a) *Paying for Welfare: The 1990s*, Hemel Hempstead: Harvester Wheatsheaf.

Glennerster, H. (1992b) *Paying for Welfare: Issues for the 90s*, Welfare State Programme Paper No. 82, London: London School of Economics.

Glennerster, H. and Midgley, J. (1991) *The Radical Right and the Welfare State*, Hemel Hempstead: Harvester Wheatsheaf.

Gordan, D. and Adelman, L. (2000) *Poverty and Social Exclusion in Britain*, York: Joseph Rowntree Foundation.

Graham, H. (1983) 'Caring: a labour of love', in J. Finch and D. Groves (eds) *A Labour of Love: Women, Work and Caring*, London: Routledge & Kegan Paul.

Graham, H. (1991) 'The informal sector of welfare: a crisis in caring?' *Social Science and Medicine*, 32, 507–15.

Gray, J. (1999) *False Dawn. The Delusions of Global Capitalism*, London: Granta.

Greenwood, R. (1983) 'Changing patterns of budgeting in English local government', *Public Administration*, 61, 149–68.

Greenwood, R. and Stewart, J.D. (1974) *Corporate Planning in English Local Government*, Birmingham: University of Birmingham, INLOGOV.

Greenwood, R., Walsh, K., Hinings, C. and Ranson, S. (1980) *Patterns of Management in Local Government*, Oxford: Martin Robertson.

Griffiths Report (1988) *Community Care: An Agenda for Action*, London: HMSO.

Gyford, J. (1991) *Citizens, Consumers and Councils*, Basingstoke: Macmillan.

Hadley, R. and Clough, R. (1996) *Care in Chaos: Frustration and Challenge in Community Care*, London: Cassell.

Hall, P. (1976) *Reforming the Welfare*, London: Heinemann.

Hall, S. (1989) 'The meaning of New Times', in S. Hall and M. Jacques (eds) *New Times*, London: Lawrence & Wishart.

Hall, S. (1998) 'The great moving nowhere show', *Marxism Today*, November/December, 9–14.

Hallett, C. (1982) *The Personal Social Services in Local Government*, London: Allen & Unwin.

Hallett, C. (1991) 'The Children Act 1989 and community care: comparisons and contrasts', *Policy and Politics*, 19, 4, 283–92.

Harris, J. (1995) 'The Labour process perspective and front-line management in local authority social work. A case study', Ph.D. thesis, University of Warwick.

Harris, J. (1996) 'Bureau-professionalism and new managerialism in social work', paper presented at the *Fourteenth Annual International Labour Process Conference*, Birmingham: University of Aston.

Harris, J. (1998) 'Scientific management, bureau-professionalism and new managerialism. The labour process of state social work', *British Journal of Social Work*, 28, 839–62.

Harris, J. (1999) 'State social work and social citizenship', *British Journal of Social Work*, 29, 915–37.

Harris, J. (2001) 'Better government for older people: citizens' participation in social policy at a local level', in P. Salustowicz (ed.) *Civil Society and Social Development*, Bern: Lang.

Harris, J. and McDonald, C. (2000) 'Post-Fordism, the welfare state and the personal social services. A comparison of Australia and Britain', *British Journal of Social Work*, 30, 51–70.

Harris, J. and Yueh-Ching, Chou (2001) 'Globalisation or glocalization? Community care in Taiwan and Britain', *European Journal of Social Work*, 4, 2, 161–72.

Harris, P. (1999) 'Public welfare and liberal governance', in A. Petersen, I. Barns, J. Dudley and P. Harris (eds) *Poststructuralism, Citizenship and Social Policy*, London: Routledge.

Healey, D. (1989) *The Time of My Life*, London: Michael Joseph.

Henwood, M., Wistow, G. and Robinson, J. (1996) 'Halfway there? Policy, politics and outcomes in community care', *Social Policy and Administration*, 30, 1, 39–53.

Heron, C. (1998) *Working With Carers*, London: Jessica Kingsley.

Hill, M. (1993) *The Welfare State in Britain: A Political History Since 1945*, Cheltenham: Edward Elgar.

Hills, J. (1997) *The Future of Welfare: A Guide to the Debate*, York: Joseph Rowntree Foundation.

Hills, J. (1998) *Thatcherism, New Labour and the Welfare State*, CASE Paper 13, London: London School of Economics.

HM Government (1999) *Caring About Carers. A National Strategy for Carers*, London, Stationery Office.

Hoggett, P. (1991) 'A new management in the public sector?' *Policy and Politics*, 19, 243–56.

Hoggett, P. (1994) 'The politics of the modernisation of the UK welfare state', in R. Burrows and B. Loader (eds) *Towards a Post-Fordist Welfare State?* London: Routledge.

Hoggett, P. (1996) 'New modes of control in the public service', *Public Administration*, 74, 3, 9–32.

Hoggett, P. (2000) 'Social policy and the emotions', in G. Lewis, S. Gewirtz and J. Clarke (eds) *Rethinking Social Policy*, London: Sage.

Hoggett, P. and Hambleton, R. (1987) *Decentralisation and Democracy*, Bristol: University of Bristol, School of Advanced Urban Studies.

Home Office (1998) *Getting it Right Together: Compact on Relations Between Government and the Voluntary and Community Sector in England*, London: Home Office.

Hood, C. (1991a) 'Contemporary public management: a new global paradigm?' *Public Policy and Administration*, 10, 2, 104–17.

Hood, C. (1991b) 'A public management for all seasons', *Public Administration*, 69, 3–19.

Hood, C. (1995) 'The "new public management" in the 1980s: variations on a theme', *Accounting, Organizations and Society*, 20, 2/3, 93–109.

Hood, C., Scott, C., James, O., Jones, G. and Travers, T. (1999) *Regulation Inside Government: Waste-Watchers, Quality-Police and Sleaze-Busters*, Oxford: Oxford University Press.

House of Commons, Social Services Select Committee (1985) *Community Care*, London: HMSO.

Howe, D. (1986) *Social Workers and Their Practice in Welfare Bureaucracies*, Aldershot: Gower.

Howe, D. (1992) 'Child abuse and the bureaucratisation of social work', *The Sociologist*, 40, 3, 491–508.

Howe, D. (1994) 'Modernity, postmodernity and social work', *British Journal of Social Work*, 24, 513–32.

Howe, D. (1996) 'Surface and depth in social work practice', in N. Parton (ed.) *Social Theory, Social Change and Social Work*, London: Routledge.

Hugman, R. (1991a) *Power in Caring Professions*, Basingstoke: Macmillan.

Hugman, R. (1991b) 'Organization and professionalism: the social work agenda in the 1990s', *British Journal of Social Work*, 21, 199–216.

Hugman, R. (1996) 'Professionalization in social work: the challenge of diversity', *International Social Work*, 39, 2, 199–216.

Humphries, B. (1997) 'Reading social work. Competing discourses in the *Rules and Requirements for the Diploma in Social Work*', *British Journal of Social Work*, 27, 641–58.

Hunt, G. and Campbell, D. (1998) 'Social workers speak out', in G. Hunt (ed.) *Whistleblowing in the Social Services: Public Accountability and Professional Practice*, London: Edward Arnold.

Huntington, A. (2000) 'Children and families' social work – visions of the future', in I. Paylor, L. Froggett and J. Harris (eds) *Reclaiming Social Work: The Southport Papers*, vol. 2, Birmingham: Venture Press.

Hurd, D. (1988) 'Citizenship in the Tory democracy', *New Statesman*, 29 April.

Ife, J. (1997) *Rethinking Social Work: Towards Critical Practice*, Melbourne: Longman.

Ignatieff, M. (1991) 'Citizenship and moral narcissism', in G. Andrews (ed.) *Citizenship*, London: Lawrence & Wishart.

Improvement and Development Agency (2001) *An Inspector Calls: A Survey of Local Authorities on the Impact of Inspection*, London: IdeA.

Jessop, B. (1994) 'The transition to post-Fordism and the Schumpeterian workfare state', in R. Burrows and B. Loader (eds) *Towards a Post-Fordist Welfare State?* London: Routledge.

J M Consulting Ltd (1999) *Review of the Diploma in Social Work*, Bristol: JMC Ltd.

Johnson, L. (1991) *Contracts for Care: Issues for Black and Other Ethnic Minority Groups*, London: National Council of Voluntary Organisations.

Johnson, N. (1993) 'Welfare pluralism: opportunities and risks', in A. Evers and I. Svetlik (eds) *Balancing Pluralism: New Welfare Mixes in Care for the Elderly*, Aldershot: Avebury.

Johnson, N. (ed.) (1995) *Private Markets in Health and Welfare*, Oxford: Berg.

Johnson, N. (1999) 'The personal social services and community care', in M. Powell (ed.) *New Labour, New Welfare State? The 'Third Way' in British Social Policy*, Bristol: Policy Press.

Johnson, T.J. (1972) *Professions and Power*, London: Macmillan.

Johnson, T.J. (1995) 'Governmentality and the institutionalisation of expertise', in T. Johnson, G. Larkin and M. Saks (eds) *Health Professions and the State in Europe*, London: Routledge.

Joint Reviews (1999) *Making Connections: Learning the Lessons from Joint Reviews 1998/9*, London: Department of Health, National Assembly for Wales and Audit Commission.

Joint Reviews (2000a) *People Need People: Releasing the Potential of People Working in Social Services*, London: Social Services Inspectorate and Audit Commission.

Joint Reviews (2000b) *Promising Prospects. Joint Review Team Fourth Annual Report 1999/2000 English Authorities. Summary*, London: Social Services Inspectorate and Audit Commission.

Jones, C. (1983) *State Social Work and the Working Class*, London: Macmillan.

Jones, C. (1989) 'The end of the road? Issues in social work education', in P. Carter, T. Jeffs and M. Smith (eds) *Social Work and Social Welfare Yearbook 1*, Buckingham: Open University Press.

Jones, C. (1993) 'Distortion and demonisation: the Right and anti-racism', *Social Work Education*, 12, 3, 9–16.

Jones, C. (1994) *The Making of Social Policy in Britain, 1830–1990*, 2nd edn, London: Athlone Press.

Jones, C. (1995) 'Demanding social work education: an agenda for the end of the century', *Issues in Social Work Education*, 15, 3–15.

Jones, C. (1996) 'Anti-intellectualism and the peculiarities of British social work education', in N. Parton (ed.) *Social Theory, Social Change and Social Work*, London: Routledge.

Jones, C. (1999) 'Social work: regulation and managerialism', in M. Hexworthy and S. Halford (eds) *Professionals and the New Managerialism in the Public Sector*, Buckingham: Open University Press.

Jones, C. (2001) 'Voices from the front line: state social workers and New Labour', *British Journal of Social Work*, 31, 547–62.

Jones, C. and Novak, T. (1993) 'Social work today', *British Journal of Social Work*, 23, 195–212.

Jones, D. (1999) 'Practice with standards', *Professional Social Work*, December, 4–6.

Jones, M. (2000) 'Hope and despair at the front line: observations on integrity and change in the human services', *International Social Work*, 43, 3, 365–80.

Jordan, B. (1989) *The Common Good: Citizenship, Morality and Self-Interest*, Oxford: Blackwell.

Jordan, B. (1991) 'Competencies and values', *Social Work Education*, 10, 1, 5–11.

Jordan, B. (1994) *Putting the Family First: Identities, Decisions, Citizenship*, London: UCL Press.

Jordan, B. (1998) *The New Politics of Welfare*, London: Sage.

Jordan, B. and Jordan, C. (2000) *Social Work and the Third Way: Tough Love as Social Policy*, London: Sage.

Joyce, P., Corrigan, P. and Hayes, M. (1988) *Striking Out. Trade Unionism in Social Work*, Basingstoke: Macmillan.

Keat, R. (1991) 'Consumer sovereignty and the integrity of practices', in R. Keat and N. Abercrombie (eds) *Enterprise Culture*, London: Routledge.

Keat, R. and Abercrombie, N. (1991) (eds) *Enterprise Culture*, London: Routledge.

Keat, R., Whitely, N. and Abercrombie, N. (eds) (1994) *The Authority of the Customer*, London: Routledge.

Keefe, A. (2000) Letter to *TOPSS England Regional Training Forums*, 27 July.

Kelly, A. (1992) 'The new managerialism in the social services', in P. Carter, T. Jeffs and M. Smith (eds) *Social Work and Social Welfare Yearbook 3*, Buckingham: Open University Press.

Kingdom, E. (1996) 'Gender and citizenship rights', in J. Demaine and H. Entwistle (eds) *Beyond Communitarianism: Citizenship, Politics and Education*, Basingstoke: Macmillan.

Knights, D. and Sturdy, A. (1990) 'New technology and the self-disciplined worker in insurance', in M. McNeil, I. Varcoe and S. Yearly (eds) *Deciphering Science and Technology*, Basingstoke: Macmillan.

Labour Party (1991) *Citizen's Charter: Labour's Better Deal for Consumers and Citizens*, London: Labour Party.

Labour Party (1992) *It's Time to Get Britain Working Again*, London: Labour Party.

Labour Party (1997) *New Labour: Because Britain Deserves Better*, London: Labour Party.

Laffin, M. and Young, K. (1990) *Professionalism in Local Government*, Harlow: Longman.

Land, H. and Rose, H. (1985) 'Compulsory altruism for some or an altruistic society for all?' in P. Bean, J. Ferris and D. Whynes (eds) *In Defence of Welfare*, London: Tavistock.

Langan, M. (1993) 'The rise and fall of social work', in J. Clarke (ed.) *A Crisis in Care? Challenges to Social Work*, London: Sage.

Langan, M. (1998) 'Radical social work', in R. Adams, L. Dominelli and M. Payne (eds) *Social Work. Themes, Issues and Critical Debates*, Basingstoke: Macmillan.

Langan, M. (2000) 'Social services: managing the third way', in J. Clarke, S. Gewirtz and E. McLaughlin (eds) *New Managerialism, New Welfare?* London: Sage.

Langan, J., Means, R. and Rolfe, S. (1996) *Maintaining Independence in Later Life: Older People Speaking*, Oxford: Anchor Trust.

Leach, S., Stewart, J. and Walsh, K. (1994) *The Changing Organisation and Management of Local Government*, Basingstoke: Macmillan.

Leat, D. (1995) 'Funding matters', in J.D. Smith, C. Rochester and R. Hedley (eds) *An Introduction to the Voluntary Sector*, London: Routledge.

Lee, S. (1997) 'Competitiveness and the welfare state in Britain', in M. Mullard and S. Lee (eds) *The Politics of Social Policy in Europe*, Cheltenham, Edward Elgar.

Le Grand, J. (1990) *Quasi-Markets and Social Policy. Studies in Decentralisation and Quasi-Markets No. 1*, Bristol: School for Advanced Urban Studies, University of Bristol.

Le Grand, J. (1993) *Quasi-Markets*, Basingstoke: Macmillan.

Le Grand, J. and Robinson, R (1984) (eds) *Privatisation and the Welfare State*, London: Unwin Hyman.

Leonard, P. (1997) *Postmodern Welfare. Reconstructing an Emancipatory Project*. London: Sage.

Levitas, R. (1996) 'The concept of social exclusion and the new Durkheimian hegemony', *Critical Social Policy*, 16, 5–20.

Lewis, G. (2000) 'Introduction: expanding the social policy imaginary', in G. Lewis, S. Gewirtz and J. Clarke (eds) *Rethinking Social Policy*, London: Sage.

Lewis, J. (1993) 'Developing the mixed economy of care: emerging issues for voluntary organisations', *Journal of Social Policy*, 22, 2, 173–92.

Lewis, J. (1995) *The Voluntary Sector, the State and Social Work in Britain*, Cheltenham: Edward Elgar.

Lewis, J. (1997) 'Gender and welfare regimes: further thoughts', *Social Politics*, 4, 160–77.

Lewis, J. (2000) 'Gender and welfare regimes', in G. Lewis, S. Gewirtz and J. Clarke (eds) *Rethinking Social Policy*, London: Sage.

Lewis, J. and Glennerster, H. (1996) *Implementing the New Community Care*, Buckingham: Open University Press.

Lewis, J. with Bernstock, P., Bovwell, V. and Wookey, F. (1996) 'The purchaser–provider split in social care: is it working?', *Social Policy and Administration*, 30, 1, 1–19.

Light, D.W. (2001) 'Managed competition, governmentality and institutional response in the United Kingdom', *Social Science and Medicine*, 52, 1167–81.

Lister, R. (1990) 'Women, economic dependency and citizenship', *Journal of Social Policy*, 19, 445–67.

Lister, R. (1997) *Citizenship: Feminist Perspectives*, Basingstoke: Macmillan.

Lister, R. (1998) 'Vocabularies of citizenship and gender: the UK', *Critical Social Policy*, 18, 309–33.

Lister, R. (2000) 'Gender and the analysis of social policy', in G. Lewis, S. Gewirtz and J. Clarke (eds) *Rethinking Social Policy*, London: Sage.

Lloyd, J. (1997) 'A benefit cut in search of a policy', *New Statesman*, 19 December, 12–13.

Loader, B. and Burrows, R. (1994) 'Towards a post-Fordist welfare state? The restructuring of Britain, social policy and the future of welfare', in R. Burrows and B. Loader (eds) *Towards a Post-Fordist Welfare State?* London: Routledge.

Local Government Management Board (1993) *Fitness for Purpose. Shaping New Patterns of Organization and Management*, Luton: LGMB.

Local Government Management Board (1995) *Gearing Up to Govern*, Luton: LGMB.

Local Government Training Board (1985) *Good Management in Local Government. Successful Practice and Action*, Luton: LGTB.

Loney, M. (1986) *The Politics of Greed: The New Right and the Welfare State*, London: Pluto.

Lund, B. (1999) 'Ask not what your community can do for you: obligations, New Labour and welfare reform', *Critical Social Policy*, 19, 4, 447–62.

Lymberry, M., Charles, M., Christopherson, J. and Eadie, T. (2000) 'The control of British social work education: European comparisons', *European Journal of Social Work*, 3, 3, 269–82.

Lyotard, J.-F. (1984) *The Postmodern Condition: A Report on Knowledge*, trans. G. Bennington and B. Massumi, Manchester: Manchester University Press.

McCurry, P. (1999) 'The light at the end of the tunnel', *Community Care*, 5 August, 10–11.

McDonald, C. (2000) 'The third sector in the human services: rethinking its role', in I. O'Connor, P. Smyth and J. Warburton (eds) *Contemporary Perspectives on Social Work and the Human Services: Challenges and Change*, Sydney: Longman.

McDonald, C., Harris, J. and Wintersteen, R. (forthcoming) 'Contingent on context? Social work and the state in Australia, Britain and the USA', *British Journal of Social Work*.

McDonald, C. and Jones, A. (2000) 'Reconstructing and re-conceptualising social work in the emerging milieu', *Australian Social Work*, 53, 3, 3–11.

MacDonald, K. (1995) *The Sociology of the Professions*, London: Sage.

Mackintosh, M. (2000) 'Exchange and the metaphor of exchange: economic cultures in social care', in G. Lewis, S. Gewirtz and J. Clarke (eds) *Rethinking Social Policy*, London: Sage.

McNally, S. (2000) 'Professionalism and user advocacy', in N. Malin (ed.) *Professionalism, Boundaries and the Workplace*, London: Routledge.

Malin, N. (2000) 'Professionalism and boundaries of the formal sector: the example of social and community care', in N. Malin (ed.) *Professionalism, Boundaries and the Workplace*, London: Routledge.

Marquand, D. (1988) *The Unprincipled Society*, London: Fontana.

Marquand, D. (1996) 'Moralists and hedonists', in D. Marquand and A. Seldon (eds) *The Ideas that Shaped Post-War Britain*, London, Harper Collins.

Marsh, P. and Triseliotis, J. (1996) *Ready to Practise. Social Workers and Probation Officers: Their Training and First Year in Work*, Aldershot, Avebury.

Marshall, T.H. (1950) *Citizenship and Social Class*, Cambridge: Cambridge University Press.

Marshall, T.H. (1963) 'Citizenship and social class', in *Sociology at the Crossroads*, London: Heinemann.

Marshall, T.H. (1965) *Social Policy*, London: Hutchinson.

Marshall, T.H. (1975) *Social Policy in the Twentieth Century*, London: Hutchinson.

Marshall, T.H. (1981) *The Right to Welfare and Other Essays*, London: Heinemann.

Marsland, D. (1996) 'Community care as an alternative to state welfare', *Social Policy and Administration*, 30, 3, 183–8.

Marwick, A. (1990) *British Society Since 1945*, London: Penguin.

Maud Report (1967) *Report of the Committee on Management in Local Government*, London: HMSO.

May, M. (2001) 'Protecting the "vulnerable": welfare and consumer protection', in M. May, R. Page and E. Brunsdon (eds) *Understanding Social Problems: Issues in Social Policy*, Oxford: Blackwell.

Midgley, J. and Jones, C. (1994) 'Social work and the radical right: the impact of developments in Britain and the United States', *International Social Work*, 37, 115–26.

Minford, P. (1984) 'State expenditure: a study in waste', *Economic Affairs*, 5, 2, 9–15.

Minichiello, V., Browne, J. and Kendig, H. (2000) 'Perceptions and consequences of ageism: views of older people', *Ageing and Society*, 30, 3, 253–78.

Mishra, R. (1984) *The Welfare State in Crisis*, Brighton: Wheatsheaf.

Mishra, R. (1993) 'Social policy in the postmodern world', in C. Jones (ed.) *New Perspectives on the Welfare State in Europe*, London: Routledge.

Mishra, R. (1999) *Globalization and the Welfare State*, Cheltenham: Edward Elgar.

Mooney, G. (1997) 'Quasi-markets and the mixed economy of welfare', in M. Lavalette and A. Pratt (eds) *Social Policy: A Conceptual and Theoretical Introduction*, London: Sage.

Morris, J. (1993) *Community Care or Independent Living?* York: Joseph Rowntree Foundation.

Mouffe, V. (2000) 'For an agonistic model of democracy', in N. O'Sullivan (ed.) *Political Theory in Transition*, London: Routledge.

Muetzelfeldt, M. (1992) 'Economic rationalism in its social context', in M. Muetzelfeldt (ed.) *Society, State and Politics in Australia*, Sydney: Pluto.

Muetzelfeldt, M. (1994) 'Contracts, politics and society', in J. Alford and D. O'Neill (eds) *The Contract State: Public Management and the Kennett Government*, Melbourne: Deakin University Press.

Myers, F. and MacDonald, C. (1996) '"I was given options not choices": involving older users and carers in assessment and care planning', in R. Bland (ed.) *Developing Services for Older People and Their Families*, London: Jessica Kingsley.

National Council for Vocational Qualifications (1988) *The NCVQ Criteria and Related Guidance*, London: NCVQ.

National Council for Voluntary Organisations (1989) *Contracting In or Out? The Contract Culture: The Challenge for Voluntary Organisations*, London: NCVO.

Newman, J. (2000) 'Beyond the new public management? Modernizing public services', in J. Clarke, S. Gewirtz and E. McLaughlin (eds) *New Managerialism, New Welfare?* London: Sage.

Newman, J. and Clarke, J. (1994) 'Going about our business? The managerialisation of public services', in J. Clarke, A. Cochrane and E. McLaughlin (eds) *Managing Social Policy*, London: Sage.

Nixon, J. (1993) 'Implementation in the hands of senior managers: community care in Britain', in M. Hill (ed.) *New Agendas in the Study of the Policy Process*, Hemel Hempstead: Harvester Wheatsheaf.

Nocon, A. and Qureshi, H. (1996) *Outcomes of Community Care for Users and Carers*, Buckingham: Open University Press.

Nolan, M. and Caldock, K. (1996) 'Assessment: identifying the barriers to good practice', *Health and Social Care in the Community*, 4, 77–85.

Novak, T. (1995) 'Thinking about a new social work curriculum', *Social Work Education*, 14, 1, 4–10.

O'Brien, M. and Penna, S. (1998) *Theorising Welfare: Enlightenment and Modern Society*, London: Sage.

O'Connor, J. (1973) *The Fiscal Crisis of the State*, New York: St. Martin's Press.

O'Connor, M.E. (2000) 'Aspects of Managerialism', paper given at the conference *Managerialism, Contractualism and Professionalism in Human Services*, Melbourne: Deakin University, Centre for Citizenship and Human Rights.

Offe, C. (1975) 'The theory of the capitalist state and the problem of policy formation', in L.N. Lindberg (ed.) *Stress and Contradiction in Modern*

Capitalism: Public Policy and the Theory of the State, Lexington, MA: Heath Press.

Offe, C. (1983) 'Some contradictions of the modern welfare state', *Critical Social Policy*, 6, 7–16.

Offe, C. (1984) *Contradictions of the Welfare State*, London: Hutchinson.

O'Hagan, K. (1996) *Competence in Social Work Practice*, London: Jessica Kingsley.

O'Higgins, M. (1992) 'Effective management: the challenges', in T. Harding (ed.) *Who Owns Welfare? Questions on the Social Services Agenda*, Social Services Policy Forum Paper No. 2, London: National Institute for Social Work.

Oldman, C. (1991) *Paying for Care: Personal Sources of Funding Care*, York: Joseph Rowntree Foundation.

Oliver, D. and Heater, D. (1994) *The Foundations of Citizenship*, Hemel Hempstead: Harvester Wheatsheaf.

Ong, B. N. (1985) 'The paradox of "wonderful children": the case of child abuse', *Early Childhood Development and Care*, 21, 27–36.

Orme, J. (2001) 'Regulation or fragmentation? Directions for social work under New Labour', *British Journal of Social Work*, 31, 611–24.

Orme, J., Bywaters, P. and Preston-Shoot, M. (2001) Joint University Council, Social Work Education Committee, Briefing Paper, available online: http://www.swap.ac.uk/resources/news/preston.htm

O'Sullivan, N. (2000) 'Introduction', in N. O'Sullivan (ed.) *Political Theory in Transition*, London: Routledge.

Packman, J. and Jordan, B. (1991) 'The Children Act: looking foward, looking back', *British Journal of Social Work*, 21, 4, 315–27.

Pahl, J. (1994) '"Like the job – but hate the organisation": social workers and managers in social services', in R. Page and J. Baldock (eds) *Social Policy Review 6*, Canterbury: Social Policy Association.

Papadakis, E. and Taylor-Gooby, P. (1987) *The Private Provision of Public Welfare. State, Market and Community*, Brighton: Wheatsheaf.

Parker, G. (1999) 'Impact of the NHS and Community Care Act (1990) on informal carers: briefing paper for the Royal Commission on Long Term Care for the Elderly', in G. Wistow and M. Henwood (eds) *Evaluating the Impact of Caring for People with Respect to Old Age*, London: Stationery Office.

Parker, H. (ed.) (2000) *Low Cost but Acceptable Incomes for Older People: A Minimum Income Standard for Households Aged 65–74 Years in the UK*, Bristol: Policy Press.

Parry, N. and Parry, J. (1979) 'Social work, professionalism and the state', in N. Parry, N.M. Rustin and C. Satyamurti (eds) *Social Work, Welfare and the State*, London: Edward Arnold.

Parsloe, P. (1981) *Social Services Area Teams*, London: George Allen & Unwin.

Parsloe, P. and Stevenson, O. (1978) *Social Services Teams: The Practitioners' View*, London: HMSO.

Parton, N. (1996a) 'Social theory, social change and social work. An introduction', in N. Parton (ed.) *Social Theory, Social Change and Social Work*, London: Routledge.

Parton, N. (1996b) 'Social work, risk and "the blaming system"', in N. Parton (ed.) *Social Theory, Social Change and Social Work*, London: Routledge.

Pascall, G. (1997) *Social Policy: A New Feminist Analysis*, London: Routledge.

Payne, M. (1994) 'Partnership between organisations in social work education', *Issues in Social Work Education*, 14, 1, 53–70.

Payne, M. (1995) *Social Work and Community Care*, Basingstoke: Macmillan.

Peters, T. and Waterman, R. (1984) *In Search of Excellence: Lessons from America's Best-Run Companies*, New York: Harper & Row.

Phillips, M. (1993) 'Oppressive urge to end oppression', *Observer*, 1 August.

Phillipson, C. (1994) 'Community care and the social construction of citizenship', *Journal of Social Work Practice*, 8, 103–12.

Pierson, C. (1994) 'Continuity and discontinuity in the emergence of the post-Fordist welfare state', in R. Burrows and B. Loader (eds) *Towards a Post-Fordist Welfare State?* London: Routledge.

Pierson, C. (1998) *Beyond the Welfare State: The New Political Economy of Welfare*, 2nd edn, Cambridge: Polity Press.

Pinker, R.A. (1979) *Social Theory and Social Policy*, London: Heinemann.

Pinker, R.A. (1992) 'Making sense of the mixed economy of welfare', *Social Policy and Administration*, 26, 273–84.

Pinker, R.A. (1993) 'A lethal kind of looniness', *Times Higher Education Supplement*, 10 September.

Pithouse, A. (1987) *Social Work: The Social Organisation of an Invisible Trade*, Aldershot: Gower.

Plant, R. (1992) 'Citizenship, rights and welfare', in A. Coote, (ed.) *The Welfare of Citizens*, London: Rivers Oram Press.

Pollitt, C. (1990) *Managerialism and the Public Services*, Oxford: Basil Blackwell.

Pollitt, C. (1994) 'The *Citizen's Charter*: a preliminary analysis', *Public Money and Management*, April–June, 9–14.

Potter, J. (1994) 'Consumerism and the public sector: how well does the coat fit?', in D. McKevitt and A. Lawson (eds) *Public Sector Management: Theory, Critique and Practice*, London: Sage.

Power, M. (1997) *The Audit Society: Rituals of Verification*, Oxford, Oxford University Press.

Prime Minister (1991) *The Citizen's Charter: Raising the Standard*, London: HMSO.

Preston-Shoot, M. (1996) 'A question of emphasis? On legalism and social work education', in M. Preston-Shoot and S. Jackson (eds) *Educating Social Workers in a Changing Policy Context*, London: Whiting & Birch.

Prior, D., Stewart, J. and Walsh, K. (1995) *Citizenship Rights: Community and Participation*, London: Pitman.

Ranson, S. and Stewart, J. (1994) *Management for the Public Domain*, Basingstoke, Macmillan.

Rees, S. (1995) 'The fraud and the fiction', in S. Rees and G. Rodley (eds) *The Human Costs of Managerialism. Advocating the Recovery of Humanity*, Leichhardt: Pluto Press.

Rhodes, R.A.W. (1992) 'Local government finance', in D. Marsh and R.A.W. Rhodes (eds) *Implementing Thatcherite Policies: Audit of an Era*, Buckingham: Open University Press.

Richards, S. (2000) 'Bridging the divide: elders and the assessment process', *British Journal of Social Work*, 30, 37–49.

Richardson, S. and Pearson, M. (1995) 'Dignity and aspirations denied: unmet health and social care needs in an inner-city area', *Health and Social Care in the Community*, 3, 5, 279–87.

Ritzer, G. (2000) *The McDonaldization of Society* (New Century Edition), Thousand Oaks, CA: Pine Forge Press.

Roche, M. (1987) 'Citizenship, social theory and social change', *Theory and Society*, 16, 363–99.

Rogowski, S. (2001) 'Where has all the idealism gone?' *Community Care*, 18 January, 15.

Rose, N. (1996) 'The death of the social? Re-figuring the territory of government', *Economics and Society*, 25, 3, 327–56.

Royal Commission on Long Term Care (1999) *With Respect to Old Age*, London: Stationery Office.

Rummery, K., Ellis, K. and Davis, A. (1999) 'Negotiating access to community care assessments', *Health and Social Care in the Community*, 7, 291–300.

Rustin, M. (1994) 'Flexibility in higher education', in R. Burrows and B. Loader (eds) *Towards a Post Fordist Welfare State?* London: Routledge.

Salamon, M. (1998) *Industrial Relations Theory and Practice*, 3rd edn, Harlow: Prentice-Hall.

Sapey, B. (1997) 'Social work tomorrow: towards a critical understanding of technology in social work', *British Journal of Social Work*, 27, 803–14.

Satyamurti, C. (1981) *Occupational Survival*, Oxford: Blackwell.

Schorr, A.L. (1992) *The Personal Social Services: An Outsider's View*, York: Joseph Rowntree Trust.

Scottish Office (1999) *Aiming for Excellence: Modernising Social Work Services in Scotland*, Edinburgh: Scottish Office.

Seebohm, F. (1989) *Seebohm Twenty Years On. Three Stages in the Development of the Personal Social Services*, London: Policy Studies Institute.

Sibeon, R. (1990) 'Social work knowledge, social actors and deprofessionalisation', in P. Abbott and C. Wallace (eds) *The Sociology of the Caring Professions*, Brighton: Falmer Press.

Simiç, P. (1995) 'What's in a word? From "social worker" to "care manager"', *Practice*, 7, 3, 5–17.

Simpkin, M. (1983) *Trapped Within Welfare. Surviving Social Work*, 2nd edn, London: Macmillan.

Smale, G., and Tuson, G., with Biehal, N. and Marsh, P. (1993) *Empowerment, Assessment, Care Management and the Skilled Worker*, London: HMSO.

Smith, C., Knights, D. and Willmott, H. (1991) *White-Collar Work. The Non-Manual Labour Process*, Basingstoke: Macmillan.

Social Services Inspectorate (1991a) *Care Management and Assessment: Practitioners' Guide*, London: Department of Health.

Social Services Inspectorate (1991b) *Care Management and Assessment: Managers' Guide*, London: Department of Health.

Social Services Inspectorate (1992) *Implementing Caring for People: Assessment Circular*, London: Department of Health.

Social Services Inspectorate (2000) *Modern Social Services: A Commitment to People. The Annual Report of the Chief Inspector of Social Services 1999– 2000*, Department of Health.

Spicker, P. (1995) *Social Policy: Themes and Approaches*, London: Prentice-Hall.

Stacey, M. (1981) 'The division of labour revisited, or overcoming the two Adams', in P. Abrams, R. Deem, J. Finch and P. Rock (eds) *Practice and Progress: British Sociology 1950–1980*, London: George Allen & Unwin.

Stanley, N. (1999) 'User–practitioner transactions in the new culture of community care', *British Journal of Social Work*, 29, 417–35.

Stewart, J. (1983) *Local Government: The Conditions of Local Choice*, London: Allen & Unwin.

Stewart, J. (1989) 'The changing organisation and management of local authorities', in J. Stewart and G. Stoker (eds) *The Future of Local Government*, London: Macmillan.

Stewart, J. (1992) 'Guidelines for public service management: lessons not to be learnt from the private sector', in P. Carter, T. Jeffs and M.K. Smith (eds) *Changing Social Work and Welfare*, Buckingham: Open University Press.

Stewart, J. and Stoker, G. (eds) (1994) *The Future of Local Government*, Basingstoke: Macmillan.

Tanner, D. (1998) 'Empowerment and care management: swimming against the tide', *Health and Social Care in the Community*, 6, 6, 447–57.

Tanner, D. (2001) 'Partnership in prevention: messages from older people', in V. White and J. Harris (eds) *Developing Good Practice in Community Care: Partnership and Participation*, London: Jessica Kingsley.

Taylor, M., Langan, J. and Hoggett, P. (1995) *Encouraging Diversity: Voluntary and Private Organisations in Community Care*, Aldershot: Arena.

Taylor-Gooby, P. (1985) *Public Opinion, Ideology and State Welfare*, London: Routledge & Kegan Paul.

Taylor-Gooby, P. (1987) 'Welfare attitudes: cleavage, consensus and citizenship', *Quarterly Journal of Social Affairs* 3, 199–211.

Taylor-Gooby, P. (1993) 'Citizenship, dependency and the welfare mix: problems of inclusion and exclusion', *International Journal of Health Services*, 23, 455–74.

Taylor-Gooby, P. and Lawson, R. (1993a) 'Introduction', in P. Taylor-Gooby and R. Lawson (eds) *Markets and Managers: New Issues in the Delivery of Welfare*, Buckingham: Open University Press.

Taylor-Gooby, P. and Lawson, R. (1993b) 'Where we go from here: the new order in welfare', in P. Taylor-Gooby and R. Lawson (eds) *Markets and Managers: New Issues in the Delivery of Welfare*, Buckingham: Open University Press.

Thompson, N. (1993) *Anti-discriminatory Practice*, Basingstoke: Macmillan.

Thompson, P. and Ackroyd, S. (1995) 'All quiet on the workplace front? A critique of recent trends in British industrial sociology', *Sociology*, 29, 4, 615–33.

Thompson, P. and McHugh, D. (1990) *Work Organisations. A Critical Introduction*, Basingstoke: Macmillan.

Timms, N. (1991) 'A new Diploma for Social Work, or Dunkirk as total victory', in P. Carter, T. Jeffs and M. Smith (eds) *Social Work and Social Welfare Yearbook 3*, Buckingham: Open University Press.

Titmuss, R. (1963) *Essays on the Welfare State*, London: Allen & Unwin.

Titmuss, R. (1970) *The Gift Relationship: From Human Blood to Social Policy*, London: Allen & Unwin.

Training Organisation for the Personal Social Services (1998) *The Pursuit of Competence and Confidence: Report of a Joint Department of Health and Training Organisation for the Personal Social Services [England] Conference*, London: TOPSS.

Training Organisation for the Personal Social Services (1999a) *Modernising the Social Care Workforce: The First National Training Strategy for England*, Leeds: TOPSS.

Training Organisation for the Personal Social Services (1999b) TOPSS England Training Strategy for Social Care – Reports on Workforce Groups Issued, Leeds: TOPSS, press release mscw/99–2.

Tulle-Winton, E. (1999) 'Growing old and resistance: towards a new cultural economy of old age?' *Ageing and Society*, 19, 281–99.

Twigg, J. (1989) 'Models of carers: how do social care agencies conceptualise their relationship with informal carers?' *Journal of Social Policy*, 18, 53–67.

Twigg, J. (1992) *Carers: Research and Practice*, London: HMSO.

Twigg, J. (1998) 'Informal care of older people', in M. Bernard and J. Phillips (eds) *The Social Policy of Old Age*, London: Centre for Policy on Ageing.

Twigg, J., and Atkin, K. (1994) *Carers Perceived: Policy and Practice in Informal Care*, Buckingham: Open University Press.

University of Warwick (1978) *Preparing for Social Work Practice. A Contribution to the Unfinished Debate on Social Work and Social Work Education*, Coventry: University of Warwick, Department of Applied Social Studies.

University of Warwick (Local Government Centre) (2001) *Improving Public Services: Evaluation of the Best Value Pilot Programme. Final Report. Executive Summary*, London: Department of the Environment, Transport and the Regions.

Wagner Report (1988) *Residential Care: A Positive Choice*, London: HMSO.

Waine, B. (2000) 'Managing performance through pay', in J. Clarke, S. Gewirtz and E. McLaughlin (eds) *New Managerialism, New Welfare?* London: Sage.

Walker, A. (1989) 'Community care', in M. McCarthy (ed.) *The New Politics of Welfare. An Agenda for the 1990s?* Basingstoke: Macmillan.

Walsh, K., Deakin, N., Smith, P., Spurgeon, P. and Thomas, N. (1997) *Contracting for Change: Contracts in Health, Social Care and Other Local Government Services*, Oxford: Oxford University Press.

Warde, A. (1994) 'Consumers, consumption and post-Fordism', in R. Burrows and B. Loader (eds) *Towards a Post-Fordist Welfare State?* London: Routledge.

Warde, A. (1996) 'The future of the sociology of consumption', in S. Edgell, K. Hetherington and A. Warde (eds) *Consumption Matters*, Oxford: Blackwell.

Warner, N. (1994) *Community Care: Just a Fairy Tale?* London: Carers' National Association.

Webb, D. (1991) 'Puritans and paradigms: a speculation on the form of new moralities in social work', *Social Work and Social Sciences Review*, 2, 2, 146–59.

Webb, D. (1996) 'Regulation for radicals: the state, CCETSW and the academy', in N. Parton (ed.) *Social Theory, Social Change and Social Work*, London: Routledge.

Webb, A., Day, L. and Weller, D. (1976) *Voluntary Social Service Manpower Resources*, London: Personal Social Services Council.

Webb, A. and Wistow, G. (1982) 'Over and under', *Social Work Today*, 11 May, 11–13.

Webb, A. and Wistow, G. (1987) *Social Work, Social Care and Social Planning: The Personal Social Services Since Seebohm*, Harlow: Longman.

Welsh Office (1999) *Building for the Future*, London: Stationery Office.

Wenger, G.C. (1984) *The Supportive Network: Coping with Old Age*, London: George Allen & Unwin.

White, M. (2000) 'Performance assessment', *Community Care*, 19 October, 2–3.

White, V. and Harris, J. (1999) 'Social Europe, social citizenship and social work', *European Journal of Social Work*, 2, 3–14.

White, V. and Harris, J. (eds) (2001) *Developing Good Practice in Community Care: Partnership and Participation*, London: Jessica Kingsley.

Wilding, P. (1992) 'The British welfare state: Thatcherism's enduring legacy', *Policy and Politics*, 20, 201–12.

Williams, F. (1989) *Social Policy: A Critical Introduction*, Cambridge: Polity.

Williams, F. (1992) 'Somewhere over the rainbow: universality and diversity in social policy', in N. Manning and R. Page (eds) *Social Policy Review 4*, Canterbury: Social Policy Association.

Williams, F. (1994) 'Social relations, welfare and the Post-Fordist debate', in R. Burrows and B. Loader (eds) *Towards a Post-Fordist Welfare State*, London: Routledge.

Williams, F. (1996) 'Postmodernsim, feminism and difference', in N. Parton (ed.) *Social Theory, Social Change and Social Work*, London: Routledge.

Wilson, E. (1977) *Women and the Welfare State*, London: Tavistock.

Wilson, G. (1993) 'Money and independence in old age', in S. Arber and M. Evandrou (eds) *Ageing, Independence and the Life Course*, London: Jessica Kingsley.

Winchester, R. (2000) 'Report calls for rethink on inspection', *Community Care*, 21 September, 10–11.

Winchester, R. (2001) 'Can residents stop the great homes sell-off?' *Community Care*, 1 March, 11.

Wistow, G., Knapp, M., Hardy, B. and Allen, C. (1994) *Social Care in a Mixed Economy*, Buckingham: Open University Press.

Wistow, G., Knapp, M., Hardy, B., Forder, J., Kendall, J. and Manning, R. (1996) *Social Care Markets. Progress and Prospects*, Buckingham: Open University Press.

Wootton, B. (1959) *Social Science and Social Pathology*, London: Allen & Unwin.

Younghusband, E. (1978) *Social Work in Britain, 1950–75*, vol. 1, London: Allen & Unwin.

Zifcak, S. (1994) *New Managerialism: Administrative Reform in Whitehall and Canberra*, Buckingham: Open University Press.

Zuboff, S. (1988) *In the Age of the Smart Machine: The Future of Work and Power*, New York: Basic Books.

Index